REDISCOVERING CHRISTIANITY: ORIGINS AND A NEW ERA

REDISCOVERING CHRISTIANITY: ORIGINS AND A NEW ERA

PATRICIA BUDD KEPLER

ISBN:	Softcover	979-8-3694-2353-0
	eBook	979-8-3694-2352-3

Art Work: Thomas Budd Kepler

Print information available on the last page.

Rev. date: 08/01/2024

To order additional copies of this book, contact:
Xlibris
844-714-8691
www.Xlibris.com
Orders@Xlibris.com
789440

CONTENTS

DEDICATION AND APPRECIATION

This book is dedicated to my sons, Thomas Budd Kepler, James Blain Kepler, and John Harold Kepler, to my grandchildren, Manda Roy, Lenora Martinelli Kepler, Kieran Martinelli Kepler, James Everett Kepler, Alyssa Blain Kepler, Alana Erickson Kepler, April Erickson Kepler and my great grandchildren Addalyn Kepler Fleck and Atlas Kepler Fleck, and to my sisters, Theresa Budd Schulz, Mary Budd Bradshaw and my late brother, Harold J. Budd Jr.

Each of them in their own way has contributed to the writing of this book. My sons, grandchildren, and sisters have commented on and done basic editing of chapters. Thomas Budd Kepler has edited several of the chapters and encouraged me throughout the process of getting this book into print. I could not have done it without him. Many dear friends have also read and commented on sections of the book. I am especially appreciative of the support and expertise of Judith E. Michaels, friend and colleague in Ministry.

I alone take responsibility for the content of this book though I attribute to my family and friends the depth and love of life that came from them and set the context of my life and faith.

My late husband, Thomas Fitch Kepler, was with me as this book was conceived and accompanied me in the early years of writing. His faith is part of my story.

To all, I offer my deepest gratitude and eternal love.

A PRE-PRELUDE

The other day, I was having a conversation with one of my grandchildren about religion when I realized she did not really know much about Christianity, the faith into which she was born. I began to wonder about other young people like her. How would they learn the basics of Christianity if they did not go to church? And even then, their education could be spotty. This book was conceived that day. I decided to write down the basics as I know them.

She and all my grandchildren and their parents are very loving and ethical. Has Christianity contributed to their values and who they are? I wondered if those values would be passed on to new generations if their religious roots were lost.

I decided to write about those roots as they are recorded in Scripture. I could not possibly trace Christianity for the 2,000 years that followed in the vast variety of Christianities around the world. But I did know something about the Bible and the different ways people see it.

But I could not stop with the basics. Christianity is not frozen in time, it evolves. I would go from the basics to the present and anticipate the future. How has Christianity evolved over time and how prepared is it to contribute to tomorrow's world?

I realized that I was writing for myself and my peers as well as generations following us; people of faith who, like me, must answer to them and the world.

I am writing about my evolution of faith, my feminism, and growing pacifism, as I look at the changing culture around me with new spiritual eyes.

I know that what we mean when we say we believe in God is more than an abstraction. It can help define us, connect or divide us, and affect our loyalties and actions. Our views of God matter whether we can articulate them or are even aware of them. It is important to call into consciousness the views of the Divine we all have or do not have.

Liberal Christians in my generation pursued social justice issues and peace with passion. But we had only begun to do the challenging work of revising our theology when right-wing Christianity gained political power.

As I was looking at the basics of Christianity, I would have to get back to looking at the theological questions our work for justice and peace required. Our theology needed to be revised and renewed. I am in good company. Many Christians are wandering into that deep water. I would join them.

I was ready to review the Scriptural foundations of faith, if only briefly, see how they have informed us and left open questions for us to address as we evolve and journey into the new era already dawning. I can only explore these things as a citizen of the United States though the voices of friends from many countries are ringing in my ears.

I love it that Jesus fully embraced his faith, even as he challenged it and opened doors for new generations to carry it on in the power of the Spirit. He worked and prayed for the Realm of God to come on earth as it was in heaven. He believed that the Spirit that lived in him would live on in those who followed him.

So it is that this book begins each chapter with a review of faith according to the witness of Scripture which all Christians see as foundational. That is followed by modern day challenges and questions that ask how God's Spirit is moving us toward God's new creation emerging in our time in religious and secular people, in communities longing for a world that supports life and enhances it.

Old paradigms are shifting. What new ethical imperatives are emerging? How is God surprising us with new revelations? How is

God's Spirit breathing life into our world exhausted by wars and often beset by fears?

The systems of the past are making a last attempt to hold on and prevail while new ways of thinking and being are developing. That leads us into difficult times of transition. Our experiences and concepts of God are changing as we come to terms with the realities of this era.

We are living in a period when our understanding of both God and humanity is shifting. We are finally forced to face the fact that in this world, God does not control everything. Power is in human hands as well. We need more than ever to draw closer to God's righteousness so that the image of God in us can have room to act and grow in the future before us.

We are living into the age of the Spirit when the power of the Holy Spirit is moving and connecting with the spirit of human beings.

I write about these things with great hope. I have no illusions about our human nature, but I have faith that the light of God resides in us and can shine through us. I have no illusions about God's power. Human beings have agency. But our life spans are short, and our institutions exist but for a time. God's Spirit wills life and love for the world, spans the ages, and transcends them.

When we listen attentively and see with clarity, we hear the angel songs and are amazed and filled with wonder at the beauty of the earth and aware that there is a universe out there whose breadth and depth is hard to imagine. I trust that beyond all time and space is a creating energy that gives life and loves creation with an intensity that can bring life into being.

PRELUDE

So here I am writing about God in a time when it seems that God is, on the one hand, not very popular, or, on the other, the power behind right-wing political movements. That is, if you listen to the press and pay attention to popular culture.

I am writing about God and us and our world because there is more going on behind the scenes than is obvious and I want to look behind that curtain because that is where the future lies.

The testimony of Christianity through the centuries is that God and people belong together. God and all creation are part of a great ongoing love story with all the ups and downs that implies. The plot is thickening in our time and new challenges and questions are emerging about our human relationship with the Holy.

My underlying theory is that God is in relationship with us, moves with us as we change, and enables us to meet the challenges of time in ways that are life giving and renewing if we are open to them. We must be willing to engage with the Holy not only with our hearts, but with our minds and spirits. We need to repeatedly liberate God from our limited perspectives, and that can liberate us to be more open to the divine that lives in and around us. And though God is with us in our world, God is also Mystery and beyond what we can know.

While humanity is not as great a mystery as God, though we encounter each other every day in very mundane ways, as people we have depths that are hard to plumb and a reality beyond simple definitions. There is a mystery deep within our human beings.

I share the visions of the authors of the first creation stories in Genesis in the Hebrew Bible: we are created in God's image with the freedom to know and choose between good and evil. We are not strangers to God, we are offspring, heirs with Jesus Christ, from a Christian perspective.

As we look at Christianity's roots and explore its future, we will talk about God, Jesus Christ, the Spirit, Scripture, and the Church. In each chapter, after setting the basics, we ask questions that emerge as we look to the future.

Religion has a deep ethical component that has a social impact on our lives for better or worse. We cannot talk about God or no-God without also talking about human behavior and the social systems that engage and shape our lives. Everything is related, connected.

RISING QUESTIONS

Many of the assumptions and patterns in life that we once took for granted shift beneath our feet. I find questions about God and faith rise to the surface as we change and the world around us changes. We can hold on to the past or we can listen for angel voices telling us that we are birthing the future.

We are entering an age that is moving away from patriarchy and other hierarchies and care for creation is essential for survival. We are entering an electronic age with artificial intelligence and robots, and we are living in a time when everything in the world is more interconnected than ever, violence is more deadly than ever, and space is our frontier and for some, our playground.

The new world that is emerging is affecting our understanding of God and humanity. The power dynamics between human beings are changing. The stakes are high. Power to destroy on a small scale has always been in human hands. Now we have the power to destroy on a global scale. And where we once had to look into the faces of those with whom we were in combat, the victims of our destruction can now remain faceless and to the offensive warrior, nameless.

The religion I embraced once said that God holds the ultimate destiny of the world in "his" hands. Now, humanity has the power to destroy the world. Do we hold the world in our hands? Have we outgrown God? Or have we entered a time when we are finally in ultimate need of claiming the depth and breadth of holiness in humanity and discovering the power of God's lifesaving presence? Empires and conquering powers are a thing of the past though nationalisms prevail. Political economic empires are being manipulated by international corporate giants.

Can we see the wonder of love in God and humanity, and can God's love and humanity's compassion save the world together? Can love be expressed in faithfulness to God's law, be in touch with reality, and act with a pragmatism that serves justice and peace?

There are big, worldview questions before us. They affect every level of life as we know it and our understanding of and relationship with God. At one level, we may find it discomforting to ponder these questions or be too engaged with survival to entertain them. Those who are called to take them on are called to be heralds of God's new creation and resources of hope for the future.

As we explore Christianity and beliefs about God in the Twenty-First Century, we each come from a subjective place: our personalities, context, experiences, and our stage of life affect our spiritual journey. The diversities we represent can enrich our engagement even if at times they drive us apart. We must be ourselves and honest with each other.

We are sharing a radical turning of time. We all live in the same world on a small planet named earth. We need each other. We need a holy Spirit beyond ourselves to help guide us and speak to our human souls.

THE BIG PICTURE

We live life in concentric circles that begin with all embracing world views and end in the intimacy and particularity of home. Between the big picture and everyone's home reality, there are the various spheres in which we live.

There are times in history when the big picture is fairly static even though it is in motion. This is not such a time. The big picture is changing. As it changes, it affects every sphere of life including our daily lives and our beliefs in God.

Christians have always given lip service to the idea that God's liberating Spirit is constantly breathing new life into creation and taking us into new dimensions, into the heart of mystery, and into the arms of salvation amid the realities of everyday life. Now it is time to take those ideas seriously. The new Order of God is at hand. It is not the end of the world. Though the possibility that we could blow ourselves up or slowly destroy our natural habitat exists. If we avoid that, a promising new frontier lies ahead.

Most Christians have always believed that God wills humanity's wellbeing and is a God of love and grace who calls us to love one another. Now we need to take a serious look at what it really means to love in both an intimate and global way.

We will have to revisit the place God's Law has in our lives and how it connects with love. We will have to revisit the connection between Law and Love to disarm and contain evil.

In fact, clarifying what we mean by love is important in the present for both people who believe in God or wonder if they do, and those who do not.

LESSONS FROM A PANDEMIC

Some of the writing of this book took place during the years of our worldwide Covid pandemic. That pandemic pointed to both how connected we are as human beings and how divided our small world is. The pandemic sheds light on the power of nature and sheds light on this new era.

Years ago, the worldwide viral threat to human life that Covid-19 posed would have been considered science fiction. Or even an act of God. Though there have been plagues, it is the global nature of Covid-19 and how fast it spread that was new.

Many people are still worn out, traumatized, and mourning as we reach for life that seems normal again. We may never be able to determine the full effect of the Covid years.

In prior eras, we would not have been able to develop vaccines that could protect us from the virus.

In the early years of Covid, there were heroes among us and compassionate people ready to help others. There were people who had to keep the social wheels of society going, who had little choice but to work while others were isolated. There were the doctors and nurses putting their own lives at risk to treat extremely sick people. There were also the deniers who said it was nothing more than a virus when people were dying. They would not get vaccinated, did not trust the science of vaccines, and those would not wear masks. And there were those for whom vaccinations and masks were not available.

From a faith perspective, even when God seemed dead or irrelevant, for some, there was hope and healing in God's presence and people who mediated God's love. When our human capacities for coping are strained by disasters, we need somewhere to turn, some way to reclaim life again. If God's Spirit can breathe new life and resilience into creation, God becomes a possibility.

One thing we learned about humanity is that ordinary human life goes on even during disaster. We still must eat, wear clothing, care for children, do chores, try to make ends meet, treat other health issues, and earn livings as we can, though jobs were lost. Every day we keep going though our patience has an endpoint. Some people and parts of society are lost.

Through that time, we had a President who was a Covid minimizer and fake-news perpetrator, for whom truth was meaningless, who claimed to be a Christian, who was militant and ultra nationalist and deeply divided the nation. And yet, for some, he became a messianic figure.

Now, this is a challenging and crucial time to be reflecting on our relationships with one another and the connectedness of our world, our interior landscapes, and the nature of God. We are facing a new reality as we emerge from the war on Covid-19 and its aftermath. It is one more sign that we are entering a new era when the world is smaller than ever.

We are also facing old realities, inequalities between nations and people meant that some had better access to resources and medical supplies and treatments than others. Some scapegoating went on as China, where the virus was first detected, was blamed. And, in fact, there were some isolated groups of people that Covid did not reach.

Scientists tell us that this will not be the last virus to run wild and amok in our world.

TOM'S QUESTION

During the writing of this book, my husband, Tom, became sick. After living through Covid in the isolating first two years of the pandemic, his atypical Parkinson's and cancer worsened. He died just as we were preparing for hospice care. He lived with great grace throughout his illness and had no fear of death. He was at peace. During this time, I worked intermittently on this book as I was his primary caregiver, which I could not have done without the caring help of our sons and their families.

Tom was more of a skeptic than I am. He had a scientific bent and in his last years, he tended toward thinking that if something could not be proven, it did not exist. He was dedicated to the teachings and life of Jesus and took them seriously as a guide for life. As a Presbyterian Minister, he had pursued a tent-making ministry for most of his life. He was committed with his full being to peace and justice and not interested in abstract theology.

His primary theological question at the end of his life, was, however, abstract. "What does anyone mean by God, anyway? It was a question that emerged out of his experience of our changing times and his questioning of his own old-world view. He preferred asking that question to answering it.

That question, as hard to answer as it is, seems appropriate and essential to reflect on now. It is a question I ponder as I write this book.

In this book, his question and my emerging faith concerns have led to this, my halting attempt, not to produce answers but to at least explore the questions with you. "What do I/you/we/our churches mean by God anyway…or Christianity?"

Obviously, I, or anyone else for that matter, can only take a stab at tentatively answering this life-changing question as we reflect on faith, past and present, each from our own perspective. Everyone's answer is important and valuable even if it is inevitably partial, limited, and incomplete. God will always be beyond even our imaginations.

We can believe that God is with us and makes God's self-known, often in surprising ways, and yet, when it comes to talking about God and it comes down to articulating what we mean by God, it is hard. I find myself producing well-worn phrases and thoughts. Like the priest in Graham Greene's, "The Living Room," who was trying to talk with his niece about God's will. He despairingly said, "my tongue is heavy with the petty catechism."

This book does not address the issue of whether there is a God. I leave that question to the philosophers. I assume God. I experience God. I take seriously the testimonies in Scripture of those who have experienced God and the writings of others who experienced God, each in their own era. It is ours to seek to know more of God alive in us and in our world today and try to find words for what we mean by God.

The home of my faith journey has been the Presbyterian Church in the United States. Within that tradition, I write from a feminist liberal perspective that developed in the liberation movement years of the late fifties, sixties, and early seventies. I was a Minister and employed mother of three sons during that time and that meant I was living outside of tradition's box. I was also a wife though separated from my husband for two years during that time before we got back together. I experienced life as a single mother during those two years.

The movement years are over, but the influence they had on our lives and society is not. The issues they addressed are still with us. Our consciousness is raised around human rights issues and environmental concerns are central. There are, as always, new ethical issues continually emerging.

It is time to ask, whether, in all our movements toward identity formation, social justice, peace, and saving our planet, we have liberated ourselves from idolatrous notions of God. God is always in need of being freed from the theologies that are restricted by our specific contexts and limited minds. It is time to ask how God's Spirit is moving us toward liberating our concepts of God and our labels for and stereotypes of each other.

While the God of our lives is always as close as our own heart, God is also beyond us, even more incomprehensible than the universe is when we try to contemplate its billions of years and infinite number of galaxies. There is a sense in which being an agnostic is the most honest approach to faith. But we do not need to be clueless. We have the testimony of past generations and the lived life on earth of Jesus as guides. We can rely on them as a foundation for our faith.

However, the fact is that Being, God's being and the true being of any one of us is never fully known or knowable. Yet, there are some things we dare to believe and feel. Christians believe that God was incarnate in Jesus, and we take his teachings as guidance for living. The cross on which he died has become a symbol for Christianity and the resurrection that overcame death, a symbol of God's unending love and overcoming of earth's limitations and evil.

As we proceed, we want to try to discern what it means to relate to God, how God was experienced in Biblical times, and how that connection can translate into our own time and find expression through us in the coming age that is upon us.

There is a global movement toward this new age, uneven and different as it is in every culture. And every era in time continues to exist in and contribute to emerging eras just as human life stages inform each other and circle back and forth between stages.

The question, never mind its placement in an era, is a timeless one: "What do we mean by God anyway?" Or by that One who is ultimate in our religious system - if there is anything ultimate beyond our own egos?

An auxiliary question to "What do we mean by God anyway?" is "What do we mean by human beings anyway?" The two questions are connected. What is it about God and humanity that, when in right relationship, can be an influence and energy for life? How can human beings' experience of the Holy be a positive force in creating a just and livable order in each new age?

VIOLENCE AND RELIGION

As I am wrapping up this book, violence is exploding in the land where Judaism, Christianity, and Islam were born. It is now Israel and what is left of the Palestinian Territories. War has broken out if war can be waged between totally uneven powers. It is more like a David and Goliath scenario. 1,400 Israelis were killed at the hands of Hamas, a Muslim Gazan right wing militant group. As I write, over 35,000 Palestinians in Gaza were killed by Israeli forces and forced starvation is taking place. The possibility of genocide or ethnic cleansing of Gaza is feared.

This is one issue that does not split the left and right easily. There are Christians and Jews who stand with Israel unconditionally and those who hold Israel accountable for protecting human rights. The situation is not complex but the different motives driving where people stand are and public knowledge is driven by propaganda.

The tragedy unfolding before our eyes raises the question in bold relief of what God and ethics we believe in and what difference they make in our actions. It also raises the question of whether the conflicts in the world are about God at all or if God's name is being taken in vain as we pursue material and military goals and sheer power.

There are many people courageously calling for a ceasefire and an end to the suffering and killing of the Gazan people and calling for a negotiated peace in the Middle East. Their voices are a sign of hope and faith in the universal righteousness of a Divine Power and testimony to the humane in humanity.

We cannot help but be aware of the times when religion, and God, in the name of religion and its adherents, have been a destructive force in the world. For religion to be a positive force in history, our God perceptions matter and our perceptions of ourselves and humankind make a difference.

As we wrestle with the question of what we mean by God, and what difference it makes, sometimes the things that are most clear and important at first, are what we *do not* mean by God. Since religion can be a force for good or for destruction and everything in-between, being sure about what or who God is and is not ls consequential. God is not a God of violence.

As we search to understand faith, we have to say with the Apostle Paul that we see "through a glass darkly." That did not stop Paul from witnessing to the God of Jesus Christ, nor does it need to stop us. Seeing at all through the glass is a gift. So, we dare persist in trying to talk about what we see.

A PERSONAL CAVEAT

As I was writing, I often found myself resisting putting my thoughts about God and humanity down in black and white. My professional and personal life has made me acutely aware of the limitations of putting faith into writing. Such writing will always be incomplete, subject to change, and often controversial.

I have written and delivered thousands of sermons over the years, each a short reflection on some aspect of faith. Writing this book forced me to weave my thoughts together. Especially now, it is important to examine our beliefs about God and a life of faith.

It is important for those to whom faith is central in life to leave a legacy of faith for new generations. That is what those before us have done. I treasure more than I can say the human love that has sustained and upheld me from past generations and contemporary ones and given my life meaning as I have pursued questions of faith. Through the love that we share, we come to know how sacred and precious life is.

When we are talking about faith, we are talking about worldviews inevitably lived out in specific and diverse ways by all of us.

When I told the Minister of the church where I worship, the Rev. Dr. Allen Fairfax, that I was writing this book, he told me a Karl Barth joke. Barth was a renowned German theologian who died in 1968 at the age of eighty-two. It was said of him, "God allowed Karl Barth to live such a long life because God wanted to find out who He (God) was."

I am not writing to tell anyone, especially God, who he/she/it is. I am writing to try to articulate my own belief and share my thoughts and experiences of God as well as my questions in a time when some people are wondering why anyone would believe in God anyway. I am writing to invite you to explore your own beliefs and allow them to evolve.

Many people find it hard, as I do, to articulate what they believe about God in a coherent way in today's world, though some scholars could tell you in detail what other people have believed.

ETHICS AND FAITH

There is another reason it is important to speak of our faith. Different religious perspectives lead to different actions in the world. There are also many secular ethical values that support some life while destroying other life and other secular ethical values that seek to protect all life. Both can have roots in religious perspectives and contexts. It matters what religious perspective we take into the future.

I support the ethics of righteousness, justice and peace, the search for integrity and wisdom. What are the religious roots of these values and how can we advance them across cultures?

How will religious beliefs have to evolve to support a world committed to wholeness, to justice and mercy, to peace with compassion? Can these ethics hold in the future if their religious roots, their source, are cut off from them? At least a remnant needs to retain religious roots that evolve with God over time.

Imperfect as people of faith are, we are asking God questions and ethical questions that are at the heart of religion, theology, and culture. We need a place, a way, to talk about that which lies beyond our material reality and is greater than, beyond our time-bound institutions and knowledge.

It is only when people of faith know where they stand that they can face the divisions between them and be held accountable for their actions. People of faith live and work with those who, in secular contexts, hold values that also support or destroy life. We collaborate with secular powers every day of our lives.

In many ways, it would be easier for those with a social conscience to remain silent on the question of God while holding fast to life-affirming ethical issues. It might even be easier to deny God than wrestle with the question, "What do you (or anyone) possibly mean by God, anyway?"

ALL FAITHS HAVE ROOTS

The fact that belief in God is both personal and communal means it has roots in one faith or another. While we are looking at the God question from our own Christian perspective, we are addressing issues that become communal and we are called to be in dialogue with those who are asking similar questions or ones like it, in their own context.

Believing in the presence of God and God's goodness and love has sustained and supported many of us throughout our lives. It has challenged and changed us. We speak of these things so they can challenge, contribute to, and give hope for the future and hope to those to whom the future belongs.

I have already said I have no interest in proving God. If God exists, God exists, of course, no matter what we believe or think. Ancient people took a sacred transcendent force or forces beyond themselves for granted. Modern people can ask if that force even exists. Many of the powers our forebears assumed to be in God's province are now in human hands, including the ability to wipe out human life on earth as we have noted. We are truly on the brink of a new age.

Some think that we have outgrown a need for God, who can seem just a construct of human minds and now outmoded. Some have found ultimate value outside of traditional religious contexts. Some say they are "spiritual" but not "religious." Some still have a faith that believes God controls everything. Some have faith and believe in humanity's free will. Some are prone to follow charismatic leaders while some are prone to be suspicious of all authority. Some never think about God. Some have felt that God is irrelevant in the face of real life and political systems. Some see religion as destructive in history. Some see it as a useful tool. And on and on.

Wherever we are on that spectrum, in our individual lives and in our communities, in this new age, it is more important than ever to recognize the false gods and seductive idols to which we give ultimate meaning. They endanger life on earth. There is peril in seeing as ultimate that which is finite.

The Mysterious Holy can be seen as a relic of the past or an Advocate and Energy for life in the present, and a hope and light for the future in a world desperately in need of mooring.

God can be a God who moves with us into our new age in ways that sustain and enhance life or a God who leads us into battle on the eve of destruction. We must choose. Already, we are sounding the drums of war. We are called to choose life, to be part of Christianity's rebirth and progenitors of humanity's redemption, wise as serpents and gentle as doves as Jesus called his followers to be.

We could try to keep the God we worship locked in the dusty bins of the past and throw away the key, but God's Spirit will always break free.

As deeply indebted as we are to the saints in all religions who have kept faith alive in the past, our gratitude will be meaningless unless we are willing to be saints and prophets in our time, walking with wisdom and wonder, courage and strength, and open eyes, into the unknown era before us.

How individuals encounters God on their journey will differ. Sometimes the Holy will come to us through other people, sometimes we have a more direct encounter with the Divine, sometimes we see God in the grandeur of creation or in a beloved animal. Sometimes God seems silent, and we wait. Sometimes God is there in conflict as we try to find our way. Sometimes God seems like an illusion.

As we contemplate God, let it be with abandon and caution, with respect and familiarity, with acknowledgment of our roots and respect for the faith of others that liberates.

We are in continuity with all that has come before us. Even if we want to make a clean break from it, we emerge from the past and are partially created by it. It is a resource and teacher. But we must move on. Life is a journey, and we are on a road never traveled and yet strangely familiar. Our individual and collective relationship with God is evolutionary and sometimes revolutionary.

CHAPTER 1
AN OVERVIEW

FAITH AS EVOLUTIONARY

Our understandings of God evolve as the world evolves and eras change. God, in relationship with us, moves with us and changes us, that God who is God in and beyond all time. Faith and our understanding and experience of God, along with that of religious communities and institutions move through the ages, all in their own way, all in their own context, all at diverse paces.

While society is evolving, we, as individuals, are going through life stages. One hopes that faith matures with us until we reach life's end. As human beings and part of creation, we are always becoming, always in process, always in motion, and sure to die at some point. During change, we try to weave the resources and learnings from the past into the present.

Throughout the Chapters that follow, we ask whether and when our God has been too small, too parochial, or too grand. While we can open our hearts to the depths and possibilities toward which the Holy Spirit leads us, we can never, like Goldilocks, find a place to rest that is "just right." We are called by the Spirit to reach for a faith able to withstand the new questions that arise as our lives and world change that is "good enough."

"According to the Bible, the knowledge of God is not reached by abstract speculation, as in Greek philosophy, but in the actual everyday business of living, in social relationships and in current historical events. God is not known by thinking out ideas about God, but by seeking and doing God's will as made known to us by prophetic men and women and by our own consciousness of right and wrong." (Alan Richardson, "A Theological Word Book of the Bible" p.89).

While God is not known through our thinking about God, we need to be conscious of just what it is we do think about God because it affects how we see God's will as we live and interact with our world. Our consciousness affects our conscience.

A NEW ERA

At the end of the Twentieth Century and well into the Twenty-First Century, we are entering a new era in human history. This new era poses new challenges for all religions, including Christianity.

Today the radical changes on the horizon signal a major shift in human existence. We are living in an electronic information era and in an age of deep social change. An article in the Boston Globe on December 22, 2022, is entitled "Is this the dawn of a new age on earth?" A panel of three dozen scientists from around the world are on the verge of calling this, in geologic time, the Anthropocene, the age of humans: a time when humans impact the world as never before.

These times open the door for changes in disciplines as different as science and art, astronomy and religion, politics, and education. These times have already led to deep and frightening political conflicts as we go through times of transition.

We could be on the verge of an artistic era and time of great creativity as envisioned by Gibson Winter, a noted sociologist and ethicist, or we could elicit times of war and global climate change such as the world has never known; or a new era could turn us all into the robot-like beings of dystopian fiction that could blur the lines between the real and fictional, or into more compassionate humane people.

In the twenty-first century, we live in a time of aroused social consciousness when we are finally addressing issues of systemic oppression: movement away from patriarchy, hierarchies, racism, ethnic divisions, childhood slavery, and movement toward addressing causes of vast income gaps and hunger in the world. In these times, the environment and climate change are in focus and the future of life on earth is at stake.

We also are living in an age when new individualisms are emerging that could signal new freedoms, self-assertions, and ethical sensitivities, or escape from the complex need to deal with communal systems. It is too soon to tell.

Autocrats and dictators filled with self-interest are emerging who are making a mockery of morality as they come into power and attract passionate followers in nations around the globe. With weapons of war in existence that could annihilate life as we know it, levelheaded leaders, and citizens able to resist the temptations of power and profits are desperately needed to lead the world away from violence.

In this new era, humanity's modern technologies can be harnessed for the good: to feed the world, to fight disease, to expand educational opportunities, to protect human rights and freedoms and blend individual fulfillment with the common good. Insights of modernity can be complemented by the insights of Indigenous peoples and their connections with the earth, early cultures, and respect for ancestors.

In this new age of reality and pseudo-reality, of materialism, artificial intelligence and all that accompanies it, religion could contribute to advancing our humanity. It could also hide its head in the sand and become irrelevant.

Electronic technology is redefining communication and information. More information than we can manage is at our fingertips and so is misinformation. Science is scrambling to keep up with nature's unfolding and the new horizons made possible by our computer age. Musicians, artists, writers, teachers, people in many different working roles are all contributing to understanding and working with the reality of a new age and its inevitable continuity with and tension with that which has come before.

As we go on to explore what we mean by God, we see that faith takes place in the context of history that changes through generations. While some things about faith are valuable through time, holding on to other aspects of faith can be dangerous. We want to identify what needs to be changed and what needs to be reaffirmed for the good of individuals and society.

Some say we are living in a post Christian/post religious age. Are we? Perhaps religion is just now coming into its own, maturing, able to be in dialogue with other disciplines and culture. Being at home in a secular world without being seduced by it, religions could help humanity turn toward life.

Now is a time to ask as never before, with deepest longing, if there is a spiritual force that lives beyond us that is also in us, that supports love in its many forms as new frontiers open and new ethical issues arise before old ethical issues are solved. Now is the age of the Spirit.

CHRISTIAN BASICS AND THE TRINITY

Pursuing questions about God, humanity, and faith in a new age, we need to review the foundations of Christianity as it is written about in Scripture because that is where it begins. In each Chapter in this book, we review the basics, the roots. For some, these will be well known. For others, new information. For still others, a different take on basics than their own.

Of course, there is not one Christianity, but many Christianities. However many versions of Christianity there are, there are some essential things we agree on. We share the same roots. The central beliefs we share provide an outline for this book.

We share a belief that God is One. We share a belief that God was incarnate in Jesus Christ, a historic Jewish leader who lived in Palestine. He was both divine and human. Christians focus on the life of Jesus and on his death on a cross. They believe in his resurrection from the dead and his ascension to God and his return as the living Christ. We believe that God is with us in the world as the Holy Spirit. We see our One God manifest in the Trinity.

The Trinity is a complex concept that emerged formally out of heated debates in the early Christian Church as to who Jesus was and is. Some denied Jesus' full humanity. Some denied his divinity. The Trinity made it clear that the Church believes Jesus to be both fully divine and human, an incarnation of God and one of us. The Spirit, the third "person" of the Trinity, also identified by some as Wisdom, was already present in Judaism. It was reemphasized as an energy and life force, a life-giving power in the time of Jesus, living in Jesus and the early church.

These words from Ephesians to early Christians in the New Testament show how naturally they perceived God as present in Jesus and the Spirit.

"I bow my knees before the Father from whom every family in heaven and on earth takes its name. I pray that, according to the riches of his glory, he may grant that you may be strengthened in your inner being with power through his Spirit, and that Christ may dwell in your hearts through faith as you are being rooted and grounded in love. I pray that you may have the power to comprehend, with all the saints, what is the breadth, length, and depth, and to know the love of Christ that surpasses knowledge, so that you may be filled with all the fullness of God." Ephesians 3:14-19

These verses more than any theological treatise describe how the Spirit and Christ are seen as woven into the fullness of God in and for humanity.

God the Creator and Parent, Jesus Christ, the Word of God and the Spirit, the Breath of God, are seen as all existing eternally, and throughout time, as expressions of the One God, the Holy One, Sacred Being, Divine Love. The Trinity is not a mathematical formula, it is a statement of faith and a theological affirmation in Christianity.

The Trinity: God as Three in One can sound like nothing more than theological jargon. It is, however, at its core, a claim that God, mysterious and undefinable in the abstract, is and always was and will be, present in the world through time, is and was present in Jesus Christ and the Holy Spirit. God is in the world and exists in and beyond time.

God is also active in humanity. God is creative energy and, though a life force beyond time and space, is very present with us in this world, unfolding in time and space, transcendent and alive in creation.

God is in relationship with human beings, is one with whom we can have a personal and communal relationship, a deep and loving connection.

Human beings are limited by time and space despite adventures into outer space. All individuals die. God exists through all generations and all time and sees the whole picture.

Though Jesus is central to all Christianity, that does not mean that all Christians share the same beliefs about Jesus or experience him the same way. We do agree that he is still alive in the world, and that in him, there is new life and hope for individuals and humanity,

Christians believe the Spirit moves in individual lives and communities of faith to inspire, empower, challenge, and support them as they continue the work of Jesus Christ, ushering in God's ever new creation.

Christians have the Bible in common as a testimony to faith, both the Old Testament (the Hebrew Bible) and the New Testament are part of the Canon. A thread running through Scripture is God's relationship with humanity in history.

Finally, Christians have in common that they gather in community for worship, fellowship, and live out their faith, affirming an inner spirituality.

Though we differ dramatically about God's will and what ethical positions are in harmony with God's righteousness, Christians believe that there is an ethical dimension of faith and that the "Kingdom (Realm) of God" is here and coming, embodying God's love for creation.

Christians believe that there is life after death but disagree on who gets to that life and how. No one can really describe fully what it is.

MANY CHRISTIANITIES

Having stated these basic beliefs that are differently perceived by Christians, we recognize the many faces of Christianity. In addition to the main branches of Christianity, Roman Catholic, Orthodox and Protestant, there are fundamentalists, evangelicals, conservatives, traditionalists, liberals, charismatics, progressives, and combinations of these that cut across religious institutions. There are so many differences among Christians that one wonders if we are all even worshiping the same God and share the same faith. "What do we mean by God anyway?"

Keeping the range within Christianity in mind, this book is written from a primarily Protestant perspective though the questions it raises are meant for all Christians.

In the United States, Christian religious groups rise and fall in popularity. In conservative political times in the United States, Christian liberalism seems to all but disappear and the "Christian right" is front and center, seeming to define Christianity, especially in the media.

In more liberal political times, progressive Christianity flourishes. In the Liberation Movement years of the fifties, sixties, and seventies, the liberal church was in the foreground and more conservative churches were declaring that religion and politics should not mix. When the "right" gained political power, they changed their mind about political and religious power mixing. They became a political force.

I live in the U.S. Northeast where Roman Catholicism is the majority Christian face of religion and Unitarianism and Congregationalism is strongest on the Protestant side. (Some Unitarians would not consider themselves Christians while others do.)

Orthodox Churches have their centers of influence. Charismatic churches dot the landscape and their influence waxes and wanes. Independent megachurches exist alongside "Mainline Churches." Religious cults have followings and identifying them as cults enables them to be put in perspective.

Beyond the spheres of cultural and political influence, all varieties of Christians continue to worship and act in their communities whatever the national climate.

There are those who declare the Unites States to be a Christian nation. While Christianity has been the dominant religion in the States, we are constitutionally organized on the separation of church and state.

Increasingly, other religions have had an impact on society in the States. Judaism has always had a visible existence and increasingly, Islam has become more visible. Buddhism, with its emphasis on meditation, is now part of the religious scene. Our attention in the States is being drawn to the multicultural face of Christianity and to the multifaith nature of our culture. This is happening amid a growing agnostic, atheist, and organized Humanist influence.

Christianity is a worldwide religion and is strong and growing in some countries around the world while it is waning in the West.

In these times, basic and evolving Christianity needs to be clarified, mainline churches need to cooperate and become more unified and become an international force for peace in the name of Jesus Christ.

There have been and continue to be times when religious and secular forces join for the good of all humanity. And then there are Christian churches that collude with secular States in promoting injustice. In this new era, we will want to welcome cooperation between religious and secular forces when they are able to work for the common good without fostering religious nationalisms or ideologies. Of course, the question arises as to how the common good is defined.

Christianity, like all Religions, is of both the heart and the mind. All Christian churches have a place in people's lives because they offer comfort and solace and strength for individuals in their everyday living, and in the facing of difficult times, including death. Matters of the heart. Christianity is also an outlet for art, play, and joy, and can provide individuals with the experience of community.

In matters of the mind, Christianity provides an opportunity to explore the meaning of life and a relationship with a Divine Presence.

It also seeks to explore and act on the more reason for discussing these matters together. That leads us into the discipline called theology.

As we move on, a few words about theology, the discipline that addresses the nature of God and thereby also, the nature of humanity and the world we live in. It translates what the heart knows and, at other times, provides revelations for changes of heart.

DOING THEOLOGY

The discipline that deals with God-talk is theology. Theology is something in which all Christians engage whether we recognize it or not. While theology can be complex and dense in its academic form, it really belongs to all Christians and is expressed in our worship, in our views of ourselves and one another and the world. It is expressed in how we live in the world. It is all connected to how we understand God, and God's will and power.

On the one hand, theology deals with matters of life and death and is a human attempt to find ways to speak about God who is never fully knowable. It is also about ways to understand ourselves and find meaning in life.

Theology is an invitation to play with concepts of the Holy in thought, in art, in liturgy, and in social systems, giving words to what is experienced existentially and can never be fully defined.

Theology gives us a way to talk about the connections between the human and divine, from past to present, connections that carry, at their core, the seeds of the future.

Churches differ on where the responsibility for defining theology lies, with the institution or with individuals or with both. In many Christian sectors, institutions mediate theology and determine doctrines (where they exist.) Christian communities and individuals decide how seriously to take those doctrines, religiously speaking.

Theology is more art than science though its pursuit at the academic level entails the rigorous study of Scripture and Church History, Social

Ethics, and Psychology. It stands on its own and at the intersection of these disciplines.

In this book, as we engage in God-talk, we are having a theological discussion about how we see the past and envision the future of faith as it is evolving. Marshall McLuhan, a Canadian philosopher was once popular for his idea that "The medium is the message." In the religious world of today, I also believe that "The message is in the message." Words and concepts matter.

In each Chapter, after a brief review of Christian basics as they relate to God, Jesus, the Holy Spirit, Scripture, and Community, we will ask which of these basics proved grounding for all times, and which are evolving through time. We will review the basics as we find them in Scripture. Then we will raise theological questions that seem important to our new era.

CHAPTER 2
GOD

"God is a Spirit and those who worship God must worship in spirit and in truth." *Presbyterian Shorter Catechism*

"Beloved, let us love one another, for love is from God; everyone who loves is born of God and knows God." 1 John 4

"I do not see a man-made world; I see a God-made world." Helen Keller

As we embark on this journey into the heart of Christianity, we know that God talk can be very personal and very multifaceted. God is revealed in separate places, times, and contexts, and that leads to the development of specific religions that evolve through time including some that are not theistic.

Christianity, developed in the Middle East toward the end of the Roman Empire. The calendar of the Western world measures time from the birth of Jesus.

The birth of Judaism dates back thousands of years with the call to Abraham and before that, the Creation stories and the story of Noah and his descendants.

The God of Judaism and Christianity engages in the world and in the lives of human beings. God can seem as close our own breath and still far beyond the reaches of our imagination and comprehension. And yet, we dare to ask what we mean by God. We begin knowing that there are many answers to this question.

God is being, is energy, is goodness, is wisdom and a holy presence in this world. God is love, and is as invisible as love is, but both God and love are very real. God's love finds a dwelling place in human hearts and finds an expression in people's lives.

God is present in time and space and yet encompasses all time and place and is also beyond them. We can experience God in our beings that, while embedded in our material world, can connect with God's Spirit. We can experience God in nature, in the world around us, and in the unfolding of the universe. It is our human hope in faith, that the realm where God is, is also our human destiny, in the present and beyond death.

Human beings can reflect Divine light in the world and embody God, through showing acts of kindness and compassion, seeking justice and peace, proclaiming, and protecting the sacredness of life. And just plain showing resilience and perseverance in living everyday life.

When we refer to God it is often in anthropomorphic terms because we are physical beings and that brings us closer to God. Speaking of God as one of us is one way of communicating our connection with the Holy. God's arms uphold us. God's love surrounds us. God touches our hearts. God speaks with us, and we respond to God's words. We communicate with God in prayer.

There are many ways of experiencing God. Robin Chernoff in her book, "Holy Unexpected," says God is a current that one can step into, almost by accident and get caught up in. She also says, "God in my veins."

Sue Monk Kidd says "The joyful experience of God makes it impossible to separate loving God from loving others. We are nearest to God when we love. *(God's Joyful Surprise*, p.242)

The Psalmist writing the 23rd Psalm, speaks of God as "my shepherd." The Apostle Paul sees God in Christ as God's wisdom and power.

People through the ages have worshiped God(s) in communities of faith and witnessed to God in the living of their lives. People have told stories about God and at times expressed their acute feelings of the absence or silence of God.

Some find strength within to pursue, without a belief in God, what people of faith see as God's justice and righteousness, God's grace, and mercy.

People have also used God for political and personal ends that are antithetical to God's righteousness, making a mockery of God.

PART 1

STEPPING INTO THE STREAM THAT IS GOD

There is a much-loved hymn taken from a Psalm that begins, "As a hart longs for living streams, so longs my heart for God." While we are longing for God, it is said that God longs for us, pursues us like "the hound of heaven." God and people are seen as meant for each other. God seeks out beloved creation and human beings, who are created in the image of God in spite of imperfection and sin and living in a world where evil exists.

Just as the crystals hanging in my window reflect the light of the sun, casting their rainbow colors everywhere in our living room, human beings reflect God's light into which we cannot gaze directly. The glory and mystery of God are alive in the world, and we can catch glimpses of them everywhere though we are aware that fully knowing God is impossible. And that is enough.

In her book "Dwelling, a Spiritual History of the World," Linda Hogan, a native American, shares a beautiful image. She stops in a walk in the forest to drink from a stone cup that holds water that reflects the sky. "Bending over the stone, smelling the earth up close, we drank sky off the surface of the water." (p. 42)

As the water, the stone, the earth, reflects the vastness of the sky, all creation and human beings reflect God. We drink God from the reflections of God.

Discovering God, reflecting on God is prelude to simply acknowledging that God is, or could be as much part of our lives as the air we breathe, greater than the sky, even though God, unlike the sky can only be seen in reflected beauty.

Eventually, we must try to talk about our thoughts and experiences of God with words. How we talk about God matters and influences how we see our world. We experience God not only personally, but in community because we are social beings.

Though we all talk about God from our perspectives in place and time, God does not belong to any one person or group of people in any time or place. God is the God of ages, whom people have experienced in every time throughout the world. God is the God of ancients and the One who is constantly making all things new in every age.

As we speak of God, we will speak of the God who is worshipped in Judaism and more particularly, in Christianity, and then in Islam.

GOD IN SCRIPTURE

In both Judaism and Christianity, we lean heavily on Scripture for an understanding of God's embodiment in time and history. Stepping into Scripture is like stepping into a stream that reflects God.

In the Hebrew Bible, we witness the development of a religion that worships God as One. God, who is One God, is established in the face of other religions who worshipped many gods and rulers who were considered gods.

In that Scripture, we move from the creation stories and the formation of the first woman and man to the growth of families and tribes who worship this One God. We come to know a God who is in a covenantal relationship with a people chosen to establish a religious community. Their history tells of a peoples' relationship with this one God as it unfolds and evolves in the pages of the Bible.

The Israelites found ways to talk about and with God as they experienced God in worship, in their culture and rituals, and in their history. For Christians, the Jesus story is a continuation of their story to which is added the culture and history of Gentiles who joined the Jewish followers of Jesus as the early church was born.

In trying to speak about who God is in this book, we begin with the naming of God and trace the evolution of God in a people's lives as it is recorded in the stories, psalms, prophecies and wisdom of the Hebrew Bible. That is where the testimony begins for both Jews and Christians.

A brief review of ways of naming God introduces us to the beginning of the foundations of the Jewish Faith and of Christianity.

NAMING GOD AS ONE

The Hebrew Bible, known by many Christians as the Old Testament, was first handed down through oral tradition and then committed to writings that were eventually gathered and codified as Scripture.

The early God of the Israelites was monolatrous, that is, the true God among many gods. This was a change from the worship of a pantheon of gods in earlier cultures in the Middle East. Elohim, a plural name for God, sometimes translated as "they" was an early name for God.

Over time, the Hebrew people began to worship a monotheistic God, One God, before whom there were no other gods. When Moses, who was called by God to lead the Hebrew people out of slavery in Egypt, asked what he should call the Holy One, the answer came, "I am who I am." (Exod. 3:14) Some translate, "I am who I am becoming."

A four-letter name for God, YHWH, emerged that reflects the sheer beingness of God, the holiness, the one whose name must be held in awe. In the Hebrew language, only consonants are printed, vowels, when used are marks above them. Without vowels, these letters are not pronounceable. God's name was so holy it could not be pronounced.

Over time, YHWH came to be pronounced as Yahweh and eventually was transformed to Adonai, Lord, or Lord God.

God was also known by the Israelites, as the God of the ancestors, of Abraham, Isaac, and Jacob. God in history. God of blood line. God in a covenantal relationship with a people.

In addition to names for God, there are countless images and metaphors and stories in Scripture that speak of who God is. They communicate attributes of God's nature and through verbs, the nature of God's action in the world.

Metaphors such as Shepherd, Rock, Almighty, Redeemer, Holy One, Sovereign, Maker, Father, King, Lord, Mother Hen, are all examples of ways of seeing and naming God in Scripture that have survived until modern times. In new ages we can expect to add new images.

The Hebrew people saw God's self-revelation in dynamic interaction with them. God speaks, appears in dreams, is present in a guiding cloud, and in a burning bush that is not consumed.

Running through Scripture are threads that point to God's nature. God is Being, God is Mystery, God is Sovereign, God is Righteous, God is Just, God is Great. God who is transcendent is in relationship with creation and in that relationship, God is loving, righteous, just, steadfast, merciful, faithful, and sometimes angry and wrathful.

God is creator and creating energy. God is righteous and has built morality into the bones of the human world. Through the ages, ancient adjectives and verb phrases have been used and new ones appear that reflect these attributes.

Names, metaphors, verbs, and adjectives for God matter. They are suggestive of how those who use them see the Divine, themselves, and the world. They influence how people relate to the world around them. With words, Scripture points to both experiences of the Holy even as we know that the Holy One lies beyond words and naming.

As times change, God 's interaction with his people changes to meet their needs and evolving realities, speaking to and within them. At other times, God's revelation transcends human cultural and historic limitations. Divine revelation is always mediated by human beings, "earthen vessels" as Scripture, at one point, refers to humanity.

Of course, God can be experienced in more than words. God can be experienced in worship and art, in music and dance. God is known in hearts and spirits as well as in minds. A people's expression of faith has depth, intensity, and artistry.

Physical places are created for the worship of God. At first, the worship of God centered around stone altars and later, the Ark of the Covenant, and then the Temple and synagogues. Each tell their stories about people's connection to God in covenantal community.

As the religion of the Hebrew people develops through thousands of years, the fundamental testimony of Scripture is that God is real, is being, is an energy persisting through time in relationship with beloved creation. God is a living relational, dynamic, force for good.

God who wills life for creation, sets the ethical boundaries of creation. When followed, these boundaries lead to life. Pushing against those boundaries or defying them and the God who set them in place leads to tragedy, violation of creation, and destruction.

THE EMERGENCE OF A RELIGION

Naming God, and a people's evolution in faith, take form together. Faith is lived and recounted in stories, rituals, laws and rules, poetry, history, prophesy, wisdom which are recorded in the Hebrew Bible and continue in religious observance.

As we seek to understand how God is seen and worshipped in the Christian tradition that centers on Jesus, we turn to his Jewish roots and the Scriptures he studied and knew so well, which formed him.

The Hebrew Bible begins with two creation stories in Genesis and goes on to describe the emergence of generations, tribes and nations who populate the earth.

Early in Genesis, after the second creation story and Adam and Eve's life in the Garden of Eden and then their fall from Paradise by defying God and coming to know good and evil, there is another less known account of how the human race comes into being and falls from God's grace. The "sons of God and the daughters of human beings" unite. This leads to moral problems and God sees the sickness of humanity and the evil in their hearts. (Genesis 6)

What follows is the often-told story of the flood and Noah's survival. God despairs over evil in the world and seeks a new beginning for creation. God wipes out every living creature on earth but saves Noah, his family, and two of all other animals.

When the flood is over, the arc of a rainbow appears, and dry land is found, Noah builds an altar and offers burnt offerings to God. God promises to never destroy the earth again. God says,

> *I will never again curse the ground because of humankind because the inclination of the human heart is evil from youth; nor will I never again destroy every living creature as I have done.*
> *As long as the earth endures,*
> *seedtime and harvest, cold and heat,*
> *summer and winter, day and night*
> *shall not cease.* Genesis 8:21b-22

It is in these great mythic stories that the reality of a people's experience of God in relation to themselves and the world around them is expressed.

As the Biblical story continues, God calls a people to be in a new covenant with him, beginning with a call to Abram and Sarai his wife. God calls Abram, Sarai his wife, along with their whole extended familial and servant network, to set out on a journey of faith. Abram responds in faith and his name is changed to Abraham. It is the beginning of a new era. God vows to give him a promised land.

Abraham and Sarah have a son, Isaac, after she has passed her childbearing years. Before Isaac is born, Hagar, Sarah's servant bears a child by Abraham who is named Ishmael. After some complex family dynamics, Hagar and Ishmael are sent away, out into the dessert, but with God's protection and promise that Ishmael would be father of another great nation.

In their time, Isaac and his wife, Rebekah, gave birth to Jacob and Esau. Their stories and those of their offspring are filled with human emotion and intrigue. Their family history reads like a novel.

God is known through these stories as the God of Abraham, Isaac, and Jacob. The God of the ancestors. The stories of the patriarchs and their wives eventually lead to Moses and the complex story of the Hebrew people's relationship with Egypt. It is a long story. At first, they are saved from famine by one of their own, Joseph, who is adopted by Pharoah's daughter. After a time and a change in Egyptian rulers, they become an enslaved people.

God, acting through Moses, liberates them from slavery and leads them in an exodus from Egypt to freedom. God is their liberator.

The Israelites are on their way to becoming a people and Scripture has been tracing the birth of a religion. The Israelites, under the leadership of Moses, are given the Ten Commandments, and these solidify them as a faith community. God is there in these Ten Words. God is giver of Divine Law.

After their escape from Egypt, they journey through the wilderness for forty years to a new land and their history moves on. We recount these stories of the early years of the Hebrew people's relationship with their God because they are so important to all that follows and the Ten Commandments, made in covenant with them, are central to their faith and to the faith that follows.

TIMELESS TRUTHS AND TEMPORAL TEACHINGS

The Ten Commandments have stood the test of time in Judaism and Christianity and offer insight into the nature of God and human nature. The Hebrew people were becoming a people in a new way after their escape from slavery in Egypt. They were given the Ten Words by which to live faithfully in relation to God, and peaceably together with each other as they moved into the future.

Through time, those commandments have remained relevant as a guide for religious and social behavior. They were honored by Jesus. They are very general, and though they need to be interpreted afresh in each age, their moral insights provide a moral, social and personal foundation. The Commandments that applied originally to the Hebrew people and resonated with some of the moral laws in societies around them had significance for Christians as the church emerged. They are a guide to the moral bones of creation, religiously speaking.

The God who wills good for humanity gave laws for living in social community that set boundaries essential for humanity's and creation's survival. They make common sense.

The first four Commandments that have to do with humanity's relationship with God are specific to religion but have implications for the wider social order. They point to the fact that loyalty to the Holy is meant to be above all human loyalty and be held as sacred. They assume that the Holy alone can be trusted with unconditional love. A Power that transcends any human power at any given time is meant to protect people from anyone or any group or any obsession that would claim absolute control over life. It makes clear the danger of idolatry.

"I am the Lord your God who brought you out of the land of Egypt, out of the house of slavery; you shall have no other gods before me." Exodus 20:2

The Commandments, like the Creation Stories, describe God as setting the boundaries in creation, in relation to God and to human society. In the beginning, the commandments applied only to free Jewish men. Over time that was challenged. It was challenged by Jesus. They came to apply in the Christian tradition equally to men and women, free and slave, Jew and Gentile. And they were not to be worshipped for themselves but were created for the good of humanity.

In the Bible, the Ten Commandments are followed by specific purity and ritual laws. A reading of these shows that while observance of some of them can be an important part of communal religious identity through time, others are impossible to keep in changing times and places.

The ritual and purity laws set forth in the Hebrew Bible provide an insight into how religions and societies can be both unchanging and changing over time. Rituals can help bind a people together and provide a way to express faith.

Purity laws need to change over time. They can become inhumane as eras evolve and can lead to problematic ideas about God and harmful treatment of people. For instance, in early Hebrew laws there are rules that allow parents to kill children for disobeying them and rules that isolate women during menstruation and rules that call for the stoning of women for adultery or men for blasphemy. The purity laws are found in Leviticus.

The written word reveals both the culture of a people and the evolution of their faith, their universal insights that transcend time and temporary rules.

Commandments, to be effective, need to be honored. God directs the appointment of leaders who judge people on the keeping of the law. These leaders are to be just and impartial and shall not accept bribes. God remains the ultimate judge.

GOD RELATES TO PEOPLE IN TIME

From the first five books of the Bible that establish the religion of the Israelites flow books of history, poetry, story, prophesy, and wisdom--a rich collection of thirty-nine books that cover centuries.

As God and people interact in Scripture, insights about God and human nature unfold side-by-side, both are evolving, both have timeless elements as well as elements confined to certain times.

In Scripture, we are introduced to Divine qualities already mentioned, such as timelessness, faithfulness, righteousness, justice, mercy, wisdom, sovereignty, and power. We have spoken of God as Liberator and Law Giver. God is also described as Warrior, a violent actor in history who engages in battle on behalf of the Israelites.

Over time, conflict arises over how human beings see and speak of God. God's self-revelation is ongoing and emerges out of the times and places in which people live. It is understandable that the ways people have of describing God often mimic human qualities and emotions. There are times when perceptions of God transcend human limitations, times when people can hear God through and beyond the social givens of time.

In the pages of the Hebrew Bible, God raises up great leaders from Moses to the Prophets. God lifts up Judges, Priests, Prophets, and Kings. These leaders emerge, each with their own strengths and Achilles' heels. God engages with them, sometimes directly, sometimes through angels or through other human beings.

King David is a central figure in the history of Israel's journey with God. It is through David that a golden era in their history takes place. David, who begins as a shepherd boy, becomes a kind of Messianic King. The restoration of David's Kingdom becomes a national dream.

Even great leaders, like David, who accomplish great feats, have times when they go astray. Biblical stories are complex, psychologically intriguing, and revealing of God's faithful relationship with humanity through all circumstances and seasons.

Through both great and corrupt leaders, history unwinds, the present is judged, and the future unfolds. The Kingdom divides into Israel and Judah; each is eventually carried off into exile. Judah eventually returns to Jerusalem.

God's faithfulness through time is established, and the Hebrew people and their leaders face the temptation of worshipping other gods and idols. The prophets call them back to worship their God, to whom Scripture bears witness. While the people are sometimes faithful and sometimes rebellious, God remains faithful and offers hope for the future.

THE REALITY OF ERAS

Scripture is set in an era when "land and blood" defined history and the people living it. It is set in patriarchal and authoritarian times when slavery and the violence of war and brutal punishments for breaking laws were assumed and unchallenged.

In those times, God is referred to mostly with masculine pronouns and is in places seen as intervening in violent ways in history with an avenging and punishing spirit. God is seen as intervening in national conflicts, giving and taking land, and either causing or requiring the death of the enemy.

In early Scriptural times, God who calls a particular people engages in coming to their aid and providing for them. God engages in battles between his people and other nations, between their gods and the God of the Hebrews. The God of the Hebrew people both fights for them and demands faithfulness from them. And God calls upon them to visit death on their enemies. We can see in God the reflections of early society's worldview and resulting behaviors, some of which are not unfamiliar today.

For example, in one story there is a contest between the priests of Baal and the priests of Yahweh to find out who is the real God. They each set up a sacrificial altar and call their God to send down fire. Only Yahweh sends fire. Unable to call down fire from the heavens, the priests of Baal are driven off to the river and said to be slain by Yahweh. When we tell this story today, we usually stop short of the drowning of the priests of Baal.

Behind this story is the struggle of the Hebrew people to worship God as One surrounded by cultures who worshipped a pantheon of gods. Even though God is, over time, revealed in Scripture as righteous, just and merciful, concerned even for the enemy, in this early story, God is depicted as killing the enemy. While that is not the story's main point, it depicts a God who, being written about in violent times, takes on the characteristics and behaviors of the times.

As centuries move on, the people's perception of God evolves. The people are divided, they end up in exile. God cannot save them. But, over time, there is reconciliation and promise. The fact that God is involved with creation remains constant though it takes on a new character. God is always "doing a new thing."

As has been noted, the Hebrew Bible takes place over many centuries. Society changes over those centuries. The Hebrew people's perceptions of God evolve with the changing circumstances of historic eras. Life is in motion.

As we think and read about God in Scripture, we can be aware of how much cultural times and human nature effect perceptions of the

Divine. All religious communities and all people have a time bound existence that affects their view of the world, God's activity in it, and their ability to experience God. They also have the capacity at luminous times, to experience God beyond time and space.

Even though all human perceptions of God are imperfect, the Spirit can give insights that transcend human cultural limitations even while speaking directly to those cultures.

Over time, perceptions of God as recorded in Scripture begin to move away from a warrior God to a God who is less violent and wills peace. And God's mercy begins to shine through God's wrath. God is Merciful.

There are stories where God desires to save the enemy. One story that shows God as a merciful God comes to life in the somewhat humorous and unique story of Jonah who tries to run from God rather than prophesy to save the city of Nineveh, a perceived enemy of his people. God is asking Jonah to call them to repentance and salvation. Jonah has no desire to save the enemy. He ends up in the body of a whale who spits him out on the shores of Nineveh. Jonah is saved, God prevails, Jonah preaches, and the people of Nineveh choose life and are saved. God is gracious. Jonah pouts.

In the Jonah story, God pursues a leader from his chosen people to bring about change for the good even in the enemy.

This fanciful story tells a timeless truth about how the God of the Hebrew people cares about the salvation of another people, the Ninevites. Here, God is God of all creation, is impartial.

In religions there is an ongoing dialogue between the practices of a specific religion and its traditions, and the call to honor the God of all creation. From the particular, the universal evolves and vice-versa. The Hebrew people become carriers of God's presence in the world.

Through human being's developing understanding of who God is, and who people are meant to be, glimpses of eternal truths break through. Scripture tells an evolving story of the relationship between God and humanity.

Just because our human understanding of God is evolving does not take away the wonder of meeting God where we are. It enables human beings to learn from the past without idealizing it.

In Scripture, we find many different perceptions of who God is and how God acts in the world over centuries. These changing perceptions in no way need to negate a people's faith in God or suggest that God is made up by human minds. It simply means that the world is changing and that affects our relationship with God. As the world changes, God is creating still.

As our perceptions of God change, some things that God is not become clearer.

THE GOD OF THE PROPHETS

Over time, prophets emerged in the Hebrew Bible who were led by God to call people back to the God whom they had forsaken for the false idols they had turned to in exile. Prophets proclaimed God to be a God of righteousness and justice, a God of mercy and grace, who calls people to have hope and practice the social justice that is indispensable to their faith. Prophets began to see a God who wills peace.

> *God 'shall judge between many peoples,*
> *and shall arbitrate between strong nations far away.*
> *they shall beat their swords into plowshares and their spears*
> *into pruninghooks,*
> *nation shall not lift up sword against nation,*
> *neither shall they learn war anymore.*
> *They shall each sit under their own vines and fig trees,*
> *And no one shall make them afraid, For the mouth of the*
> *Lord of hosts has spoken.* Micah 4:3-4

The God who destroys the enemy fades into the background. God is a God of mercy and peace. God is still a righteous God and just, but vengefulness is not at the heart of God's being. God calls people back to life from the pursuit of all things that corrupt the heart.

God beyond human understanding is engaged in the real and complicated life of humanity and their lived history. God wills creation's good. God comes with salvation in hand to overcome all that leads to destruction. God breathes life into creation and is in creation, again and always. It is up to the people to choose the way of life or the way of death.

What becomes clear in the prophets is that there are some ways of worshipping that are not of God, which are destructive. Idolatry was a key concern in the Hebrew Bible.

The prophets lead away from some ancient ways of seeing God toward emerging revelation. Today, we can with the prophets turn toward a God of righteousness and justice who does not condone violence. We can no longer ignore destruction once perceived as an act of God: the flood that destroyed the earth, death of innocent first-born Egyptian children because Pharoah would not let God's people go. Any killing of enemies at the instruction of God is not of God. Those were human interpretations of events and an understanding of God born of earlier times and contexts.

We cannot rewrite Scripture, but we can interpret it. We can acknowledge that our human understanding of God evolves. While God is always more than we can comprehend or name, as society changes some things that God cannot be, and human beings cannot claim God to be and survive, become clear.

While God's being is constant, God in relationship with creation is in motion. We cannot say that God was never perceived as a warrior, but we can simply acknowledge that God as the God who loves all creation and wills its survival is a God of peace and not destruction. Our perceptions of God reflect our changing consciousness which evolves as eras change. Self-revelations of God emerge as we can comprehend them.

While human reason has trouble imagining a God both just and merciful. God has no trouble being both just and compassionate. God's love embraces life and gives life, even in the face of death and evil. And God desires steadfast love from God's people.

Animal sacrifice for the sins of the people was once practiced to atone for sins and as peace offerings to God. Eventually the practice of animal sacrifice was abandoned. God desired the sacrifice of contrite hearts and a seeking after divine knowledge.

> *I have hewn them by the prophets,*
> *I have killed them by the words of my mouth,*
> *and my judgment goes forth as the light.*
> *For I desire steadfast love and not sacrifice,*
> *the knowledge of God and not sacrifice.* Hosea 6:5,6

Over time, perceptions tilt away from a punishing God to a God who forgives and calls people to forgive as they are forgiven. The admonition to do to others as one would have them do to you. It doesn't admonish people to do to others as they have done to them. Take revenge.

The movement toward God's mercy and forgiveness in no way implies that sin does not have consequences. The consequences are seen as lying in the very order of creation. When foundational moral laws are broken, destruction in some form is inevitable

The Biblical testimony is that if you kill someone or break other commandments, there is great suffering which spreads like a ripple through the water. The process of breaking the spiraling effect of sin is in people's hands. Sin calls for repentance, reconciliation, reform, and grace which God longs for and enables.

Prophets speak through time of the things that lead to life. They call people back from the brink, restoring life after great harm is done. They attempt to stem movement toward harm. It is God who calls the prophets to their mission. God's Spirit and human beings acting in concert together can move in hope toward a redeemed future.

Old ways of seeing the world and God persist or are glossed over, even as new ways emerge. Clinging to old ways in new times is not harmless. At the same time, the good and transcendent in old ways can be preserved. Liberation from slavery, as expressed in the Hebrew people's flight from Egypt can be celebrated even as the deaths of innocent Egyptian children in the process need to be mourned. The means were a problem.

Throughout history the issue of ends and means is in play in relation to God and God's people. The evolving realization is that life-giving ends must be achieved through means that do not violate life. Ethics applies to means as well as ends, goodness and justice are in the process as well as the objective. God's goodness pervades both process and ends.

WHEN HUMAN BEINGS ARE A GOD PROBLEM

As history moves and humanity's context and consciousness changes, our understanding of God's being and actions can shift. While human consciousness shifts, there are some human traits that show up in Scripture that seem to persist through time that make changes in religious understanding difficult. Changes in consciousness are slow and selective as one era emerges from another.

While the concept of a warrior and punishing God could seems archaic today, modern culture has made violence a form of entertainment and human wars continue to be waged, a militant and vengeful God seems natural. It is a human problem, not a God problem. Human sin distorts our perceptions of God. That was true in Biblical times and is true today. Scripture gives us insights into humanity as well as Divinity.

Human traits such as a need for power, a fear of helplessness, and a need for an all-powerful force beyond us, political or spiritual, seem to call for an all-powerful people along with an all-controlling God. An all-powerful God was in the minds of those who wrote parts of the Hebrew Bible eons ago. The concept survives in the minds of some present-day believers as well.

In times of trouble and need, we call upon God for help and want God to save us. We want God's power to come to our aid. If we cannot be all powerful, at least we can have a God who is. If God does not meet our expectations, we seek leaders endowed with God's perceived omnipotence. We want to slay the enemy. We make idols of wealth, power, or ideologies. At times, we are trapped by oppression and disasters.

We confuse power over and power with. We assume powerlessness is the alternative to power over others leaving one feeling hopeless, helpless, or victimized. Over time, God is a God who desires power to be shared and used for humanity's good.

There can be great strength without dominating power, but we must imagine it and want it. Assuming that God is all powerful in human affairs can be a problem of human perception and not a God problem. God is, of course, greater than any human force on earth, *beyond* as well as *in* our material realm. But that does not equate with having absolute power in human affairs in the world.

Time after time, human beings go astray in Scripture, are blind to their own sin, are unable to cope, and act in ways that sabotage their own good or harm others. God does not abandon them but calls them out and calls them back to living with integrity.

A human trait that persists through time that is often prelude to destructive behavior is the desire to be better than others, to lord it over others, a desire for supremacy often fueled by a sense of or fear of inferiority. Prejudice toward "the other," rubs off. This trait causes us to need a God who makes us better than others, makes us right, and the only carriers of the truth, the chosen, or the saved and elect. There is a difference between being chosen by God for a special mission or just cause and being Gid's one and only recipients of truth and salvation.

The pursuit of idols who satisfy instant desires or confirm that which we want to believe, or help us fit in with the society around us. We want a God who makes life easy, and stays put in time. In Scripture we find a God who is always faithful yet changing to meet the needs of evolving time. A creative, ever creating God.

Once oppressive forces take hold in life, it is often hard to find ways to get out from under injustice and ward off tyrants without resorting to force. Life becomes complicated and unmanageable. Non-violent resistance has been one path to change embraced by those who understand God as non-violent.

We know that violence leads to violence. God's Spirit is always at work on behalf of peace and protecting life. It needs to work through wise and sane minds and hearts.

God is a presence who is with us as we confront our demons, our temptations, evil. We can find hope and strength in the Spirit of God. There are destructive hierarchies to be foiled, hearts to be saved, vision to be cleared, truth to be told, bodies to be healed, mouths to be fed, creation to be protected, prisoners to be released, discriminations to be turned around. And ordinary lives to be lived.

Beyond issues of power, competition, violence, and greed, there is beauty to be enjoyed, playful spirits to be set free, and love to be shared.

The seeds of goodness in life are planted by God from the beginning, by a God who is just, righteous, and impartial even though calling certain groups of people to carry new revelations in the midst of social change.

There are human traits, such as compassion, a longing for justice, and pursuit of mercy that exist in humanity and survive through time and when nurtured by God's Spirit can develop through time and enhance our relationship with and understanding of God along with our self-understanding.

All our human traits, life affirming and destructive, are expressed in our communal as well as our personal lives. These traits compete for a place in our worldviews and value systems, and in our actions in religious and secular communities.

While in Judaism and Christianity, the fact of God's existence is a given, perceptions of who that God is varies within these traditions. Our understanding of God's changelessness needs to be accompanied with the understanding that God moves with humanity through time.

We cry out, "Will the real God please show up!" "Will the holy human appear?"

God's reply to Moses," I am who I am becoming," can be God's word to us as we reach out for God. And with the Psalmist, we can, in praising God, catch a vision of God's love and our own capacity for worship.

Psalm 145

I will extol you, my God and Sovereign,
And bless your name forever and forever.
Every day, I will bless you,
And praise your name forever and ever.
Great you are, and greatly to be praised.
God's greatness is unsearchable.
One generation shall laud your works to another,
And shall declare your mighty acts.
On the glorious splendor of your majesty,
And on your wondrous works I will meditate. (Verses 1-5)
God is gracious and merciful,
slow to anger and abounding in steadfast love.
God is good to all,
Whose compassion is on all God has made.

GOD THROUGHOUT TIME

The God of ancient peoples is the same God who is worshipped today, and is perhaps, more multifaceted.

The God who is the "Rock of Ages," is also the God who is making all things new. The God who is a God of righteousness is also a God of beauty. The God who never sleeps celebrates Sabbath. The God, who is Spirit, honors and enjoys that which is material, of the earth. The God whose creating work is never done is also a playful God. The God who is worshipped in religious communities is also the God of secular culture.

The door to God opens to generation after generation as ages unfold. There are always things to discover about God from the past and new insights to embrace in the present.

As human scientific and cultural knowledge develop and political and economic boundaries shift, and creation unfolds, God's Spirit is alive and active. Every year we are discovering more about the incomprehensibly great universe. It is hard to imagine where heaven is now, or God.

We know that heaven is more a metaphor than a physical place and God is alive in this world as well as, somehow, beyond or in the vast universe. Hell could be as much a state of being as a place in the underworld. Sometimes, hell seems to be on earth.

Like the people of the Hebrew Bible, when we speak of God with us, we want God to be personal, to relate directly with us, to hear us when we pray. Wherever in the beyond God is, God's dwelling place is also with creation, with each of us in this small planet of ours.

The Hebrew people in Scripture dreamt that one day, people would love God with heart, mind, and soul, and God's way would be written in human hearts.

> *This is the covenant that I will make with the house of Israel after those days, says the Lord; I will put my law within them, and I will write it on their hearts; and I will be their God, and they shall be my people. No longer shall they teach one another, or say to each other, know the Lord, for they shall all know me, from the least of them to the greatest, says the Lord; for I will forgive their iniquity, and remember their sin no more.* Jeremiah 31:33, 34

Having the law written in human hearts does not imply that then there will be no need for God. It implies the opposite, God and humanity will be one and able to work together in harmony for the good of creation, joined in the creative process.

God's free Spirit is calling us to liberate the God of our too-broken hearts and too-small dreams and open ourselves to the Holy Spirit. We have been assured repeatedly; we are loved by real God. God's love is real. Isaiah catches a vision of the possibilities of joy and peace when creation is in harmony with God.

> *For you shall go out in joy,*
> *And be led forth in peace.*

The mountains and the hills before you
Shall burst into joy.
And all the trees of the field shall
Clap their hands. Isaiah 55:12

We are not ever called to remake our image of God to conform to modern patterns and philosophies of thought. We are called upon to catch Isaiah's vision for our own time and seek the God who wills it: "to be led forth in joy and go out in peace."

Those who responded to God's call-in ancient times are succeeded by people of faith in modern times who, responding to God, can discover, work toward, and share more abundant life. People, each in their own era, will see God differently, and yet it is the same God they honor. And people around the world, each in their own way, will respond to God in the context of God's call to them.

We are all challenged to add new metaphors to time-honored ones, or uncover images ignored by history and long forgotten and thereby serve all humanity.

This is a lot of God talk. Sometimes, God-thought is too much for our human minds and hearts to deal with and we just want to avoid it. When that happens, we can take a breath or a break from God. God will call us back.

GOD'S UNIVERSALITY

God was perceived by the Hebrew people as their God and they saw themselves as God's chosen people, God's particular people. Over time, three other major monotheistic religions developed, Christianity, Islam, and the Baha'i Faith and before them was Zoroastrianism.

Each in turn saw themselves as chosen of God. Christians often see themselves as God's elect, saved by faith in Jesus Christ. Muslims see Mohammed as the ultimate prophet and the Qur'an as God's Word. Those in the Baha'i Faith, who recognize all religions as valid see themselves as possessing an ultimate revelation. Each in their own way believes themselves to have the truth about the Divine. Which would be fine if we could take out the little word "the." Each has truth and truths.

These monotheistic faiths, even when they see themselves as having true revelation, believe God to be the God of all creation. There is an inevitable tension between a people's belief that God has a unique relationship with them and yet cares about all creation. The problem often gets solved by offering a way for others to join one's own faith.

In these differing faith traditions, and Eastern religions we have not spoken about, religion developed in a geographical place at a particular time. Each tradition grows out of its context and has its own truths to share. God, while choosing some people for a special mission, loves all humanity.

Different peoples could find God in their own vernacular. And when those nations close to each other were fighting over power, God could be coopted to lead in battle on behalf of opposing regional forces who saw God as on their side.

As faith groups spread throughout the world, their reach expanded and so did their encounter with other religions. And political systems and nations rose and fell. Now we are realizing that the world is interconnected, the universality of God is an essential attribute of the Holy that needs to be taken seriously. Religious arrogance and discrimination are practiced at humanity's peril.

Religious communities, regional in origin and specific in time, tend to immigrate to new places for a variety of reasons. As religions expand geographically, their particularity faces new challenges and other religions. They also face internal conflicts and external secularism.

The major monotheistic religions including Judaism and Christianity developed in the Middle East at a time when their cultures were isolated from distant cultures. That is no longer true.

Once religions live side-be-side, it is harder to coexist when people believe they are the only chosen of God, the only saved, the only ones possessing the truth.

Where one religion seeks to be dominant in a nation, that leads to the question of whether they are worshipping a political, partisan, nationalistic or institutional version of God.

As the world becomes smaller, it becomes clearer that a Holy Presence does not give or take land or show favoritism to some peoples or build nations. It is simply hard for religious people to believe that what they believe about God is true without believing it is the whole truth about God. Sometimes ethnic identity trumps religious identity and the problem of being chosen or even victimized exists in a non-religious form.

Since God's fullness is beyond human knowledge, God cannot be limited by any religious or ethnic group that claims to have received God's favor in ways that give them the rights of privilege and power.

Religions can believe that God has revealed and continues to reveal God's very self and will to them without violating other people's claim that God has also revealed God's self to them. But it is not easy. We need to liberate God from our parochialisms while embracing our own truths. Would it be unrealistic to explore ways in which our different perceptions of God are of the same God?

As religions continue through time, they take on institutional form and institutions began to define faith and at times merge with secular powers. It becomes possible for religious faith identities to yield to purely cultural identities. How does one separate religious truths from political agendas when they merge?

Or when a religion becomes a cultural identity, how do you find the religion? One could be Roman Catholic, lapsed in faith, or Jewish without religious belief, or Protestant by birth and agnostic by faith. This complicates loyalties and identities. This complicates the religious landscape. And our understanding of what we mean by God.

Of course, all religious organizations have their view of faith and of God's revelation and relation to them. And all religious organizations have internal divisions. All religions have a range of conservative and liberal expressions, and a variety of institutional forms, often, with each group claiming ultimate or ethical truth.

When religious expressions become exclusive, militant, nationalistic, and discriminatory or predatory, they fly in the face of any claim that they worship a God who is righteous, just, and loves creation.

On the other hand, when religion becomes a matter of individual spirituality apart from any institutional identity, it loses its call to effect change in the world for good even though individuals can act out their ethical imperatives. Individual spirituality loses the mosaic of insight that comes from participating in religious communities where the exchange of ideas enriches, deepens and even challenges our understanding of God.

God can be, and always will be, worshipped by different religious bodies and their believers and denied by others. It is essential to remember that God is beyond all human knowing and all religious institutions, and Divine revelation takes place in and speaks to people in particular geographical settings and times.

If God is truly God, God must be God of all humanity. And before God, we must all be of equal worth. Yet, there are those who see God as creating a hierarchy of human value. This flies in the face of the belief that before God we are all more alike than different even if we have different visions of God and a wild variety of human identities.

GOD OF PARTICULARITY

With the universality of God in mind, different expressions of faith can enrich the whole and contribute to the beauty and inclusivity of a God who is freed from the suffocating claims of groups who see God as existing only in their belief systems. A God who calls to the diversity and depth of all creation.

In the course of time, God has visited humankind and individuals and groups within it, with insights and wisdom, with focused love and specific calls. In his book, "My Faith as an African," Jean-Marc Ela speaks of the need for faith to speak a word of liberation to Africans that gives hope in their context and vernacular, shedding the arrogance of colonial powers on religious expression in Africa.

In this Chapter we have been speaking of the God of the Jewish people who became the God of Christians. Within Judaism and Christianity are all types of people in many nations.

God's word needs to speak to people where they are: be it to Africans or Central Americans developing liberation theology, people of diverse sexual orientations seeking acceptance in religious community, people pursuing feminist, womanist, or Black theology, All are seeking to bring the church into the present so it can live into the future: all people seeking freedom from violence in its many forms, in search of theologies of peace that give life.

God's word comes to those abusing the human rights of others in the name of God, imploring them to listen, reform and stand down.

Universal and particular revelations of God go hand-in-hand. God needs to be set free from our limited human perspectives to show us our commonalities. God Most Merciful is with all of creation and each part of creation in its unique expressions. God's Spirit is loose in the whole wide world.

We do not worship God in general. We worship God in the context of one faith or another. We worship as individuals in community. We claim faith as our own and try to understand it in depth. From that personal place, we can honor everyone's right to do the same and offer them the respect we want for ourselves.

In Part 2, we go on to look at the God of the Hebrew people in the context of Christianity.

PART 2
A CHRISTIAN UNDERSTANDING OF ONE GOD: BEGINNING WITH THE FIRST PERSON OF THE TRINITY

As the early church evolved and Jews and Gentiles came together to form communities of faith, they began to see Jesus as not only from God, but as one with God. And they experienced the Holy Spirit as the empowering energy of the risen Christ. This laid the groundwork for the eventual development of the doctrine of the Trinity which we spoke about in the previous chapter.

Once Jesus Christ was seen as part of the Godhead and the Spirit became prominent in the life of Christians, God had to have a special identity as the "first person of the Trinity." In that context, God was often spoken of as God the Creator and God the Father. It is to these two expressions for God that we now turn our attention.

As we go on to explore God as Creator and Father, it is important to remember that Christians see that God is One. The Trinity is the way of recognizing Jesus Christ and the Spirit as Divine. The Trinity is not a mathematical formula it is a creative way of expressing anew God's real presence, God's self-revelation that is ongoing. There is wisdom in the ancient belief that God can be manifest in all of creation.

GOD THE CREATOR

In the beginning, God created...
So begins Genesis, the first book of the Bible.
"I believe in God the Father, Creator of heaven and earth…"
So begins the Apostles Creed. *

From ancient times until today, God as Creator has been an image that is a cornerstone of faith. Speaking of God as Creator we mean that God existed and exists beyond time and space and was before all things were. God created ex-nihilo, out of nothing. God called all things into being.

Scripture says that God brought about our material world, which, though finite and limited, is in relationship with an unseen reality beyond it. Humanity is created to have a longing for that which is greater than itself, for the Source, for the One, for the deep unknown in whose image we are created, who is our home. That transcendent One has an ongoing love for and relationship with creation. Humanity, though created to be in relationship with God, can also see itself as having no need for God. The tension is there.

When speaking of God as Creator today, it is in the context of our knowing about evolution and how slowly over billions of years the world developed. People as we know them did not come along until about 250,000 years ago. While some still resist the concept of evolution, it is an accepted scientific fact, though details are still being worked out. Evolution reminds us that creation continues through time. It is hard to imagine creation taking place over billions of years. The Psalmist says, "A thousand ages in thy sight are like an evening gone." Make that "a billion ages in thy sight."

Almost all religions have some version of a creation story through which they describe how they see creation, and humankind coming into being from a faith perspective. Scientists talk about the beginning of our created order from a distinct perspective. They deal with observable or discoverable material reality. Facts and probability.

Religions and sciences give us different lenses through which to look at the beginning of our world. Both religion and science help us reflect about life on earth and tell us something about who we are.

Of course, there can be no physical proof of a Divine Force at the earth's beginning. What people of faith believe is that the God who transcends time and space relates to us in time and space, is a creating relational power. There are no explainable details.

Because the creation stories in the Bible are myths, their authors are able to paint a big picture about how they see God and the world at its beginnings from the perspective of how they were experiencing life in the present. They were recording their beliefs. They had a poetic vision. They believed in a force they called Elohim or Yahweh whom English speakers call God today.

What is most important is that the writers of the creation stories saw themselves, and all of creation as connected to God. They saw God as creating the world as good, and God as a moral force. They saw themselves in Adam and Eve, everyone having common ancestors. They saw themselves in God's image. They saw themselves as stewards of creation. They also saw themselves as capable of defying God's intended order and God. And they saw God as never abandoning creation as humanity came of age.

All these years later, we ask ourselves if we can see the world as they saw it. Can we believe in a moral order and the connection between God and humanity? Can we believe in ongoing creation and revelation? Can we see goodness in creation and see ourselves in God's image even though, like Eve and Adam we lost paradise long ago?

When our granddaughter, Lenora, was five, we were walking from her house to the church a half-a-block away. I was holding her hand. She looked up at me and said, "Gram, I believe in God, but I don't believe God created the world." Her statement came out of the blue. She was, at that early age, trying to reconcile faith and science.

At five, Lenora was on to something. She just knew that she could believe in God even if God did not create the world in a material sense. Her parents are scientists. Of course, she knew about evolution. In hindsight, I am amazed by her leap of faith. "I believe in God, but I don't believe that God created the world."

We can indeed believe in God without being able to understand God as creating the world through billions of years. Who can even imagine billions of years, yet alone, a time before time. Some of us may have to settle for seeing God as a creating power, acting in time, caring about creation and admit that that is what matters to us, whatever happened at the beginning. Though the unfolding of creation is awe inspiring.

God at home in creation. Alyssa Blain Kepler

There was a period when religious institutions saw science as a threat to religion. Today, religion and science can be seen as natural partners. The insights religion and science bring to bear on life, though different, can be compatible. We can explore science at the same time that we can embrace religion. They belong together even though some religious fundamentalists still think they are at odds. And some scientists think people of faith have left their minds behind.

The fact is that some scientists are people of faith who believe that God is at work in the world and in the work they do. And there are some scientists who are no more informed about religion than religious people are about science.

Both religion and science have elements of art at their core: questioning, observing, imagining, discovering, interpreting, and at play in the world we live in. Creation is a process. The Creator God is creating still, is energy, is involved with and evolving in life on earth as it unfolds. And both religion and science pose ethical issues as they evolve in time.

Humanity participates in creation. We are all creators in our own times and places. In making moral decisions, we affect our destinies. In making and appreciating all forms of work and art we connect with the creative process. We give birth to and nurture new generations. We are co-creators with God.

What is amazing is that the ancient creation stories found in the Bible in Genesis carry truths that still ring true today, even in our technological world. Let us take a closer look at those stories to see the ways in which they speak to us through time.

In the first chapters of Genesis there are two creation stories, each with a different emphasis.

Revisiting the Creation Stories

The first creation story in Genesis begins with these words.

"In the beginning, when God created the heavens and the earth, the earth was a formless void and darkness covered the face of the deep, while a wind swept over the face of the waters. Then God said, 'Let there be light', and there was light. And God saw that the light was good, and God separated the light from the darkness. God called the light Day, and the darkness God called Night. And there was evening and morning, the first day." Genesis 1.

Poetic words. After that come the next six days of creation. On the sixth, humanity was created.

"Then God said, 'Let us make humankind in our image, according to our likeness; and let them have dominion over all the wild animals of the earth, and over every creeping thing that creeps on the earth.'

So God created humankind in their image, in the image of God, God created them, male and female God created them." Gen. 1:26,27

Then, at the end of creation, God surveys their handiwork, "God saw everything that he had made, and, indeed, it was very good.'" Gen. 1: 31a. (Notice that God is referred to with both plural and singular pronouns. The Hebrew word used for God in this story is El or Elohim which can be a plural name for God. It is the oldest name for God and was used as eras were changing.

God gives human beings stewardship over all of nature, to care for it and derive sustenance from its fruit and vegetation.

This story is both poetic and powerful. All humankind was created in God's image, and at each phase of creation, Elohim looks out at creation and sees that it is good.

There is another creation story that begins in Genesis 2. This story tells us more about the origins of the social structures of creation as they were seen at the time of its writing. This story could well be describing the beginning of a new social era, the patriarchal age.

This story describes the relationship between God and humanity as life emerges.

In this account, Adam is created and then Eve is created out of Adam's rib. Another translation says that God created a human being and then divided that one into male and female. Either way, we hear of Adam and Eve and their story at the beginning of time.

After they are created, they live in Paradise, the Garden of Eden. As the story unfolds, Paradise ends for them because, with the urging of the snake, they ignore God's admonition not to eat of the tree of the knowledge of good and evil. They eat the fruit of the tree and moral choice enters the lives of human beings and with it, the possibility of sin and death.

There is a second tree, the Tree of Life which they do not touch. It is left standing in the Garden and is guarded by angels with flaming swords.

After they eat the forbidden fruit, first Eve and then Adam, they are banished from the Garden of Eden. They discover their nakedness and hide from God and a curse falls on them. They are told that because of their disobedience, men would rule over women and women would bear children in pain. Men, for their part, would work by the sweat of their brow until death when they would return to dust. Patriarchy takes hold.

Their idyllic and dependent, symbiotic relationship with God is broken. However, God does not abandon them. They remain connected to God with the ability to choose their own path. Love enters in.

Responsibility has entered in. They have a voice within the confines of the curse.

Adam and Eve leave paradise and find themselves in a world that is finite, materialistic, physical, and wrought with dangers as well as blessings. They can never return to God's womb, to paradise.

This story, being about humanity's birth, is a little like our birth. When we are born, we separate from the safety of our mother's womb. In the beginning we are very dependent on parents for survival. The womb is the paradise in which we grow. But then we must leave the womb. We enter the world and have a new kind of freedom. Over time, that freedom involves making moral choices. If we are fortunate, we make choices surrounded by the love of our parents.

There is amazing wisdom in these creation stories and insight into the moral world and our human condition. These myths tell life lessons that evolution does not address. Interestingly, in the second creation story, there is an open door for moving toward a new creation, "the tree of life" stands waiting in the Garden. Evolution is somewhat mechanistic and fatalistic. Faith introduces consciousness, responsibility, and conscience and posits a universal and transcendent, ongoing connection with the Holy Parent, the God who would never abandon creation.

Those ancient people saw creation as good and understood something about what we have come to call sin. In both stories, God is a creating and sustaining power. Human beings are in God's image and yet, free agents. What we have come to call "original sin" or "the fall" is in place. We are all born into a world in which sin is a reality.

The desire to know the difference between good and evil is an essential element in the Creation stories. It opens the door to responsibility and freedom: the ability to try to discern what is life-giving and make moral choices, to have agency, to exercise choice.

The fruit of the knowledge of good and evil, once God's alone, becomes humanity's as well. Humanity loses its innocence and gains moral knowledge and responsibility. In the relationship between God and humanity, life in the real world begins. And discerning good and evil is a mark of divinity.

Both creation stories imply that there is a moral ordering to the universe that when followed enables life to flourish and God and humans to be in harmony, naked together and unashamed. But life becomes a struggle after the fall from the safety of the womb. The relationship with God is no longer symbiotic: men and women are alienated in what is described as a patriarchal culture, and all people eventually die.

Once out of the garden, other alienations follow. Sibling rivalry turns deadly when Cain kills his brother Abel as he competes with him for God's favor. In the living of life, there are ways to live that sustain existence and honor God but there are also ways to live that are destructive. As generations slip into generations, the Creator and the Created engage together in the ongoing dance of life, death, and life.

Obviously, these early creation stories are not written to be taken literally. That would rob them of their power. They are told by our ancestors to reveal their deepest perceptions about how they see God and creation: how they experience God and being human. And they convey their belief that a moral order exists in human life. What is amazing is how relevant they still are.

The creation stories, while not the first Biblical stories written, are the first stories in Scripture and are foundational for all that follows. They are amazingly apt for all time. Etched as they are into the consciousness of humanity through time, they are poised to take on new meaning. They ring with ancient truths and knowledge of humanity that are seen through different eyes in each age.

I have had an experience of how these stories can come alive. I remember standing in a big open field after just having led an intense workshop. I was one of the leaders in an Ohio Synod School that included people of all ages. The natural setting of the school was serene and beautiful. At that moment, no one else was around.

I looked up at the sky, which was shimmering with stars. It drew me in, and I felt part of that vast universe of creation. And then, I had an overwhelming feeling that I am like God. I do not know where that feeling came from. It scared me at first. I thought it was a thought I was not supposed to have. Wasn't this the ultimate sin in Genesis? Being like God by eating from the tree of knowledge? The story was living in me.

But then a profound sense of peace came over me. I am like God. That does not mean I am God. There is a difference. In that moment I knew I was in God's image, connected to all of humanity, and even to the stars. The ancient myth had a new meaning.

After some time, when I was working on feminist issues, I remembered the creation stories again. I was amazed at how concisely and simply patriarchy was described in the second creation story after Adam and Eve's expulsion from Eden. I became gratefully aware that their fate after expulsion from paradise was not their original condition it was like a curse. It could change. It was changing and we are change agents. We are creating the future. We see the Spirit moving with us toward an era when patriarchy does not define our human societies. We are reversing the curse.

God and Humanity as Co-Creators

As human beings, we are a creative force in the world. We are made to connect with and share in God's continuing creative activity. We do so caring about the survival and salvation of creation. We can take heart in the stories of people who have walked with God, people whose lives have been and are, touched by God, people who have carried the awareness of God in their being. People who have rebelled against God and yet, often found their way back. Now it is the turn of new generations to continue the story.

We can find hope and courage in believing that creation is ongoing in the loving and nurturing presence of God. A force greater than evil and disaster is at work. God beyond time moves within history in all times. The Holy One is connected to creation and loves us where we are. God loves us and all creation.

Thinking about God and creation, let your thoughts turn to human creativity and the creation of children. Birth seemed like a miracle to me every time our sons were born. I was in total awe. Life forming in me out of an egg seeded by my husband and coming out of my body as a person! My husband and I played only a small part as creators, though we provided the raw material for our sons, which came together from his and my forebears.

Miracle as that was, the ongoing miracle of creation is in the development of a child through nurturing and care. Birth is a beginning, creation is ongoing, a work of art in process. If God is Creator, God must be Nurturer too. The desire of a person or people to love a new baby, to raise it as their own is what really gives life whether a child is one's biological or adopted child. Without care a baby dies or suffers for a lifetime, sometimes wreaking havoc in the world. And it is a miracle that each child is a unique person.

Not all people become parents but there are children who need their care. Nurturing is a social responsibility. We create the societies we live in to support and nurture life, or not. We never get it completely right; it is a complicated process. But we know in our hearts what people need for survival and thriving.

The creation stories in the Bible are prelude to all that follows. When we speak of God as Creator, we are not just referring to the beginning of time, but to the nurturing of creation. God is Creator/Nurturer who has an ongoing, intimate, intrinsic connection with creation.

Everyone, in fact, the entire population of the world at any given time, is just a blip in time. It is through God that we enter the long stream of time. It is a statement of faith that the Holy Creative One who existed for our forebears, existed for the world and all that is in it, will be with all generations to come.

The Eternal Holy One is alive in and for us. Limited as we are, we exist in the stream of the eternal, we are a link in creation through the nurturing love of God as well as through our ancestors.

Creation is not a once and done reality. Creation is a process. It is complex. It is relational, all parts are connected to other parts. God is Artist, Nurturer, Parent, Discerner, Builder, Lover.

God is Wisdom, is enlivening Spirit, breath of life, energy, living word, liberating power. How beautiful for us to imagine and experience as we can, some force beyond everything we know, who is invisible, yet with us, beside us, caring about us, surrounding us. How blessed to be sharing in creation with that life affirming nurturing One.

Suffering, tragedy, loss, evil exist in the world. Sometimes they seem to dominate life. Destructive forces are at work along with creative, life affirming forces. God is present even when God seems absent.

God is not controlling everything; humanity and nature have agency. God is present in all seasons, creating, nurturing, restoring, comforting. It is to their Creating/Nurturing God that people of faith bear witness and whose caring they carry on. Sometimes the experience of God is direct. Very often, it comes to us in other people, in other creatures, in art, in nature. We listen and look for the good and carry it in our bodies.

My friend, Lynda Elliott, had a beautiful operatic voice. She would often say my voice sings through me. It is part of me, and it is also more than me. A gift from above.

Lynda took voice lessons and practiced endless hours even after she was singing professionally. She was responsible for the care of her great gift. That is the way it is with the gifts of creation. We need to nurture, use, and share them. Let them sing through us and to us. And of course, Lynda was a divine gift herself. It was not just her voice.

When Aretha Franklin died, Michelle and Barack Obama said that through her they had experienced a part of the Divine. In ways remarkable and ordinary, the creative Divine lives in all of us and is all around us.

God in the Creative Process Throughout Time

Creation is not static; it changes as it moves through time. Social networks that form in the human world that are diverse and complex come into being through human agency and institutions are formed. Nations and organizations within them and beyond them rise and fall as ages come and go. Some moral issues run like threads through every time while other moral issues come and go as ages change.

The Rev. Dr. Gibson Winter, ethicist, and sociologist, speaks about epic shifts in the socio-political-religious evolution of societies in his writing. In his book, "Liberating Creation," he sees the world moving out of an organistic blood and land era, into a mechanistic/ technological/ electronic era and predicts that it is on the cusp of an era of art and creativity.

Winter emphasizes the importance of preserving insights from Indigenous cultures in the modern world and sees their contributions as desperately needed for survival. The mechanistic/technological age has a need for power and hierarchy and lacks care for creation. He speaks passionately about our responsibility in today's world to care for creation and see ourselves as part of it.

Since life is not simply linear, each historic and cultural stage carries prior orientations and future possibilities with it. We spiral back, live in the present, and move forward, all simultaneously.

God connects with people of faith wherever they are through every age. Humanity is called to meet the challenges each new time carries with it in a spirit of love and hope. There is always promise and peril. Religion can serve the world well, but it also carries the potential for supporting injustices and encouraging blind obedience to authority. Not all religious expressions serve the good of creation. New ethical dilemmas are complex and multi-layered and require wisdom and levelheaded faith in changing times.

As Christians, as we circle back in time, we can find aspects of the gods of ancient people that gave them wisdom and can give us insight as we engage in the creative processes of nurturing the modern world. The amazing reality about God is the Divine ability to be present for beloved creation in every era in both ancient and modern times. God is our continuity through time and did not just appear when Judaism was born and Christianity after it.

Humanity needs to be careful to not associate God in an exclusive way with their cultures and religion. In the quest for God who is actively renewing creation, we need open minds and hearts. The entire world is groaning toward a new creation that carries earlier civilizations in its core. Those civilizations have lessons to teach about practices that harm and practices that give life. It is the work of the Spirit to carry God on its wings through time and give each generation discerning spirits.

God is our continuity whose love for creation never wavers. Winter says that we are called "to be co-creators with God at the dawning of eras." A new era is dawning.

Judaism and Christianity are just two of many religions. The sacred exists in many forms. We are increasingly aware that we are one world. There is one creation and many creations all in need of the ongoing creative, nurturing, correcting, energy of the Holy in humanity. Both religious and secular culture can be agents of the Holy, or not.

God and Nature

As we leave our exploration of God as Creator, we remember that nature can turn our spirits to God. God can be experienced through the natural world as religions before our own professed and as some native religions still attest. We human beings are part of the natural world as well as the human-made world.

There is the majesty and glory of nature in the ocean, in tall standing mountains, in cascading waterfalls and flowing streams, in expansive deserts, and wild animals. There is also nature in farmland and city parks and domesticated animals and birds that share our environment. Nature lives in the people around us and their creative expressions.

There is power as well as beauty in nature. I learned to respect the power of the ocean as a small child when our family went to the shore for vacations. In those summers, I would love to be in the ocean, and learned quickly to be aware of its dangers when I was caught up in its tides or pummeled by its waves. I also came to enjoy its buoyancy, its playfulness, its endlessness.

Standing in the wilds of nature, or in the light of the vast universe, we become aware again of how small we are as human beings and yet, how connected to and drawn into the grandeur of it all. We can feel a deep gratitude for our senses and our consciousness that allows us to marvel, wonder, and realize that we are part of it all, even, in some ways, responsible for the care of it.

Of course, we cannot speak of nature without recognizing the power that nature can assert through rain and wind and snow and blazing heat, through storms and earthquakes, and through diseases. We can try to manage nature's power or get out of its way. Responsible as we are for our environment, we have no absolute control over it. If we are in nature's way, its power can destroy. There is no room for human arrogance in the face of the forces of nature.

Did God cause the flood that Noah escaped, or did God just see it coming? Or was there a real flood and those writing about it attributed it to the greatest power they could imagine, God. They did see God as caring about human beings and other animals enough to save them through the Ark.

In the mythic story of Noah, perhaps based on some natural disaster, ancient writers of Scripture saw the hand of God in both the flood's destruction and the saving of creation for ongoing time, in fact, for the rest of time. They saw the rainbow and heard the Holy say that never again would he destroy "every living creature."

Modern humanity lives in a different time than did our ancestors. It is foolishness to not recognize that this is so. We are now aware of how much our behavior, our industry, and our actions impact nature. When the authors of Genesis imagined God as giving humankind dominion over nature, it was for its preservation, not for its devastation.

Humanity is called to responsible stewardship of creation, to a partnership with creation, so that all living things, including humanity can continue to survive.

From a religious perspective, we have a God-given, sacred, moral responsibility for the stewardship of our habitat, our dwelling. And still we tend to attribute control over nature to God as our forebears did. We can see God in nature without believing that God controls it.

(My new stove that arrives as I write, is marked with this warranty: "This stove is not guaranteed against flood and fire and acts of God." Acts of God?)

God does not manipulate natural forces. We do not have to believe that any more to believe in God. Many things once attributed to God are acts of nature or human nature. That does not minimize God, it simply recognizes the agency of creation and humanity as part of creation. Nor does it mean that God does not have the last word.

God alone, in earlier eras, was seen as having power to destroy the world. With nuclear weapons at our disposal, humanity now has the power to end human life as we know it. Human responsibility for preserving life looms large.

Every time violence breaks out in any part of the world, fear breaks out along with it. Could this be the war that leads to humanity's destruction?

The creating life-giving power of the Divine is on our side when we are on the side of life, when we are building our Arks and conserving the other animal and plant life around us. Even my beloved dog who lives with us is an expression of nature. She is akin to me and though we are different, we are both animals and we care for each other. But we have reached a point in time when we are vulnerable, when all creation is vulnerable.

We are blessed that nature offers up its bounty and beauty to us as we share this small planet that is in our hands. Nature nourishes our bodies and souls and reminds us of the vastness and diversity of creation: the wonder of it. The earth is our home. A hymn of gratitude comes to mind for the world we are given by God.

For the beauty of the earth,
For the glory of the skies,
For the love that from our birth
Over and around us lies,
God of all to Thee we raise,
This our hymn of grateful praise.
Folliott S. Pierpoint

GOD THE FATHER: GOD IN RELATIONSHIP

"Our Father who art in Heaven." So begins the prayer Jesus taught his disciples, a prayer that has been handed down to us through the ages. It is a prayer that so many know by heart. It is said wherever Christians pray, and it resonates deep into our beings.

God in the first person who is Creator is also known by Christians as God the Father.

Father as a name for God is used far more in the New Testament than in the Hebrew Bible, especially in the Gospel of John. The word Jesus often used for "Father," in Aramaic, a language Jesus knew, is "Abba," an intimate and relational way of referring to God. It is a respectful yet loving way of speaking of or addressing one's father. There is a strong connection between God creating and nurturing and God as "Abba."

In Scripture, we are not told anything about Jesus' earthly father after the birth narratives and the trip his family took to Jerusalem when he was twelve, except for a line here and there that identifies Jesus as Mary and Joseph's son. Mary is the parent who becomes central in Jesus' life during his years of ministry. Joseph had probably died by then.

Many depictions of "the Holy family" that we are used to seeing at Christmas, include Joseph. As images of Madonna and child become prominent, Joseph fades into the background. God as Father comes to the fore. Knowing God as Father was to know God as just and nurturing, it opened the door to new ways of seeing God.

Jesus' close relationship with God as Father, as Parent, was movement toward a God who was not only close to humanity and even possessive of them, but it envisioned humanity's closeness to God on a personal, familial level.

In many ways, the central role Jesus' mother, Mary, played in his life, and the presence of other women as close followers, was an affirmation of women that challenged the norms of Jesus' day and the patriarchy of the ages.

These changes were taking place in a society embedded in its time but on the cusp of change. The name "Father" as an image for God as Jesus used it, implies a close, warm, caring, trustworthy connection between God and humanity. Jesus as Son, Son of God, is one with God. People as heirs of Jesus are also children of God. This relationship with God is more personal and closer than the relationship between subjects and their Lord or King.

When I was growing up, I related easily to the Fatherhood image of God. I still do. My family system was traditional, and my mother and father conformed to typical roles for married couples as proscribed by society in their time. And yet, my father was ahead of his time in his support and mentoring me as a daughter, and always led me to believe that I could do whatever I wanted to do even though I was female. He was seeing beyond cultural norms.

My father was dynamic, strong, engaged. Though he was, as tradition would have it, our breadwinner and the head of our household, he was also a nurturing, worrying, loving parent.

Though he was clearly an authority figure, I never experienced his authority as absolute. I was never fearful of it or him. I argued with him when we disagreed. I was always able to stand my own ground with him. I felt respected by him, and I admired him. I felt protected by his concern. I could easily feel loved by a Father God.

I see the amazing, kind, and supportive fathers our sons have become. They are active, nurturing parents. God as Father is a positive image for me.

I am fortunate. Father is not a positive image for everyone as I came to learn. Some fathers are absent, some are abusive, some are violent. Some want to be present, but life and work stand in the way.

More than any individual experience of Father, the patriarchal structure of the family where the father is sole authority, breadwinner, and head and everyone else is subordinate, is a central systemic ethical problem for humanity however kind a particular father is. It is a problem for society even when there is no father in the household.

The patriarchal curse on Adam and Eve in which gender roles are segregated and Eve is subordinate to Adam described patriarchy well. As our social consciousness grows, we must face the fact that having the image of Father as the main, central, primary image for God is a two-edged sword. On the one hand, it depicts God as relational, and thereby in close connection with humanity. On the other hand, it is male. God could be Mother, or as some have come to call God, Holy Parent.

The fact that Joseph's fatherhood was almost ignored while Mary's Motherhood was elevated to almost divine status is a problem too. It leaves men out of the intimacy and nurturing of fatherhood.

God, Religion, and Social Systems: Patriarchy

Just as God as Creator leads us into a discussion with science, God as Father leads us into an ethical discussion about justice in human social systems, the place of religion in upholding or helping change established social norms and supporting or helping change psychological assumptions about human nature and relationships.

Challenging social norms and assumptions about human nature is related to our language and images for God which lead to our understanding of God's nature and characteristics. They get at the core, the root of systemic sexism and lead to racism and hierarchy as well.

Our naming of God as male with so called masculine characteristics is fixed in a Patriarchal era that is now seriously challenged as unjust. Our imagining God as King and imagining God as white, silly as that sounds, leads to multiple injustices. But because the Bible is set in Patriarchal times and the church developed in Patriarchal time, changing our ways of referring to God are hard to change.

There are great waves of backlash against social change and deep uncertainty about what is coming next as we move beyond the entrenched systems we have known and the ways we have seen ourselves, both at the heart of being and in relationships with each other. Some say it is anti-family and anti-God's Order.

Finding ways to support the family and the growth of individuals on all levels is actually on the agenda of social change as we seek an emerging human Order in harmony with God's justice now doing a new thing.

Through all social change, God's love for creation does not change. It is the source of human love and at the heart of who we are becoming in the world. God's Realm is a realm in which movement toward redemptive justice and mercy are pursued and supported.

The God of ages has no need for the power we assign "Him." As we ponder the nature of God, we are led to reflect on the nature of Divine Justice and love. As human beings struggle for power and engage in wars, that leave death in their wake, we worship a God of life who must weep at our human disregards for life.

However, religious communities have disagreed on how or even whether to turn our political systems toward peace. Jews and Christians alike have disagreed through time within their own communities about where God's Spirit is leading in the personal/social/political realities of the times in which they lived. This is still true today. In the Hebrew Bible God sent prophets and in the New Testament, God sent Jesus to make clear God's will.

In the days of the prophets and of Jesus, idolatries were challenged, prejudice against those marginalized were decried, rich people ignoring the poor were lambasted, and religion used to oppress or defraud the faithful in God's name to satisfy the personal gains of leaders, were named and decried.

Today we are challenged in profound ways to finally address social systems that perpetrate harm and death because the future of humanity is at stake. The way religious communities perceive God can be part of the problem or contribute the solution.

Our beliefs about God cannot be divorced from our ethical concerns. These ultimately include addressing the names and metaphors for God that have been held as sacred through the ages. We cannot reform our social systems without allowing God's Spirit to speak to our hearts about the fact that God is greater than and beyond all images we have for God and God's image is present in all people.

We cannot force God into our human social boxes. We need new vision to add new images and pronouns for God to add to old ones to be truly open to God and accepting of one another. We need to imagine the ordering of society beyond patriarchal paradigms.

The spiritual becomes political when it translates, as it inevitably does, into the way we live our lives and the roles and status we assign ourselves and one another in society. What does it mean to say that all human beings are in the image of God? Who then is God and who are we?

Faith calls for the liberation of God from the confines of human systems that do not allow us to seek liberation as human beings from patterns that have outlived their time. We take with us that from the past which is life-giving and add to it that which is emerging to enhance life.

Calling for and living through major social changes that seek love that is just and merciful, we can be strengthened by returning to the beginning, to Genesis 1, and claiming that all humanity and creation is good, has goodness at its core. God who made all things well is Goodness itself. While human beings live in a broken world, and are imperfect, we carry the image of God within and are connected to the divine. God wills for us a fulfilling life, wholeness and salvation. And we are each other's keepers.

God as Father can continue to have deep meaning for those who embrace it, God as Parent or Mother can have meaning for those who are stretching for justice. They are not exclusive. God as Spirit is an ongoing presence beyond our anthropomorphic metaphors

In the Gospel of John we find these words:

> *God is Spirit and those who worship God, must worship in spirit and in truth.* John 4:24

Changing the Language of God in Worship

As we speak about metaphors for God, acknowledging that the almost exclusive masculine naming of God in Scripture is related to patriarchal times, we seek to find more inclusive ways to speak of God as we move away from Patriarchy, and it is hard.

Discussing the masculine naming of God elicits strong emotions in people of faith or it can be seen as having little importance. Our relationship with God is a very personal matter and how we name God in our own prayer and meditation is a private spiritual matter. Our corporate relationship with God is another matter.

Part of the reason that shifts in our language and images for God can be so traumatic is that they are embedded in the liturgies and rituals we use for worship, our hymns, prayers, and litanies. These carry collective emotional weight as they are handed down from age to age. They are loved. And they carry institutional power. Tradition cannot be changed lightly nor should it. We are comforted and reassured by the familiar.

In our first Presbyterian Task Force on Women in 1968, the issue of language for God was the most controversial issue that we addressed as we discussed it among ourselves. We agreed when looking at justice for women and men and their roles and place in society. When we were speaking of God we were tampering with the Divine and each one's faith and view of Scripture. We were, at first, very divided.

We can assume that fundamentalists in every religious tradition will resist change in the naming of God, but it can also be hard for progressives who may claim that it is not important. For some, it is easier to give up on religion and God as hopelessly outmoded rather than wrestle with spiritual and theological change.

We are living in a time when thousands of years of patriarchy are being challenged. We cannot talk about God without acknowledging how significant this change is. Patriarchy has set the foundation for the worldviews and social ordering in which our lives and religion have taken place. We are living in a time when Patriarchy is being challenged and religions are being called upon to take a stand. Our worldviews can limit how we see God as well as human beings and our social systems. How we see God can alter our world views.

Our relationship with God cuts through time and strains toward the future while being rooted in the past. The liberation of God and human liberation are deeply linked. Institutions are called to reformation and transformation. Turning. *Metanoia.* The Spirit of God cannot be silenced, it calls us to new life, to the worship of God who goes before us into the future as well as living in the past. We can turn a responsive ear toward the Spirit's leading or not.

God, she, God, he, God, it. God, they. God is Spirit, active in the world, alive, leading toward the light, resisting all idolatrous images. We can respond to God's life-giving light. Jesus pointed out that some people would rather live in the shadows than in the light that reveals the true nature of all things.

We are pursuing this issue because we use language when we worship God. And language is shorthand for social systems and structures. We are shifting systems when we change our naming of God as masculine with so-called masculine characteristics. When our language is inclusive, we are, by moving beyond patriarchal paradigms, signaling our openness to walking with God, trusting God to guide us in the present and into the unknown future.

God is Not White or King

Along with challenging Patriarchy in God's new creation, we are addressing other structures of domination that are reflected in our social ordering and naming of God. God as King, Lord, and Master were liberating images when there were no alternatives to hierarchical human systems. God was King of Kings and Lord of Lords and that was liberating. All earthly autocrats were trumped by the Lord God. Now we have many forms of political organization. Kings, Lords, and Emperors are not the norm, though a few remain along with autocratic leaders without the official name of King.

Slavery, racism, and poverty were and still are devastating expressions of systemic hierarchies that diminish many of God's people. God is often seen, if not named, in the image of oppressing forces. For instance, seeing God as white is problematic.

A study in 2020 at Stanford University's Social Concepts Lab, referenced in an article by Ryan SK Timpte on how children see God, found that the majority of children believed God to be white and male. This affects whom they see as suitable for power and how they will relate to God, if at all, in later life.

We tend to want to make God in the power images of human times. The penchant for raw power, control, and hierarchy seems to be lurking in human psyches. Transferring it to images of God is problematic. God's self-revelation makes clear that God does not need what we mean by human power. God's power is of an entirely other kind.

Power in human terms is antithetical to the heart of God. Jesus refused to be the conquering hero kind of Messiah many people were expecting him to be.

Jesus opened the door to God in new ways that built on his faith, seeing God's power in love: love rooted in justice and expressed in faithfulness, even in the suffering of the Holy One on behalf of humanity. God's love is rooted in compassion, in respect for life, in suffering with, in willing freedom from the grasp of evil, in creating and giving life. God is with human beings who are trying to live life and survive, wanting to nurture and preserve, trying to honor the Holy and the sanctity of life in one another.

In the next chapter we will explore how Jesus embodied God's love which no earthly power could destroy even though they tried.

God is our peace, our refuge, our beloved. Religious communities through time have carried that legacy and been true to it or distorted it in devastating ways.

Our modern political systems come into view. Changes in religious images and language go straight to the core of our being, our idealized images, and our ultimate longings.

Rubem Alves, the great Brazilian liberation theologian and psychotherapist, speaking to a gathering of Presbyterian women years ago, said that when we challenge people's ideals, we are challenging that which gives them a feeling of security and identity. We threaten their whole concept of who they are and how they fit into the world, the foundation on which they build their lives.

Alves wanted those calling for change to know how seriously to take what they are doing and to never underestimate how people are affected by changing idealized images. He did not want us to be deterred by this reality, just to understand it. Idealized images are our idols.

Women and men living traditional lifestyles and those who incorporated them into their being even though they did not, had idealized images of who they were as women and men, and lived life to conform to them while the media reinforced them.

Shaking the foundations and challenging ideals that serve them may be essential to healing the world and embracing God's new creation.

We will free women and men and non-binary people to be more whole and love more deeply. We will include gender expressions and sexual orientations that are inclusive of who we are as human beings. It is the Spirit's work, but in the process, many will feel threatened, and some will strike out. Some will flee to false prophets.

As together we seek a deeper, liberating faith in coming times, we are called to be in continuity with the past without limiting God's ongoing revelation. Great discernment is called for. We have to trust the Holy Spirit to sustain us, empower us, and enable us as we move forward.

We need to be aware that the process as well as the end matters. We need to be kind as well as wise. We need to be persistent and strong without being violent. And we must guard against making idols of the liberation movements that we affirm. We may believe that God is at work in and through them and that may be so. However, God alone is worthy of our full devotion.

God and Change

God is who God is. We will not change that. We can pray to see and feel more of who God is and in that seeing, change ourselves and seek to improve our social order. As we do, it is essential that we listen to the questions of our hearts and minds. We listen for direction in deep silences and explorations. We are not inventing God or rewriting Scripture. We are trying to connect to the Sacred, to the Holy One in our own time as our ancestors did as the future opens before us and we cannot hold it back.

In today's world, we know how much we need righteousness, love, healing, hope, freedom from the things that haunt us. We need grace to survive our divided selves and society. We seek God's liberating presence. As we face transitional times, we need strength and courage and compassion for one another and a Wisdom beyond ourselves to confront evil. We need to stand up to discrimination and violence perpetrated by our friends as well as our enemies, sometimes by ourselves.

We call upon God in sighs too deep for words. Sometimes we take God as for granted as the air we breathe. Sometimes we just cry out into what seems like a void. But at some point, as we relate to God individually and in community, we need words, familiar words. We need new words and images along with the old ones. God among us calls us to engage in ongoing creation.

The fact that our perceptions of God can change with changing times could suggest that we are making God in our own images. We are, of course, susceptible to doing just that across the religious spectrum. But there is a difference between attributing our human values to God and adjusting our human values to the movements of a Holy Spirit in the face of particular situations and times, and the turning of ages. It is hard to tell the difference between our will and a Holy will greater than our own. But we must try.

Our words can turn into action, and we will be known by our fruits. Sometimes acting transcends words; responding to pain and injustice, recognizing evil, opens the door to the sacred. Acts of justice and mercy can be signs that we are on the right track. Just getting through each day, each season, with grace is, at times, enough.

The question for people of faith that the Rev. Thomas Fitch Kepler posed, "Who or what do you mean by God?" is the right question for our new age. An equally important question is, "Who do you think God is not?" The second question seems easier to answer than the first. Asked this question, here is how I would reply. The order of the statements is not important.

Who God is Not

God is not, as revelation unwinds, a God of any nation. God is not the property of any one people and does not set national boundaries.

God is not a God of violence, war, or vengeance. That does not mean that God tolerates injustice. The path to justice, however, is not through doing harm, but by pursuing peace.

God does not require the sacrifice of life to find forgiveness or salvation. God lovingly forgives us our sins as we forgive those who trespass against us.

God is not all powerful as human beings perceive power. Sheer power means nothing to God. God does not create or support human power hierarchies. God is so great that God can be vulnerable. God's power is in loving in time and living beyond time.

God does not control human behavior. God gives humanity freedom within the bounds of a moral and physical universe. God and humanity are meant to co-create on earth.

God has no gender, race, ethnic identity, no physical characteristics known to humanity. God was in Jesus who had a specific identity on earth. However, after his death and resurrection, the living Christ is beyond human boundaries.

God does not manipulate natural forces as a matter of course. Many things once attributed to God as "acts of God," are acts of nature or human nature. That is not to say that God cannot be found in nature or human nature, but both nature and human nature are forces of their own though intricately connected to God.

God is not Santa Claus, keeping a list of who is naughty and nice. God is not a wonderful figure in our childhood to be abandoned when we grow up and find out he doesn't exist. God is not a figment of our imagination.

God is not "out there" somewhere. God is in our hearts and world as well as being transcendent mystery beyond our comprehension. We are connected to God and in that connection, we are not strangers and in that connection we can be one with each other.

God is not cruel. In God's righteousness there is mercy.

****

I invite you to make your own list.

The Ongoing Quest for God

Having expressed my ideas about who God is not, I return to the question of who God is. We turn to the question Moses asked thousands of years ago: "Who should we say you are? It is the question we ask of the Holy Presence again and again. After stories, naming, metaphors, poetry, art, de-mythologizing and re-mythologizing, affirmations and denials, the answer echoes through the years. "I am who I am." We cannot define God. God is who God is. We just try to see as much as we can, experience as much as we can of the Holy through the lens of our humanity.

In dialogue and even conflict with one another, in the midst of our finitude we experience the eternal in one another.

Our world, however small in the context of the universe, is widely varied in culture, geography, and perspective. And people come from many different subjective experiences and worldviews. We are all looking at God from many angles through many different lenses.

In the midst of diversity, there is a pressing need for religious communities across the world to catch a glimpse of a common vision of the Holy as a resource, a guide, a creating energy, a moral force for the good in our time; a force for all that is life affirming and life giving.

Humanity enters a new age with power never held in human hands before. We can wreak havoc on the world with our weapons of war and our nuclear bombs, with the degradation of our climate, and our prejudices, with rage or despair or narrow hope for only our kind.

What we need in the future is the ability to combine a perception of God that does not limit God to our parochial images of Divinity, and a perception of humanity that does not limit us to stereotypical images of who we are. We need to relate to one another in love.

We lost our innocence about sin and evil long ago. God could not stop Cain from killing Abel. God cannot stop us from killing each other. God is a force making clear that we must stop ourselves and God will empower us, be with us as we move toward building a life sustaining new creation in harmony with the every creating of God.

With each new era comes a need for a dramatic shift in our ability to know God who is not only at work in the world but at play in the world. We can join God in the dance of life. Play signifies a creative openness to life and a willingness to give creation and creating a renewed chance to blossom.

God is with us in our work and daily living, and God is also our Sabbath. God is a safe haven to whom we can withdraw to gain perspective. God is "our shelter from the stormy blasts, and our eternal home," as the hymn says.

God can move in people's lives to break cycles of pain and suffering. God prevails even over death. God's Spirit can help us face the complexities of life and lead us toward love's fulfillment that is key to our survival.

However, we need to meet God as God is, and not as we want God to be. Sometimes it has seemed easier to throw God out than allow our perceptions of God and God's will to change. Or it seems easier and right to hang on to orthodoxies and keep religion separate from worldly realities: no questions, no doubt, and throw away the opposition.

Our lives are short, and we are very small in the vast reality of time and place no matter how important we think we are or how wealthy. If we seem insignificant at the foot of majestic mountains, or in the expanse of the sea, imagine how finite we are before God. And yet, God treasures us.

God is source, foundation, creativity, strength, righteousness, and beauty. God can be our guide as we face the daunting realities of being human in any age, in our age.

In all our musing about God, Scripture claims that God is with humanity in the world and humanity is meant to love God with heart, mind, and soul, because God alone is worthy of such trust.

God is Always More

God loves all humanity and all creation, and we are called to love each other as we love ourselves. Before God we are all more alike than different and, at the same time, accepted and appreciated with our differences. God comes to us as we are. Though we see God through many different lenses, what matters is that we see the Holy, even see reflections of Holiness.

All human attempts to even imagine God are limited and partial at best as we have said. No one, no faith tradition has the whole truth about God by whatever name.

We encounter God in the company of many amazing people with different religious practices and beliefs. As University Chaplain at Tufts I worked with other Chaplains and students of other faiths and with Christians of differing perspectives and Humanists who were atheists. I had to speak my own truth and listen to others speak theirs. At times, we disagreed, at other times we were as one.

At times, we worshipped together as an Interfaith community. At still other times we shared in artistic expression, in music and dance and left words behind. In ways that honored each of our traditions we agreed to honor one another's faith though we never felt called to accept religious extremism or abandon our commitments to a more humane world.

I found myself wanting to make a God collage. I share the following as one small contribution to that collage with the recognition that words are never enough.

God is Always More
Sitting in the silence of the sanctuary,
I try to feel God's presence.
I focus on the cross
That is trying to center my attention.
All I feel is emptiness.
And then it happens,
The room is filled with energy
Light of an invisible kind
A holy presence
And there are many Spirits
Filling the room and my heart.

God is Many.
Of course.
God is nothing we know
And everything we know
All colors and no colors
All nationalities and none
Gendered and ungendered
Human and Divine
Christ is,
God is,
And Spirits are
The Trinity and more.
God is everywhere and here
God is trillions of stars.
And one lit Christ candle
God is in the air
And in every breath we take
God is Love
And every love that fills the room.
God is Many
God is More
Always More
And yet One.
Always near, by our side.
God is filling the room
The One dancing in my heart.
-PBK

The most important lines may be, "God is More, Always more," and "God is near, by our side." God shines as the Light of ages and offers hope to this world.

Beyond words, imagination, or reason, God comes and dwells in human hearts. We, as human beings are most alive and life giving when our hearts are open to the Spirit of God within us. It is to Jesus and the Spirit that we now turn our attention.

CHAPTER 3

JESUS CHRIST

What has come into being in Him was life, and
the life was the light of all people. John 1:4

In Christ There is no East or West,
in Him no South or North,
But one community of love throughout
the whole wide earth.
Hymn. Words by John Oxenham

PART I

THE HEART OF THE CHRISTIAN FAITH

Jesus Christ is at the heart of the Christian faith. Christians believe that God was present in Jesus Christ, a religious Jew living in the Middle East some two thousand years ago. He began teaching and healing around the age of thirty and was so popular with the people and so threatening to the authorities, both religious and secular, that he was crucified. Christiams believe that after his crucifixion he was resurrected and is still alive in the Spirit.

Jesus blooms as the heart of faith. Lenora Martinelli Kepler

As you go on to read about Jesus, the first part of this chapter focuses on Jesus' ministry, his teachings, his healing, his encounters with those around him. The second part is about his death and resurrection.

While looking at Jesus' life, we will explore questions that emerge in the times in which we live. I will share bits and pieces of my own faith journey as they seem relevant, hoping that they will lead to reflections on your own life journey.

I am writing about Jesus in the latter part of my life. In some ways, I see Jesus differently now than I did when I was a child, teenager, or maturing woman. You will be reading through the lens of your own life stage. It is through our multiple perspectives set in time that our understanding of who Jesus was and is for us emerges.

As a child, I saw Jesus as a gentle and strong man, a shepherd, someone from God who loved me. "Jesus loves me, this I know," was a refrain we sang with gusto and often. I had two favorite pictures of Jesus. One was of him seated, surrounded by children of all colors, welcoming and loving them all. The other is of a more spiritual Jesus, guiding two children safely across a dangerous bridge.

I still love those images. As my faith has evolved over time, new images of Jesus have emerged along with old images and new questions. My life has been shaped and reshaped several times as all our lives are, by relationships, experiences, and our social contexts. Through all of life's spirals, we seek out Jesus' message for us, praying to be guided by his Spirit and drawn closer to God.

However we see Jesus today, Scripture is the primary resource for insight into who the historical Jesus was and how the emerging church saw and experienced him.

The church in its many forms believes that Jesus Christ is still alive in our midst as the living Christ and is active through the Holy Spirit. The essential nature of the historical Jesus and of the living Christ need to be consistent with each other. We begin with accounts of the historical Jesus as recorded in the New Testament.

THE JESUS STORY IN THE NEW TESTAMENT: THE GOSPELS

What we know about the historical Jesus comes to us in the Gospels: Matthew, Mark, Luke, and John. Each of the Gospels is written from a distinct perspective for a different audience.

After these four books we find the development of the early Christian community and discover how they see Jesus and learn the story of their struggles as they continued his ministry. These are recorded in the book of Acts and letters to young churches in what are known as the Epistles.

At the end of the New Testament is the Book of Revelation, a book about the early church's confrontations with the secular powers of the time, written in apocalyptic form that includes visions of a new creation.

Through the years, followers, scholars, seekers, and doubters have studied, interpreted, and debated the accounts of Jesus' life and his sayings as they are found in Scripture. New commentaries continue to be penned about the Bible and its times through the years. Some scholars have questioned the accuracy of all that is written about "the historical Jesus" while others have taken the writings literally.

Sources outside of Scripture have been plumbed for clues about Jesus' life. Some new writings have been discovered in ancient Scrolls that contain books about Jesus' life that were not included in the Canon (the texts officially designated as Scripture.)

There are a myriad of witnesses who have, through the centuries since the Bible was written, born witness to their experiences of the living Christ.

Even though debates about Jesus' life and teachings go on and people will continue to speak of their experiences of Jesus, it is crucial to go back to the source, to study what the Bible says about Jesus, for one's self. It helps to learn as much as possible about his context and the times in which he lived more than two thousand years ago.

All accounts that come down to us through the centuries portray Jesus as having an intimate relationship with God. God was at the center of Jesus' life and faith. His life cannot be separated from his faith tradition. Jesus was a practicing Jew who was versed enough in his tradition that he could be in deep and serious dialogue with religious leaders and scholars. He knew the writings that became the Hebrew Bible and often quoted from them.

As we explore Jesus' life, we begin with the Gospels. The Gospels were written between 65 CE and 110 CE, Jesus having died around 33 CE. Some of the material in the Gospels came first through the spoken word which was then written down. Other material had been circulating in writing as the early church was born. This includes early prayers, litanies, and sayings.

All the original manuscripts were written in Greek with occasional words in Aramaic. Those manuscripts have all been lost over time. Scholars work with manuscripts that were meticulously copied by hand from originals and copies of originals.

That which is recorded in the Gospels about Jesus' life is not intended as biography. His teachings have a timeless quality that relays deep spiritual truths and ethics even though they are clearly set in his time and place.

Jesus often taught in parables and told stories. His vivid encounters with individuals contain lessons meant for all time. Some of the most interesting insights into his character and mission come out of exchanges with his adversaries as well as with his disciples.

When the Hebrew Bible was written, peoples' identity was tied up with their group identity. God relates to the Israelites as a whole, and then, to and through their leaders and prophets, though there are some exceptions. By Jesus' time, that was changing. It is important that Jesus related to individuals as well as to communities and groups of people.

When individuals were beginning to have an identity of their own in addition to their group identity, an era was shifting. This set the stage for the widening of Jesus' faith and new developments for the future.

The shifting of an era opened the door, over time, to individual salvation as well as communal belonging. People could choose faith as well as belong to the faith into which they were born. In the Gospels, we find Jesus relating to individuals in all walks of life, including those marginalized and outcast in their communities and those identified as enemies of his people. He opened the door for the birth of the church.

Jesus lived in very tumultuous times at this turning of an age, and he reflected and contributed to that change. Some facts about his context can help us understand him better. We turn to that context with a very brief overview.

SETTING THE SCENE: THE CONTEXT IN WHICH JESUS LIVED

Jesus lived in Palestine, a region in the Middle East, which was populated primarily by his people, the Jews. His religious community saw itself in a special covenantal relationship with God, a people chosen for a special role in history. The center of their faith was Jerusalem where the Temple stood at the heart of worship.

Jesus embraced the roots from which he came and was schooled in and practiced his tradition. Jews in his time fell into groups like the Sadducees, Pharisees, Essenes, and Zealots. We do not know with certainty what Jesus' sectarian affiliation was, though he was well versed in the Pharisaic tradition. There were also Gentiles (non-Jews) in Palestine from surrounding countries as well as Roman occupiers.

When Jesus was born, Palestine was occupied by Rome. Before his time, Palestine had been dominated by many foreign powers, the Greeks had preceded the Romans. However, a Jewish uprising had fought off foreign rule and Palestine was independent for one hundred years, having gained full independence by 142 B.C.E. Hasmoneans, who led the rebellion for independence, ruled the country and eventually unified Jewish territories. Then civil unrest developed which led to Roman control.

"By 63 B.C. the Hasmonean rule has given in to excesses and civil war was on the horizon, Sadducees and Pharisees appealed to Rome for arbitration of the power struggles and the rivalry between various groups who sought their overthrow had brought the country to the edge of civil war. Like a bemused tiger, Rome bided its time, waiting for Israel to fall. When both the Sadducees and Pharisees appealed to Rome for arbitration of the power struggle, Rome not only arbitrated; it took over the entire country." p. 37 *Jesus: A Gospel Portrait* by Donald Senior.

Throughout Jesus' lifetime, the Roman occupation was in place and Greek and Aramaic were the spoken languages of the people. Hebrew was a liturgical language used primarily in worship and rituals.

Most Jews wanted freedom from Rome. Many longed for a leader who would organize an armed rebellion against the Roman occupiers. Many dreamt of a return to the monarchy and a King like David. Some were longing for a Messiah, an anointed one who would be Savior. Some few colluded with the Romans and in turn were rewarded by them.

The Romans wanted to keep the "peace." The High Priests were willing to collaborate with the Romans. It was a time of deep unrest and division. Those in power wanted to protect their power, both Romans and High Priests. Roman power was overextended, and governing occupied territories was challenging.

In Jesus' day, social systems like patriarchy, slavery, and monarchy were in place and taken for granted. Eliminating those systems could not even be imagined. However, Jesus often valued people as individuals beyond their given place in society. In so doing he questioned the absolute control of social designations and systems. He defied Jewish and Roman authorities and power, and popular cultural norms.

The divide between the rich and poor was chasmic in his time. There was a small middle class made up of artisans and merchants who were relatively comfortable economically. Jesus' family was likely of the artisan class in spite of some modern-day assumptions that they were poor. Most of the population was agrarian and living on the financial margins. Taxation by the Romans imposed a huge burden on the Jewish population.

Jesus was a Galilean from the north of Palestine, the area surrounding the Galilean Sea. The people there were known to be less purist religiously than those in the Judean area that included Jerusalem, and more diverse.

It is into this Palestine that Jesus was born at the crossroads of many cultures and a known trade route. The tensions and conflicts that surrounded him, both religious and political, were boiling over.

JESUS BIRTH

Jesus' parents were Mary and Joseph. Jesus was a first-born child. Joseph was a carpenter. Joseph was a descendant of King David and through him, Jesus was a descendant of David according to the genealogy in Matthew and Luke's Gospel.

Before Jesus' birth, Mary his mother is visited by an angel who tells her that she will bear a son whose name will be Jesus. She is told that the Spirit will come upon her. Her son will sit on the throne of David. He will be holy and called "Son of God."

Jesus' conception and birth has come to be known as "the virgin birth" in Christianity because in most translations of the Bible, the angel was sent to "Mary, a virgin." The Greek word translated as "virgin," could also be translated, "young woman."

The important message is that Jesus' coming birth, being announced by an angel, as it is in Luke, is that the child Mary would bear would come into the world with a special mission and identity. Her child was from God.

In the Middle East at that time in history, divine intervention in a birth signaled the birth of a child with a special mission, a prophet, a king, or the son of a god, an anointed one.

Around 1,500-1,200 BCE, a miraculous birth was said to have occurred. In Zoroastrianism, the first monotheistic religion in ancient Persia, now Iran. Zoroaster, also known as Zarathustra, its founder, was said to have been born of a virgin.

There are well-known stories in the Hebrew Bible of miraculous births. Perhaps the best known was Sarah, wife of Abraham, who gave birth to Isaac after her childbearing years were over.

Jesus' birth followed the pattern of miraculous births and was seen by the authors of the New Testament as testimony to his being the Messiah, the awaited anointed one, heir of King David's throne.

Though some Christians continue to believe in the virgin birth, many, living over two thousand years after Jesus' time, with no such tradition as virgin birth in their culture, see the virgin birth symbolically. Jesus' conception and birth can be seen as what it was meant to be in the first place, not as a scientific description but as a signal that the one being born was to be a central figure in the Jewish religion. And as the story unfolds, a light to the nations. The Messiah. Son of God.

Mary's response to the angel's news that she was to give birth to a child, "Son of God," was acceptance and a song, now known as "The Magnificat." This is part of her song.

> *He (God) has sown strength with his arm;*
> *He has scattered the proud in the thoughts of their hearts.*
> *He has brought down the powerful from their thrones*
> *And lifted up the lowly.*
> *He has filled the hungry with good things,*
> *And sent the rich away empty.* Luke 1:46-56.

As Mary was expecting Jesus, her cousin Elizabeth, beyond her childbearing years, was also pregnant with a special child of God, John the Baptist. She and Mary spent time together during their pregnancies. Elizabeth, and even the child in Elizabeth's womb, were said to see in Mary's baby a child of promise. Elizabeth's unborn baby "leapt for joy" at the thought of the coming Christ, according to Luke.

In the birth narratives, Jesus is born in a stable because the town to which Mary and Joseph have traveled late in her pregnancy is crowded with pilgrims like themselves coming to Bethlehem to be counted for the Roman census. There is no room in the inn.

After Jesus' birth, shepherds in the field hear angel voices telling of his birth and singing, "Peace on earth good will to all." The shepherds drop everything to run and find the baby.

In the Matthew narrative of Jesus' birth, Magi, wise astrologers, sometimes seen as Kings from the East, come to worship the newborn king, following a star. Scholars have suggested they may have come from ancient Persia, home of Zoroastrianism. Thus, Matthew signals that this child will have universal significance.

From the time of his birth, we are told that King Herod is wary of this child who is rumored to be the newborn King of the Jews. Warned in a dream that they are to avoid Herod, the Magi choose to return to their homes via a route that avoids contact with him. In fear for the life of their child, Mary and Joseph flee with Jesus to Egypt and find refuge there for three years. When they return home, they settle in Nazareth in Galilee. Their need to flee is a sign that trouble lies ahead for Jesus as later in life he becomes a man with influence and authority.

These Christmas stories are well known by Christians around the world. They are sung about in carols in many worship traditions and languages that retell the stories about Jesus' birth and its meaning in the world.

The Gospel of John tells of Jesus birth from a unique perspective.

"In the beginning was the Word and the Word was with God, and the Word was God. He was in the beginning with God. All things came into being through him, and without him not one thing came into being. What came into being in him was life, and the life was the light of all people. The light shines in the darkness, and the darkness has not overcome it." John 1:1-5

John speaks of Jesus' coming into the world in these more abstract terms, from the beginning associating him with God's transcendence and Wisdom.

Every element in each of the birth narratives is important for all that is to follow in Jesus' life.

JESUS EARLY LIFE

We know little about Jesus' early life. His circumcision is recorded in Luke. Then we read that he was taken to the temple as was Jewish custom for the rite of purification. There he was acknowledge by Simeon, a man "righteous and devout" who was told by the Spirit that he would not die until he had seen the Messiah. His proclamation about the baby ends with these words, "a light for revelation to the Gentiles, and for the glory of your people Israel," Simeon also predicts the opposition Jesus will face. (Luke 2)

The aged prophet Anna also recognized Jesus and proclaimed him to be "the redemption of Jerusalem." After Jesus' identity and destiny is declared, we read these words, "The child grew and became strong, filled with wisdom, and the favor of God was upon him." Luke 2:32

By the age of twelve, after a family trip to celebrate Passover in Jerusalem, Jesus is engaged in a deep discussion with religious scholars and is amazing them with his knowledge and understanding of their shared faith. Jesus had lagged behind when his family's caravan left for home. He gave his parents a scare when they discovered that he was missing. After that, we do not hear anything more about Jesus until he is about to begin his ministry at around the age of thirty.

JESUS' MINISTRY BEGINS: HIS BAPTISM AND THE TEMPTATIONS

As he is about to begin his ministry Jesus is baptized by his cousin, John the Baptist, Elizabeth's son, also born with a special mission to fulfill. John has become an ascetic, living in the wilderness, preaching repentance, and preparing the way for Jesus, the thongs of whose sandals he says he is not fit to tie.

When Jesus is baptized by John in the river Jordan, a dove descends and a voice from heaven is heard, "This is my Son, the Beloved, with him I am well pleased." Mark 1: 11

The authors of the Gospels clearly wanted to let the world know that Jesus was from God and filled with the Spirit. What he would say about God and life was reliable and to be listened to. Repeatedly in Scripture, we hear the words, "Listen to him."

When Jesus emerged as a leader, teacher, healer, he emerged as a charismatic man of such significance and stature that both the High Priests and Roman authorities feared his power. It was a power Jesus knew he had, and he had to decide how to use it.

After his baptism, Jesus retreats to the wilderness to pray and prepare for the future and his ministry. It is there that he faces three temptations. These temptations are critical to all that follows because they set the boundaries for the entirety of Jesus' identity and ministry and define how he will use his authority. They are key to understanding him and his mission.

Jesus was to become an influential leader, proclaimed by some as Messiah, by others as King, by others as a prophet. The temptations clarify that Jesus would not be a leader, Messiah, King, who would conform to people's expectations of a powerful ruler. He rejected the temptations to claim power on the world's terms. He would redefine how God and God's will and presence were to be understood.

All three Gospels, Mathew, Mark, and Luke, write about Jesus' temptations, thus magnifying their importance. Full of the Spirit, Jesus went into the wilderness for forty days and nights. There he fasted. At the end of that time, he was tempted by the devil, and waited on by angels.

The first temptation was to turn stones into bread. A famished Jesus does not yield and says, "One does not live by bread alone."

Then Jesus was shown all the Kingdoms of the world and told that if he would worship Satan, they would be his. He refuses and says, "Worship only the Lord your God and serve only him."

The final temptation is to throw himself off the highest point in the Temple to prove himself Son of God. If he were truly sent from God, God would protect and rescue him. Jesus stands his ground and replies, "It is written, do not put your God to the test."

These temptations open a door to understanding Jesus and through him, God. Jesus, throughout his life and in his death and resurrection, unveiled aspects of God's being and will that were challenging for his time, and as it turns out, for all times. He resisted the temptations of power, magic, and materialism. He redefined the ways in which he and his followers were to relate to the world and understand their ministry and relationships with people and their cultures.

When Jesus emerged from the wilderness, having faced the temptations, he entered the Temple and there he reads from Isaiah as if applying its words to himself.

> *The Spirit of God is upon me, because he has anointed me to bring good news to the poor. He has sent me to proclaim release to the captives and recovery of sight to the blind, to let the oppressed go free, to proclaim the year of God's favor.*
> Luke 4:18 and 19

So, his ministry begins. Jesus gathers twelve disciples to learn from him, to walk with him and share in his mission, and when he is gone, to carry it on. Among them were fishers, tax collectors, business owners, and at least one was a social activist.

As Jesus goes about his ministry, to the people whom Jesus healed and befriended, he was a savior and miracle worker. To the crowds who hung on to his words, he was teacher, healer, holy man. To some, we can suppose, a worker of magic. To some leading Pharisees and Sadducees and the High Priests, he was an agitator, adversary, and thorn in their sides. To the Romans, Jesus was a puzzle and to Herod, a threat.

What was it about his presence and his life and teachings that made him so popular with the people and such a menace to both the religious and secular authorities?

To truly encounter Jesus' teachings as recorded in the Gospels, only reading them will do. Here, we will explore some that seem especially important today for Christians in a new age. In our era as wars still rage it is important to remember that Jesus was a man of peace.

Living in a time when we have more ability to create images of reality through technology, and more ability to perpetrate fake news and narratives, we can hear Jesus' words calling for truth and integrity. In a time when we are breaking through the systemic stereotypes and injustices of the past, we find Jesus defying them in his time. In a time when we are in need of a solid mooring, Jesus is centered in God and calls people to love neighbor as self. Through all times, Jesus' word to us rings true.

Hopefully, as we explore who Jesus was and how he saw God and humanity, doors will open to our understanding of God for us. Let us turn to Jesus as a teacher.

JESUS' TEACHINGS ABOUT LOVE, LAW, AND LIBERATION

Jesus cried out over Jerusalem, "Would that you knew the things that make for peace." No one has complete knowledge of what those things are. But Jesus' teaching and actions lead us in the direction of peace, in the direction of a just order where all people are valued and responsible, in which we care for one another.

At the heart of who Jesus was is his intimacy with God, his love of God, his love for all humanity, and certainty that God loves all creation.

Jesus' teaching and ethics emerged out of his Jewish faith. That meant they were grounded in Jewish Scripture, in the Creation stories, the Law given to Moses at Sinai, the history of his people, the words of the prophets. In the Spirit, he lived his faith and took it to new depths in his time.

Jesus knew well the extent of human sin. He was often threatened by it. He stood up to it with boldness. He believed in transformation, forgiveness and the restoration of life and went about a ministry of healing and opening doors to new life. Jesus had an open heart for all and a wisdom that supported those in need and called out those who were harming others. Jesus was a true rabbi, a great teacher.

Jesus took the Ten Commandments, the Ten Words, each of which begins with "Thou shall not," and summarized them with a positive admonition to love.

"Love God with heart, mind, and soul. And your neighbor as yourself."

That was a way of affirming the Commandments as a foundation for love. The Commandments found in Exodus 20:1-17 begin this way:

"I am the Lord your God, who brought you out of the land of Egypt, out of the house of slavery; you shall have no other God's before me."

The next three have to do with idolatry, taking God's name in vain, and the observance of the Sabbath. They are followed by the commandments for living in community.

Christian churches have focused on love as at the heart of Jesus' teachings. Over the course of history, the Law and Love have been seen as in opposition to one another. Jesus saw them as one and the same.

Sister Joan Chittister, writing in her book, "The Ten Commandments: Laws of the Heart," speaks to the important need in the modern world of honoring the Commandments and being guided by their principles. "*These laws were clearly meant to shape a way of living, a lifestyle, an attitude of mind, a spirit of human community, a people.*" (p. 9)

Jesus honored the Commandments without having a legalistic approach to the Law and its outward observance. He saw keeping the law as a matter of the heart, as given to humanity for their own good.

Jesus lived the real depth and meaning of love. He said he did not come to abolish the law but to fulfill it. Love was a fulfillment of the Law. The commandments provided basic guidance and then there was more. Loving God with one's whole being took shape in enacting love in human relationships.

Eugenia Anne Gamble, in the book "Words of Love," says this:

> *Divine Love holds the pieces of life together. Divine Love makes the mundane sacred. Divine Love hold the Ten Words together as one great vision of human and Divine life intersecting.* p.13

In loving relationships, people honor their parents, they do not kill or destroy (body or soul), they are not unfaithful and do not betray each other, they do not steal from one another, they do not bear false witness against each other (lie), they do not covet what the other has, being jealous of the other. It is all a part of living love.

Jesus embodied love and like the prophets before him, envisioned a time when Love would be written in human hearts, the Law would dwell there.

Jesus' profound respect for the law enabled him to broaden it. He was clear that following God's will is never just about outward observance, but about that which lies inside, in the depths of the heart.

Jesus turned people's attitude about the Law around. The Law was not meant to be a burden placed on people. Jesus said that it was meant to serve humanity's common good.

Jesus rejected self-righteous, legalistic uses of the law and religion. It was only when the law was misused that love and law became opposing forces. By connecting law and active love, Jesus saw the commandments, the Ten Words, not as an end in themselves but as a means to life-affirming relationships and social orders, as love in action.

Rather than being an albatross around people's necks, Jesus taught that God's law is a freeing gift from God, embodying God's love and grace, essential to justice and a guide for loving. It was a foundation for God's new creation and indeed built into the bones of creation.

The commandments, from their inception, applied to Jewish men and their relationship to God and to relationships in the Jewish community. In his teachings and actions, Jesus demonstrated his belief that the Law is meant to apply to all people. In his treatment of women, of children, of slaves, and of outcasts, even enemies, he made clear that all are equal, all life is precious. That would mean that the Law applied to all. This was radical teaching and living.

In his actions as well as his teachings he helped his disciples understand what it is to love and whom we are to love. God's impartiality, expressed by Jesus, is made clear in the fact that all people have a rightful claim to be treated well by the laws of righteousness and an obligation to treat others well.

However, Jesus also taught that anyone who thinks they can love perfectly or keep the law perfectly is fooling themselves. No one has a pure unblemished internal landscape. That reality calls for people to be honest with themselves and compassionate with others. Jesus told people to take the log out of their own eye before judging the speck in another's eye.

Jesus knew that breaking moral laws have consequences. Sometimes those consequences are immediate in the harm they bring to self and others. Sometimes the consequences are paid for by innocent people. In judging others, we are to be merciful as God is merciful with us. But it is never all right to allow abuse to continue. Jesus himself challenged the High Priests who were placing hard burdens on their people and, in the name of God, robbing them. He named sin.

Harming others, ignoring the cries of those in need, killing; these acts need to be identified. They call for repentance and change, metanoia, turning around. Confession, then forgiveness and reconciliation.

It is important when talking about "The Law," to know that we are speaking of the Commandments and foundational moral law. We are not speaking of law as it is used in social legal systems though some commandments overlap with some societal laws. Nor are we speaking of religious rites and purity laws.

Eventually, the issue of accountability for breaking the law arises. There is accountability to religious and civic authorities, accountability to one another, and accountability to God.

Just how God is enforcer of the Law is a complex question. There is a sense in which, as we have already mentioned, breaking the Law comes with its own consequences. Then there is the idea that after death, there is a final judgment and God is the final judge.

Jesus says that all human beings break the law. He comes down hardest on those who cause other people harm and lead them astray and those who enjoy plenty while ignoring those in need. When it comes to enforcing the law, Jesus identifies sin but is not about punishment. He calls people to repentance, he heals, and he assumes that breaking the law comes with a human price. Some people are lost. In the end, God alone can be our ultimate judge.

Jesus tells the story of the prodigal son. The son takes his heritage while young, leaves home, and squanders it. He ends up having to survive by eating the scraps offered to pigs. He decides to go home and face the consequences, even if that means becoming a servant in his father's household. When the father sees him coming home, he is overjoyed. He runs to greet him and throws him a great party. His elder brother who has never wandered is put off. Where is his party? The father encourages him to welcome his brother and celebrate the fact that he and his father have been together all along.

Through this parable, Jesus says that There is salvation and restoration in the heart of God's love. God's justice and grace and forgiveness await those who "come home." Jesus taught about a God who loves all of us and wishes an abundant life for us. Like the father of the prodigal son, God loves with a parent's heart and longs for the son to repent and come home. God rejoices when sinners repent and forgives and welcomes with open arms. It is, however, up to the son to come to his senses.

Jesus calls those who are forgiven to forgive others. He taught his disciples to pray: "Forgive us our debts as we forgive others." In forgiveness there is spiritual redemption and freedom.

God's great love and grace is in establishing a moral order to begin with that calls life out of chaos and enables life in relationship to continue. God's love is in both creating a moral order and offering forgiveness and mercy when that moral order is broken. God's ongoing and faithful love is with human beings when they go astray. God seeks them out and wills their return, but the choice is in their hands.

Remember the creation story? After Adam and Even came to know the difference between good and evil, pursuing the good becomes an essential part of life, a choice. They had agency. The more power people have, the more essential discerning what is good for the world becomes. Evil explodes when, in jealousy, Cain kills Able.

Jesus' love and grace and wisdom were amazing. He did not nullify people's sin or their need for turning around and living life accountably and generously. Jesus' love called for compassion, self-awareness, and mutual respect among peoples. He knew what the "wages of sin" were. Jesus acknowledged and supported people's ability to change, turn around, be reborn. Second birth and a new consciousness, being able to see God at work in the world. In the gospel of John it means seeing Jesus as from God, hearing his words and seeing his light.

Finally, Jesus taught that gratitude is the final response to receiving God's gifts of love and healing. Jesus healed ten people with leprosy, a courageous act on his part since associating in any way with people with leprosy was forbidden. Only one of the ten came back to give thanks and praise God and that one was a Samaritan, an enemy of Jesus' people. To the person with leprosy who came back to give thanks, Jesus said, "Go in peace, your faith has made you whole." Ten healed of leprosy, one made fully well.

PURITY LAWS

Forbidding contact with people with leprosy was part of the purity law of Jesus' time. Jesus, while he honored the Commandments, challenged observance of purity and ritual laws when that observance conflicted with justice and love.

The Hebrew Bible contains the ritual and purity laws required for religious practice and proscribed punishments for breaking them. Some of the purity laws were severe and without mercy. Jesus got in trouble for questioning and defying them.

Jesus ignored those purity practices and social conventions that were outdated, inhumane, injurious or demeaning to human beings. He healed people who were considered unclean. He spoke with women in public, and even healed a woman who had had a flow of blood for years. He also defied the social hierarchical norms by honoring children and calling them to his side. In all these cases, he was condemned by those who held purity laws sacred and social conventions inviolable. He challenged those who treated them as on an equal plane with the Commandments.

When Jesus interacted with women and outcasts, he treated them as fully human and responsible. In so doing he was demonstrating what it means to love others as self. In reaching out to and loving those on the margins he neither pitied nor idealized them. He honored them enough to hold them accountable.

Jesus not only ate with tax collectors who were hated, but he also called a tax collector as a disciple. He ministered to Samaritans. He told a parable that is well known about a "Good Samaritan." The Samaritan, from a group despised by the Jewish people, was the only one who stopped and aided a man who had been mugged and was lying by the side or the road, while others passed by on the other side. He showed the injured man compassion, and treated him as a neighbor, and even paid to have him cared for.

Alongside purity laws were ritual laws which described rites of passage, religious celebrations, and ways of worship. Jesus honored these as a good Jew. However, where human well-being and religious ritual conflicted, Jesus challenged them. He got in trouble with legalistic religious authorities and practitioners.

Jesus' disciples picked grain on the Sabbath. Jesus healed a man with a withered hand on the Sabbath. He said that the Sabbath was made for humanity and not humanity for the Sabbath.

Jesus was invested in the well-being of all human beings and committed to a human society that served the good of all. He kept ritual and purity laws when they did no harm. He understood religion to be about the well being of people as central to his faith.

THE JUDGMENTAL JESUS

In the Gospels, while Jesus' compassion is at the heart of his ministry, he can sometimes come across as judgmental when dealing with his adversaries over God's way and will. In Matthew 23, Jesus confronts the scribes and Pharisees with their hypocrisy and calls them "whitewashed tombs," "looking beautiful on the outside but on the inside being filled with the bones of the dead and all kind of filth." v.27 He spoke plainly.

Jesus was clear that goodness was a matter of what lies inside of people, not a matter of external appearance. He exposed the hypocrisy of the religious authorities who were violently opposing him because they thought he was interfering with their judgments, perspectives, and authority. They tried to discredit Jesus at every turn, even trying to kill him for his teachings and actions. They experienced him as a threat to their power and religious authority.

Jesus saw the high priests as taking advantage of their people, his people. He accused them of selling ritual sacrificial birds and animals at exorbitant costs, placing heavy ritual burdens on their people's backs, and leading them astray and away from God. He was challenging their deeply problematic misuse of religion.

Some of Jesus' wisest teachings come out of encounters with the Pharisees and Sadducees. He knew them and understood them. He is not only clever and sharp in his responses to them, but he is as informed as any of them in his knowledge of his faith

Jesus is, however, a radical reformer, an advocate for those rejected by society, a teacher and healer with authority, with a prophetic voice. He was a responsible member of his religious community who answered to God and the inner voice of the Spirit. He was confronted and baited by those religious leaders whom he saw as misrepresenting God and using their religious position to solidify their personal power.

Jesus was in the world as son of God and humanity. It was of utmost importance to him and his purpose on earth that God be honored and seen as the God of all, that God's righteousness be understood, God's love believed and embraced, and humanity be empowered for the good.

God's Kingdom (Order) was coming in the midst of time. It was breaking into the world and was in process, a fulfillment of the promised Messianic age that some had longed for and expected at the end of time. Jesus was ushering it in in the midst of time while some still saw it coming at the end of time.

JESUS, THE MARGINAL, THE RICH, AND THE COMMON PEOPLE

Jesus reached out to all, including as we have noted, social outcasts, those marginalized and ostracized, and the poor who constituted much of the population.

On the other end of the spectrum from the marginalized and those of modest or ordinary means, were those in power, the wealthy. Jesus saw the spiritual pitfalls the extraordinarily rich faced. They were often not willing to share their bounty. He taught that when one is pursuing wealth or power as one's singular goal, eclipsing all others, it becomes an idolatry. It leads to a spiritual vacuum and self-destruction.

Jesus made clear that those with means need to share their wealth for their own sake. Their well-being would come in loving God more than wealth and prestige, and loving others as much as themselves. He was clear, wealth and power can destroy one's soul, one's humanity. Jesus honored people whatever their economic or social status and taught his disciples to do the same.

We have talked about Jesus' reaching out to those on the margins and calling the wealthy to account. It could seem that they were the only ones Jesus cared about or paid attention to. Jesus obviously also loved those who were neither marginalized nor rich to begin with, from his disciples to the general population. They made up most of his followers.

Jesus was wise and knew that everyone has needs, many of them invisible. He healed spirits and minds as well as bodies. Remember the temptation he faced before his ministry began to turn bread to stone? Jesus replied that human beings do not live by bread alone. Important as bread is to life, so important that it can be used to manipulate people,

Jesus knew that spiritual nourishment is important along with physical nourishment. Together they are the bread of life.

One of Jesus' teachings that was especially hard to accept is that God loves the late comers as much as those who have been in the fold and faithful throughout life. It seems unjust. There is the prodigal son, the lost sheep, the laborer last to join in the work who was paid as much as those who worked all day, the robber on the cross beside Jesus who proclaimed his faith as he was dying. All these people had a late change of heart, yet each reaped the full rewards of God's love along with those who had been faithful for a lifetime.

Remember the Parable of the Prodigal Son who was lavishly welcomed home by his father after years of sinful living? If we read to the end of the parable, we hear the father saying to the elder brother who had worked by his side for a lifetime, "everything I have is yours and always has been."

We are reminded that the faithful are not forgotten, are indeed heirs. They are, however, admonished to welcome those new to the fold and those returning. All are equally deserving of love. And being with God for a lifetime is a gift.

Jesus was opening the way for his Jewish community, faithful to God through the centuries, to be open to prodigals, strangers, Gentiles, and enemies. And, at the same time, to know themselves as loved by God as was the elder brother.

The early church, made up at first exclusively of Jewish followers of Jesus, would eventually welcome Gentiles and span two vastly distinct cultures, the culture of the Israelites, long seen as chosen of God, and Romans, Greeks, and people from other surrounding nations—late comers. The laws of love were meant to be practiced by all. Sorting out what that meant would be a challenge for the emerging Christian community.

In all his teachings, Jesus was revealing the heart of God's love and opening new visions of God's ever-creating activity and will.

JESUS AS HEALER

In the Gospels, Jesus was a healer as well as a teacher, spiritual leader, and prophet. We hear that Jesus heals a blind man, a man described as "deaf and mute," and lepers. He casts out demons and raises Lazarus from the dead as well as the son of a widowed mother. Jesus heals the woman with a flow of blood. He heals the female slave of a Roman centurion and enables a man with disabilities to walk. In fact, in one place in the gospel of Matthew it says that the crowds followed him, and he healed them all.

As we look at the healing Jesus did, it is important to be aware of the many layers his healing had.

Early in his ministry, Jesus delivers what we know as the Beatitudes. The Beatitudes give us insight into the breadth of what healing means.

> *Blessed are the poor in spirit, for theirs is the kingdom of heaven.*
>
> *Blessed are those who mourn, for they will be comforted.*
>
> *Blessed are the meek, for they will inherit the earth.*
>
> *Blessed are those who hunger and thirst for righteousness, for they will be filled.*
>
> *Blessed are the merciful, for they will receive mercy,*
>
> *Blessed are the pure in heart, for they will see God.*
>
> *Blessed are the peace makers, for they will be called children of God.*
>
> *Blessed are those who are persecuted for righteousness's sake, for theirs is the kingdom of heaven.*
>
> *Blessed are you when people revile you and persecute you and utter all kinds of evil against you falsely on my account. Rejoice and be glad for your reward is great in heaven, for in the same way they persecuted the prophets who were before you.* Matthew 5:3-11

Blessed are the poor in spirit, those who mourn, those who hunger and thirst for righteousness, the merciful, the pure in heart, the peace makers, those persecuted for righteousness's sake. Your healing will come, and you will be blessed (Makarios), made whole by God's grace. Holy.

Jesus' healing comes to enable people to know themselves as in God's care, as sacred, precious beings no matter how society sees them. Sometimes that entails physical healing and at other times, healing of invisible wounds, satisfying those longing for meaning, or assuring the fearful that they have inner strength.

Many of Jesus' healing miracles have spiritual, psychological, and social meaning as well as physical meaning. Blind eyes can see new truth and experience spiritual awakening. Deaf ears can learn to listen and hear life giving truths. People crippled by diseases can be given strength to live meaningful lives. Those overcome and paralyzed by grief can find hope. Those who have felt shamed and shunned by society are accepted by Jesus. Jesus said, "Let those who have eyes to see, see, and those who have ears to hear, hear."

Jesus searched the heart and loved from the core of his being and had healing power. He knew that all human beings need healing in one way or another at various times in their lives.

Jesus' ministry was life-giving in every way possible. He encouraged people to ask for what they needed. No matter how obvious a physical need for healing was, Jesus would often ask, "What do you want?" The person with a need had to be involved, desire healing and seek it if they could. When they could not, others could be advocates.

Sometimes, it was the faith of friends or family members who brought loved ones to Jesus or took Jesus to them for healing. When Jesus said, "Your faith has made you whole," he assumed an active role in wellness on the part of those needing healing or on the part of those who cared about them.

Sometimes, healing is from crippling anxieties and fears from which people want to be set free or be able to bear. I came across the following prayer written by an unknown author that asks for that kind of healing.

"Dear God, dispel my fear: End my anxiety. Wipe worry from my mind. May those I care about be safe. Make known the healing power of your hands. Give comfort and shelter beneath your wings. Grant restorative sleep tonight and safe passage to tomorrow. Amen."

Jesus healed people without regard for religious and cultural taboos. He ministered to all who came to him. And sometimes, he sought them out.

HEALING AND SCIENCE

Jesus' healing ministry is key to who he was and yet his healing ministry can be challenging for modern minds. People who believe all healing is possible in Jesus' name are left bereft if healing does not come. They can feel abandoned by God or guilty for not having enough faith.

On the other hand it can be hard for those with a scientific bent or questioning mind to accept the healing potential in faith.

The healing miracles set in Jesus' time took place in a non-scientific world where science and medicine were not as developed as they are today, and where the cause or the nature of sickness was seldom known. Psychological trauma, mental and physical illness were often seen as the result of sin or demonic possession.

In Jesus's day, healers of all kinds were common. Jesus was a healer among healers. Jesus saw the miracles he performed as representing God's power for healing the whole person. In his teaching, he never equated sickness and sin. He did see faith as contributing to healing.

As we read about Jesus' healing miracles and pray for healing in our own lives and in the lives of those we love, we often struggle with the part faith plays in the healing process in our modern world.

When faced with disease or addiction, disasters or pandemics, wisdom leads us to use all means available for healing. Thinking about Jesus' healing can serve as a reminder that God wills wholeness which in our modern world comes in many ways.

Every day, science is seeking out causes and cures for diseases, and doctors, nurses, and other health practitioners schooled in modern medicine are practicing the art of healing. The Spirit can be at work in the healing arts and in science.

Faith, science, and medicine can be partners in healing. However, we cannot assume that when healing does not take place, the healing arts and faith healing have failed. Or God has failed or not intervened, or worse, is punishing for sins. There are times when diseases and accidents take lives despite all the efforts to save them.

Often, people tend to assume that death is the failure of healing. Death itself can be an answer to prayer and a blessing for those for whom there is no cure for their disease, no help available. Sometimes comfort, peace, and the sense of a holy Presence, and the presence of human love is the only intervention possible. It carries its own form of healing.

The Spirit moved in many ways through Jesus and through his followers in the early church, to heal, to bring about peace and new vision. The Spirit of healing is moving still and though invisible, it can be felt. It is with us when healing is possible and when it is not possible, it is a giver of comfort and strength.

In my childish way, I struggled with how to apply Jesus' healing miracles to my life when I was about eight years old. The following experience still serves as a window on healing for me as an adult.

When I was in third grade, my Sunday School teacher told us with great passion and certainty that Jesus healed people and could heal us. I took it all in with great faith. That was the year I discovered that I was quite nearsighted. The doctor was worried. He told me I should be a farmer and not choose a profession that required a lot of reading. I was afraid I would lose my sight. Having heard that Jesus healed the blind man, I prayed every night for a miracle. I wanted normal vision again. I set a time frame for God. I would pray each night for a month. When I opened my eyes in the morning at the end of that time, I was sure God in Jesus would have restored my vision.

So, every night for a month I prayed for good vision. When the magical morning came, I opened my eyes with great expectation, and… no change. I learned, even at the age of eight, that since my vision was not fully restored, I needed a new prayer. Maybe God would help me live with my vision as it was and help me keep using my eyes, even with my serious nearsightedness. Somehow, the experience did not change my faith in God, but it did make a correction in my expectations. And I am blessed to still see well enough to be writing this book.

As an adult, I have had to deal with far more serious issues than nearsightedness. In both my personal and professional life, I have had to face illness and death, and have lived with the fear of them along with the fears of the disabilities that come with some illness or chronic condition.

I have found hope in Jesus' healing presence and strength in the Spirit in times of need. Sometimes, however, before hope comes, there is a time of darkness and doubt.

Whatever our modern take on Jesus' healing miracles is today, Jesus was seen as a healer in his time and that translates into his being life-giving in all times. It was clear that he valued life in this world, wholeness for individuals on all levels, and so did the God he worshipped and embodied.

If we go back to the temptations, we find Jesus rejecting asking God to be a miracle worker and save him if he threw himself off the pinnacle to prove his divinity. We do not pray for miracles to put God to the test. We pray to be close to God and connect God's power with our own for healing in whatever way is possible.

Jesus taught his followers to be advocates for healing others and to treasure their own lives. He saw the Divine in a human touch.

Even amid healing miracles, the people in Jesus' day were living on the other side of innocence. They had witnessed plagues, wars, famine, oppression, and death come in many ways. Jesus said these things would always be with the world even as he taught his disciples to pray for God's Kingdom to come. God's saving presence exists alongside of, or in the midst of, human sin and social evils and the inexorable reality of natural disease and disaster.

Sometimes whole groups of people are traumatized by these diseases and disasters and need to find healing and resilience and a way back to life after devastating loss.

In the cross of Jesus, we see that God in Jesus suffers with humanity, and in the resurrection, we know that God has the last word. The healing message of Jesus' life, death, and resurrection is to choose life in whatever way it is possible and pursue all that leads to life for all of creation, and trust God with life after death.

Even amid all the brokenness in the world, God's Realm is coming, it is here. God's love strengthens us, fills us with hope and gives us courage to pursue life. Even though Jesus did not see the end of war or poverty in his time, he sowed the seeds for social healing in eras to come.

FAITH HEALERS IN THE MODERN WORLD

The pursuit of healing in Jesus' name in the modern world is complicated. There are those who seem to have the gift of healing. However, the world of "spiritual healing" can also be a world fraught with fraud and sensationalism. Discernment and even skepticism is wise. True healers tend not to make a spectacle of their work or of themselves.

Through the power of prayer or through those with a gift for healing, we seek the healing of Jesus or the Spirit. As we do, we accept the reality of some physical limitations that cannot be physically healed: children with rare diseases, chronic conditions, end-of-life situations. We pray as individuals and in communities of faith because there is strength in communal caring and ritual. We pray for wholeness and healing and for strength when physical healing cannot come. And we pray and work for advances in science and medicine that can either heal diseases, hold them at bay, or extend life in the face of them.

In the cultures of some Native Americans, it is customary when a member of a family is sick for as many members as can to gather around their bed for support and healing. It has been shown that their presence contributes to recovery where that is possible and to peace when it is not.

In today's hospitals, in ordinary times, visitors may be limited and at times even not desired. And in pandemics, or when immune systems are compromised, impossible. However, in whatever way possible the support of others is important during challenges to health. We can all participate in healing.

JESUS PROCLAIMS THE KINGDOM (REALM) OF GOD

Throughout his ministry, Jesus proclaimed that God's Kingdom was at hand and breaking into the world and was yet to come in its fullness. He told stories and parables about that Kingdom. Jesus knew that the current religious and political powers would all fail: the Roman authorities ruling on the backs of the Jewish people and the High Priests taking advantage of their own people.

He saw that all human institutions were and always will be time-bound, however essential they are. God's Kingdom (Realm) was, and is, and will be, an order that runs like a golden thread through all time. It enters into time, reminding us that human power is finite. God's Order can breathe life into creation, call love out of the depths to the center of life and assure us that God is both with us and around us and in us in all circumstances.

Jesus likened God's Realm to a mustard seed. When planted and watered it grows into a great shrub that provides shade and a safe nesting place for birds.

Jesus saw God's presence with and in creation as sure and reliable. God's Realm is both in our midst and coming, the seeds have been planted. The restoration of creation is coming to fruition. In God's Order, humanity can find a safe living and resting place.

God's Realm is and will be an order in which God's righteousness and liberation, goodness and love are experienced and practiced. The order and goodness intended for creation from its beginning will be realized over time. God's Realm is to be sought after like a precious "pearl of great price."

As we speak of God's Kingdom, it helps if we translate the word "Kingdom" into modern vernacular. We know that only a few actual earthly monarchies exist and for good reason. They are built on hierarchical, feudal structures that divide human beings and create subservient populations.

In Jesus day, "Kingdom" was a shorthand way of referring to the powerful political structure of his day. "Kingdoms" with their "Lordships" were common ways of ordering society that were understood and taken for granted by most people in his time. Thus, "God's Kingdom" would be other than, more important than, more life giving than any earthly rule.

Jesus certainly did not mean to glorify or idealize rule by kings. It simply was the way of ordering secular life in his time. When those challenging Jesus asked whether his followers should obey Caesar and the way life was in his time, they asked this question: "Is it lawful to pay taxes to the Emperor?" Jesus said, "Render to Caesar the things that are Caesar's and to God the things that are God's." Matthew 22:21

Jesus recognized that humanity lives in and with political reality but also, and more importantly, recognized a higher authority, God's Order and way of life. God's creative power is at work, breaking into this world, offering ways of being and relating that honor the sanctity of life.

When Jesus spoke of God's Kingdom, there was serious debate about whether by God's Kingdom he meant the restoration of the Davidic Kingdom of the past, a new Order in this world, or the Eschaton, the end of the world.

Jesus was not about the restoration of an earthly Davidic Kingdom or about being a King as popularly understood. Earthly systems were to serve righteous ends but were not ends in themselves. Jesus made clear that his "Kingdom" was not of this world though it was in this world. He made clear that the kind of Order about which he was teaching, while it began in this world, connected with God's realm beyond the boundaries of earth.

Jesus recognized human orders as essential to societal functioning, and he saw the entire world as God's dwelling place, a place where all were welcome: newcomers, latecomers, outsiders, strangers, enemies, as well as the faithful. And he saw the possibility of God's Realm existing in the midst of, connected to earthly existence. God's Realm, by its existence, judges the Kingdoms of this world.

Jesus saw creation moving toward God's "New Creation" that would be built on love for God and love between human beings. He shared the prophet Isaiah's vision in chapter 61 which ends with verse 11:

For as the earth brings forth its shoots,
And as a garden causes what is sown in it to spring up,
So God will cause righteousness and praise
To spring up before all the nations.

Jesus gave his disciples and those who would follow a prayer to pray that begins and ends with a petition for God's Kingdom to come and God's will be done.

Our Father, who art in heaven
Hallowed be your name.
Your Kingdom come, your will be done
On earth as it is in heaven.
Give us this day our daily bread
And forgive us our trespasses.
As we forgive those who trespass against us.
And lead us not into temptation.
But deliver us from evil.
For Thine is the Kingdom and the Power and the Glory forever.
Amen

THE REALM OF GOD AND END TIMES

There was one prophetic tradition that claimed that the coming of the Messiah would usher in end times. There is allusion to this in Jesus' teaching and in the missionary work of his followers. There was discussion of a last judgment when God would separate the righteous from the unrighteous. In this "last judgment" God alone would judge humankind.

However, Jesus did not spend time teaching about the end of the world. Jesus advocated social change in this world by his actions: change that does more than rearrange power and who has it but change that redefines power. And as his adversaries said of him, "you show deference to no one; for you do not treat people with partiality."

God's Order, the New Creation of which Jesus spoke, would be an order based on compassionate ethics, common sense, the observance of just laws and the practice of inclusive mercy. A creation based on living love in a people who walked humbly with a loving and liberating God.

By their own actions, those who lived by greed, arrogance, hatred, and disdain for others would be judged in life by the chaos and harm they caused. God's power was not the kind of power exercised by corrupt and powerful demagogues. The power of God is, like God's own self, beyond the ability of human beings to fully comprehend.

God turned the tables on the world. In Jesus, the world judged God and rejected the Holy. God became vulnerable. The creating power of the universe was crucified. He did not resist. But in that death, there was life and a new opening up of the dividing wall between heaven and earth and a new vision of power.

BEYOND CHANGE: REDEFINING POWER

The Realm of God is an order in which power, as seen in human contexts, is redefined, and lived out in ways that support the sanctity of all life.

Jesus, building on his own tradition, set the stage for transformative change, liberation movements, redefining power, and moving toward a peaceable just and loving creation. He set the framework, the foundation, the boundaries for determining the means used for pursuing God's Order. Throughout his life, he tried to help people understand God's power and power exercised in God's name in a new light. God was not about conferring power on secular authorities. God was about redefining power, about the power of love.

Recounting an event in our modern era illustrates the difference between changing who has power and redefining power.

At a United Nations Conference on the Status of Women in Mexico City in 1976, the press kept referring to the feminist agenda as pitting women against men. Or pitting "first-world" women against "third-world" women, or white women against women of color.

Many feminists made clear that they were not advocating women's reversing power with men, nor were women at war with men or one another. They were about addressing systems of injustice that diminish everyone's humanity. They were about redefining power from "ruling over" to "living justly and compassionately with one another." They were calling for a new order in which the power to love and be loved, to meet everyone's needs, to restrain evil, is sought after. Institutional power is to serve these ends.

It is, of course, important to have people who have been discriminated against in positions of influence. We take that for granted. But liberation is ultimately about changing systems that demean life itself.

Jesus knew how hard it was and will always be to confront the demons that destroy life. Jesus wept over Jerusalem and cried out, "Would that you knew the things that make for peace." God's Order is one in which the things that make for peace are discerned and pursued.

God's Realm is not some Utopian dream. It is a Realm entered into and made real by human beings living in the light of God's love.

PART II
JESUS' DEATH AND RESURRECTION

In Jesus' ministry he quickly got in trouble with both the religious and secular authorities of Palestine. What got him in so much trouble that his adversaries wanted him dead?

Jesus was a threat to the religious establishment, especially to the High Priests. They saw him as undermining their authority with his controversial teaching, his truth telling about their inner moral poverty, and immoral and corrupt colluding with Rome.

Jesus was a threat to Roman authority. Rome had key Jewish leaders in its pocket. They wondered if this new "King of the Jews," so popular with the people, would undermine the occupation and stir up a rebellion. Would his uneasy relationship with the High Priests spell trouble?

Roman leaders were corrupt and had their feet on the necks of the Jewish people through taxation and all the insults of occupation. Jesus understood the injustice and bankruptcy of secular Roman authority. As he developed a huge following, he raised the fears of those in power in already unstable times.

Jesus defied many common social and religious perceptions about who and what is good. He did not accept violence or revenge as a way of life or as an activity of the Divine. He turned many values of society upside down, including who is in or out of God's favor. And who is worthy of honor and respect in society. He did this with authority and clarity of purpose.

Tensions in Palestine over Roman occupation were heightening throughout Jesus' life. Power struggles among groups in his own Jewish religious community were ongoing. A perfect storm was brewing.

In these unsettled times, the people in high places who felt Jesus was a problem wanted to act. The High Priests wanted Jesus out of the way. They called him a blasphemer. The Romans, wary of his leading an uprising or of upsetting the balance of power, struck a deal with the High Priests. They would try him. There were some among the populace who wanted Jesus to lead an insurrection and he did not. They felt betrayed.

Jesus was popular with so many people that he probably could have led a rebellion, but it would have been crushed by Rome. In fact, when there was a rebellion by the Zealots years later, it was brutally squashed and turned out to be a suicidal move.

Jesus was a man of peace and that was a threat in a time when violence was a way of life. He challenged long held prejudices and perspectives. He shook the foundations of religious and political thought.

At one point, Jesus, in a rare demonstration of anger, entered the Temple in Jerusalem and, in the outer court where worshipers bought birds and other animals to offer as sacrifices, he overturned the merchants' tables and shouted that God's house is a house of prayer, not a den of thieves.

Jesus held a revolutionary concept of God and God's inclusive love. He called for the establishment of God's Realm on earth. Jesus was a human being in whom the presence and power of God dwelt and in whom God's being shone. He was a problem for those living in the shadows of deceit, including self-deceit, and hunger for power.

After three years of ministry the tension surrounding Jesus was coming to a head. He decided to go to Jerusalem. Without wavering, he entered Jerusalem to confront, on his own, the powers that were coalescing against him.

On the eve of Passover, Jesus rode into Jerusalem on a donkey, to the cheers of the crowd who proclaimed him "Son of David, King," and shouted Hosannas. He was fulfilling a Messianic prophesy as he entered the eye of the storm that was swirling around him. He was about to redefine the meaning of Messianic King. The writers of Scripture see in his entry into Jerusalem the fulfillment of Biblical prophecy to which he gave new meaning.

> *Rejoice greatly, O daughter Zion!*
> *Should aloud, O daughter of Jerusalem!*
> *Lo, your king comes to you,*
> *Triumphant and victorious is he,*
> *Humble and riding on a donkey,*
> *On a colt, the foal of a donkey.* Zechariah 9:9

Zechariah envisioned a warrior king and yet a king with humility. What would follow was to forever change the concept of God sending a warrior King as Messiah. At least it was meant to.

We know his entry into Jerusalem as Palm Sunday because the crowds following him, were waving palm branches and shouting "Hosanna," which means "save us"!

Jesus knew his death was an almost certain outcome when he entered Jerusalem. He had warned his disciples that this day would come. He was drawing attention to himself rather than supporting a violent rebellion. He was confronting both the power of the High Priests and of Rome, and revealing their corruption and emptiness, their ultimate impotence, and their capacity for evil.

Before his ministry began, Jesus had been tempted to sell his soul to rule over the kingdoms of this world. He had refused. As he would say when on trial, his kingdom was not of this world.

His life came to an end when he was arrested for insurrection by the Roman authorities, having been accused of blasphemy and disloyalty to Rome by the High Priests, "We found this man perverting our nation forbidding us to pay taxes to the emperor, and saying that he himself is the Messiah, a king:" Luke 23:2

Finally, Jesus was rejected by a crowd given the choice of freeing him or Barabbas, a zealot. They chose Barabbas.

Jesus was beaten, tried before Pilate, and condemned to die by crucifixion. On the beam at the top of his cross were the words, "King of the Jews." It was placed there by the Romans. A final mockery.

Jesus died because of the sins of the world, both religious and secular. According to the testimony of Scripture, he forgave the people responsible for his death. As he hung on the cross, one of the seven last things he is recorded as saying is, "Father, forgive them for they don't know what they are doing." (Luke 23:34)

While cruel men mocked him as he died, and most of his disciples stood at a distance in fear, others who loved him stood by the cross in grief, his mother, Mary Magdalene, Mary the mother of James and Joseph, and many other women, and his disciple John. One of the two criminals crucified on the cross beside him asked to be remembered when Jesus came into his Kingdom. A Centurion who was a Roman soldier, standing beneath the cross, was heard to say, "Surely this was a son of God." A rich man, Joseph of Arimathea, gave him a burial place.

When Jesus died, it was written that the veil of the Temple was torn in two, that veil that kept the Holy of Holies hidden, apart from the people and available only to the high priests. The Holy of Holies sheltered the Ark of the Covenant, the Ten Commandments. Access to the holy of holies was now open to all. The divide between heaven and earth was shattered and bridged. Common ordinary people had direct access to the Holy.

The sky turned black; the earth shook. It was the end of time and the beginning of time. The Creating One gave up his life for Creation.

When the forces of evil in his society struck out against Jesus, they were striking out against the good, against God. The cross did not sanctify sacrifice, it was meant to end it, to defeat it. The forces of evil could not rid the world of Jesus' power.

After his death, Jesus' disciples mourned and felt lost, still in fear for their own lives. They gathered in the upper room where they had shared the last meal eaten with Jesus on the night of Passover.

Jesus was crucified on Friday, a few hours before the Sabbath began. Early in the morning on Sunday, some women who had followed him from Galilee went to anoint his body with oil and that is when everything turned around. The great stone in front of his tomb was rolled away and the tomb was empty.

While each Gospel recounts the resurrection slightly differently, many experienced his presence. Jesus had risen from the grave. He appeared to the disciples in the upper room. He met them on the shore and in their homes. He met others on the road to Emmaus and broke bread in their home. Jesus' story did not end with his death.

After his crucifixion, Jesus' disciples, Mary Magdalene, Mary the mother of James, and Salome, Joanna, and some other followers, experienced him as alive, resurrected. As he revealed himself to them, his disciples and others felt the indescribable wonder of his living presence. The word spread. Jesus has overcome death! He is alive!

When forty days had passed, Jesus' presence on earth and his appearances ended. Jesus' disciples and the followers who had experienced him as risen now experienced him as ascending to God. His mission was complete. His future now rested in the hands of his followers to whom Jesus had said, "greater things than I have done, you will do." After the disciples had, by lot, added a disciple to replace the disciple Judas who had betrayed Jesus, they remained together in prayer: waiting and praying.

Then, one day as they were gathered in one place, on a day now known in the church as Pentecost, the Holy Spirit descended on them like tongues of fire. They saw in the resurrection the power of God at work giving life through the Holy Spirit, and the promise of new life in the world.

This is the brief recounting of Jesus' death and resurrection and the birth of the Church. What meaning do we and the church make of the crucifixion and resurrection?

THE MEANING OF THE CRUCIFIXION

In First Corinthians, Paul wrote:

> *For Jews demand signs and Greeks desire wisdom, but we proclaim Christ crucified, a stumbling block to Jews and foolishness to Gentiles, but to those who are called, both Jews and Greeks, Christ the power of God and the wisdom of God.* 1 Cor, 1:22-24

Christ the power of God and the wisdom of God.

Over time, different theories emerged in the church about what the crucifixion and resurrection meant. Some said Jesus was sacrificing himself for the sins of the world. Others said he was demonstrating the love of God. Others said he was substituting for humanity and bearing the price of sin, a ransom to save humanity and satisfy God's justice. Some said God the Father was giving his only Son to atone for the sins of the world. People began to talk about being saved for eternal life by Jesus' blood. And there were many more theories.

There were some who began to equate Jesus with Moses. As Moses had led his people out of Egypt, the Hebrew people identified and saved from death by the blood of the paschal lamb on their doorposts, so Jesus had become the paschal lamb who saved his people from the slavery of death to the freedom of eternal life.

Jesus was seen by some of his followers as the new Adam, the new human being. Through him, some saw God's image restored in humanity. Jesus' death was reclaiming creation from original sin.

In the time when Jesus lived, animal sacrifices were offered up for the people's sin. Some said that Jesus became the sacrificial offering to end sacrifice, the sacrificial lamb. How do we see the cross today?

EVOLVING MEANINGS OF THE CROSS

Every time we hear the account of Jesus' crucifixion and resurrection, we are confronted with the question of their meaning for us today. That meaning has evolved over time. How we interpret the cross is central to how we see God and the future shape of Christianity.

Different interpretations of the meaning of Jesus' life, death and resurrection have divided Christians through the ages. It is good to be aware of them, but we do not have to choose from among them. We can ponder the meaning the end of Jesus' life has for us in our own spiritual journey and let it speak to us beyond all doctrinal beliefs.

While many have been inspired by and found grounding for their lives in believing in Jesus' sacrificial death for them and the sins of the world by the shedding of his blood, others have struggled to understand how his death could be caused or allowed by a loving God. Still others did not question the meaning of the cross and left it up to their church or theologians to ponder.

For some Christians, accepting the cross and saying, "I believe that Jesus died for my sins" leads to ultimate salvation in this world and in life to come, and escape from the torments of hell through the forgiveness of sin.

Some Christians focus on salvation and eternal life through the power of the cross but do not believe in hell. Some have a universal approach to salvation, believing that ultimately, a God of love will save everyone. Other Christians do not focus on the cross and salvation but focus more on the social gospel and transformation and justice in the world.

Since the way we see the cross affects the way we see God and our life as Christians in the world, it is important to consciously ponder its meaning and with it, the resurrection that followed.

The cross is such a universal symbol of Christianity, it may seem almost sacrilegious to talk about it in rational terms. Or impossible. And indeed, speaking of it in rational terms alone can miss the depth of its symbolic meaning or its deeply emotional and spiritual meaning. So I proceed with caution.

Of this we can be sure. What was laid bare in the cross was the human capacity for sin and evil that led to the crucifixion of Jesus, an innocent man. We also see Jesus' capacity for courageous and unbounded love and willingness to die himself rather than lead his followers in rebellions to sure death. He stood before the forces of evil with dignity and strength and died at the hands of sinful and ignorant people.

Those orchestrating the crucifixion may not have believed that God was with Jesus or in Jesus that day, or cared, though Pilate's wife had an inkling. They did know that they were crucifying an innocent man though some High Priests may really have believed that he was guilty of blasphemy.

The Apostle's Creed is universally accepted in Western Churches It states, after a statement of belief in God the Father, simply this: Following a statement of belief in God the Father:

> *I believe in Jesus Christ, his only Son, our Lord, who was conceived of the Holy Spirit, born of the virgin Mary, who suffered under Pontius Pilate, was crucified, died and was buried, descended into hell (the grave), rose again from the dead on the third day, ascended into heaven, and is seated on the right hand of God, the Father Almighty, who will come again to judge the living and the dead.*

In the creed, all that is stated about the cross is that Jesus was crucified, died, and was buried.

The belief that Jesus' sacrificial death on the cross has saving power is a traditional and fairly universal Christian belief. This belief raises the whole question of the place of sacrifice in a life of faith now and in the coming age.

In the time when Jesus lived, religious sacrifice was taken for granted and crucifixion was common in the political sphere. We no longer live in a time when Jews or Christians sacrifice animals as offerings of repentance, or as peace offerings. It is important to not assume or sanctify religious sacrifice as a means to salvation today.

As a Pastor, I have been asked by many people over the years why God needed to sacrifice his son in order to forgive our sins. Can't God forgive sins without sacrifice? Wasn't God a forgiving God before Jesus?

These are valid questions. How we answer them affects our perception of God. Must people believe that God gave Jesus to die for their sins in order to be "saved"? And is there a connection between our thinking of God's sacrificing Jesus and our belief in sacrifice as the highest form of love and loyalty. Or, at the opposite end of the spectrum, can we rationalize sacrificing others for good causes?

The questions surrounding the cross are not purely abstract. There is something basic, social, ecclesial, personal, and deeply ethical about them. Because this is so, I want to share how it is that I came to ask these questions for myself.

MY JOURNEY WITH JESUS AND HIS DEATH ON THE CROSS

Before I, personally, began asking questions about the cross, I was a teenager with a passionate faith. I went to Good Friday services from noon to three with my friends and wept with a full and grateful heart at the depth of Jesus' love and sacrifice for us, for me, and our salvation, as we remembered the last hours of his life and his last words. I had learned about that sacrifice in the church. Attending worship on Good Fridays was a profound and meaningful experience. Jesus' last words are still etched in my mind from those days.

My peers and I did not think much about what being saved by Jesus' death meant, but the thought of being loved enough that someone would die for us had a deep resonance. My friends and I wore an empty cross as a symbol of our faith. I took the familiar sight of the crucifix, the cross with Jesus on it that stood on my Catholic grandmother's dresser, as a significant symbol of her faith.

Over time, I became aware that the empty cross was a symbol of resurrection. But, of course, before resurrection there was his death on the cross. At some point, I began to become uncomfortable with the cross hanging around my neck as jewelry. Today I understand that for many the cross is a symbol that they are Christian. I also know the cross has meaning for other people because Jesus had experienced suffering and was with them, present for them in their suffering and the suffering of the world.

Over time, as I thought about the fact that Jesus as an innocent man had been put to death because he was a threat to the powerful religious and secular leaders in his day, I became aware of how many other innocent people had been killed for threatening those in power. How many innocent people had been killed in their leaders' struggle for power. How many innocent people had died because of prejudice and hatred.

In our collective memory, there were the Africans dying on slave ships, the Armenian Genocide and the Holocaust in Germany. Millions killed in wars. South Africans killed and imprisoned under Apartheid. Gazans facing genocide as I write, and so many other innocent deaths.

I wanted to think in terms of Jesus' sacrifice as putting an end to sacrifice, but it had not. For some, it sanctified it, it justified the scapegoating of some to cover up the sins of others, the sacrifice of some human beings to achieve land and power over others. It never seemed to be the powerful who were giving their lives for the powerless. And when the powerless sacrificed their lives, it was too often in vain, though noble explanations were at times attempted.

I thought about the Scripture passages, etched in my brain and pondered them. When Jesus talked about "losing our lives to find them," was he speaking of dying or suffering or sacrifice, following in his footsteps?

I could read the passage to be about an inner struggle for that which gives life: giving up idolatries, moving beyond egotisms, living a compassionate life, finding hope and finding new life through knowing God or the Spirit or Jesus a life force. Or I could see myself on a cross.

I began to think that the cross is not meant to condone suffering or glorify it. It is not meant to encourage martyrdom. Jesus' ministry was one of teaching, healing, of bringing the lost or marginalized into the fold, of rejoicing over finding the lost sheep. Jesus celebrated and affirmed life. He said he came to bring life and bring it abundantly. The cross is not meant to overshadow his life.

Long before the cross God was a forgiving God. It is part of God's being. God's forgiveness did not depend on the cross. It was there in Judaism before Christianity emerged. Jacob was stopped by God from sacrificing Isaac. The cross makes God's vulnerability and forgiveness visible and leads to God's overcoming death itself.

These thoughts were all running through my mind as I thought about the cross.

When Tom and I were students at Princeton Theological Seminary, the Choir, in which he sang, always included the following hymn in its concerts.

In the cross of Christ I glory,
Towering o'er the wrecks of time
All the light of sacred story
Gathers round its head sublime.

And the last verse
Bane and blessing, pain, and sorrow
By the cross are sanctified
Peace is there that knows no measure,
Joys that through all time abide.

John Bowring, 1825 Ithamar Conkey, 1851

When we went back for a Reunion years after graduation, some of us could no longer sing that hymn. What had happened in our theology, faith, or lives? I suppose the answer was different for all of us who remained silent as other voices sang this favorite hymn with gusto as in the old days.

For all of us who remained silent, glorying in death on a cross was a problem. We did not want pain and suffering to be "sanctified."

When I became a mother, I reflected on the cross from a different and very existential perspective. I was deeply repulsed by a Father, or

Mother God, for that matter, who would give his or her son to die, even for the sins of the world, which is quite abstract. Maybe we are not supposed to think about it.

The question looms. Should we celebrate sacrifice or sanctify it through the death of Jesus on the cross? Our hearts say that we should do everything we can to prevent untimely deaths.

My teen-age self was right to weep on Good Friday. My adult self weeps for the sacrifice of all innocent lives and I think Jesus weeps for them too.

Clearly, the forces of evil in the world, mundane as human greed and need for power, and ignorant as the zealot's desire to go to war no matter the cost, caused Jesus' death. Divine Wisdom knew it would come and was there with and in Jesus as he was crucified, suffering as so many in the world have suffered. And through it all, loving humanity, even the crucifiers. Didn't Jesus say as he hung on the cross, "Forgive them for they don't know what they are doing."

It was in seminary that I learned all the possible theories of the cross. And it was in churches and through hymns that I heard the concept that we are saved, washed, by Jesus' blood. I did not want to be saved by blood.

At some point I decided that theories of the cross were beside the point. Blood was beside the point. We were dealing with mystery and a depth that was hard to plumb. It had all ended in resurrection.

Whatever we believe about the cross we can be sure it is not meant to sanctify sacrifice.

DESANCTIFYING SACRIFICE

Sacrificial living and dying was not, is not the will or doing of a loving God. The miracle is that the God beyond all limitations took on our human limitations by being manifest and living among us in Jesus Christ. And as Jesus lived out God's righteousness. the world crucified God in Jesus who died not for the sins of the world, but because of them. And then overcame death in resurrection.

In our time, civil rights activists, feminists, pacifists, all manner of people of good will have been speaking out against all forms of violence, all violations of life. Human sacrifice is indeed a most extreme form of violence.

No individual or group of human beings should exist as a slave, servant, or sacrificial class. No person should be persecuted or killed for standing up for righteousness or for simply being who they are. It is up to us to stop the murder of prophets and the abuse of people's lives and labor. The cross is not meant to sanctify sacrifice.

People addressing injustices in human society are struggling to understand empowerment and service in new ways. Jesus' teachings feel right: mutual service, loving our neighbors as ourselves, washing each other's feet, reaching out to those in need, accepting help when we are in need, serving one another, loving family, friends, and enemies. And being mindful of the foundational moral Law that sets boundaries in human relationships, try to honor them.

The fact is that we live in a world that accepts human sacrifice in the midst of war. We accept sacrifice as a given though it is a cause for deep mourning even as we express gratitude for their sacrifice. And we note that it is the powerful and old who send the young off to war.

We know that many people work for little pay for long hours to feed families and we accept their sacrifice. For a long time we accepted slavery as a given and the servanthood of women in the home and of men sometimes working themselves to death.

When innocent lives are lost to violence for whatever reason, we are called upon to multiply our efforts to prevent more loss of life. We are called to work to end all that leads to human sacrifice and call upon God's power in love to be with us as we desanctify sacrifice.

Clearly the cross is not meant to condone suffering or glorify it. It is not meant to encourage martyrdom. It was different because it was a one-time event, and yet, it can somehow justify sacrifice. However, it can also give courage and an awareness of God's presence to those in harm's way. The cross makes God's vulnerability and forgiveness visible. And it leads to God's power over death.

Surely Jesus was not meant to be a scapegoat for the sins of the world. Taking a page from psychology and family therapy, no one wins in a family that allows one of its members to be a scapegoat for everything that is wrong within the whole family system. God as a loving Parent would not offer up a Son as a scapegoat.

The belief that God willingly sacrificed his son for humanity's salvation is dangerous. It has helped open the door for some Christians to exhibit violent behavior and justify sacrifice in God's name.

The cross has symbolic meaning as well as theological or pragmatic meaning. The full symbolic meaning of the cross may forever lie beyond our grasp. We can comprehend Jesus' suffering. We can see the forces that aligned against him. We understand the violence of the times and yet, no single doctrine can capture its meaning.

What happens after the cross is resurrection. Jesus' resurrection after death leads to resurrection not only after death, but to new life in this world and to a Life Force that overcomes evil.

RESURRECTION

God, the power beyond powers, the love behind all loving, being present in Jesus, in his life and teachings, in his healing, and in his suffering and death, confronts evil, reveals its final impotence, and unveils resurrection and victory over the forces of death.

The suffering Jesus endured on the cross is a symbol of sin having its momentary day. The cross can be seen as a Christian Passover, a release from the bondage of death to the freedom of life, a crossing over the sea that separates heaven and earth. Death did not have the last word. Jesus lives and there is new life in him.

Jesus Christ faces down the forces of evil with courage and strength. He is a life force in the midst of the powers that spawn death, even as in his humanity he prays that the cup of suffering would pass him by.

God, known as the Almighty, takes on the vulnerability of humanity in oneness with Jesus. Jesus faced death as all living creatures do. Those around him suffered the loss of him as people who lose those they love do. And then Jesus opened the door to the mystery of life beyond death and his Spirit empowered those who followed him to create new communities to proclaim the good news of God's presence, and the power of Love and resurrection life.

We are not saved by the blood of Christ, but by the breath of the Spirit's calling life forth out of the grasp of evil and death.

We can pray to better understand the cross, we can read Scripture, we can search our hearts, listen to many voices and theories but in the end, there is weeping over death and joy in resurrection. We can say no to sacrifice and yes to salvation. We witness the final impotence of the power of evil. In Christ, we see life emerge out of the tomb, and we can find the faith that leads to life. It is our Passover from slavery to the forces that destroy life to the freedom to embrace the powers of life.

Metaphorically speaking, the empty cross is transfigured, and we can see in it the Tree of Life. It is the Tree of Life left standing in the Garden of Eden in the Biblical creation story in Genesis. Once guarded by angels and inaccessible, its fruit becomes available to all of us for healing. Its leaves shade our path into the future. We cannot return to the Garden of Eden, we can never return to humanity's womb, but by the grace of God, the fruit of the tree of life is transported to this world where it opens the way forward into the future.

The tree of life is in our own gardens. It is the tree of life in the Book of Revelations for the healing of the nations.

The angels surrounding the Tree of Life with flaming swords have retreated. The tree of salvation, wholeness, redemption, reconciliation is accessible. The angels announce it, "He is not here, he is risen as he said."

In their book, *Saving Paradise: How Christianity Traded Love of this World for Crucifixion and Empire*, Rita Nakashima Brock and Rebecca Ann Parker write brilliantly about the post resurrection church. They found the church to be made up of communities of faith who affirmed beauty and hope in this world as a reflection of the resurrection life, of Paradise.

> *Paradise can be experienced as spiritual illumination of the heart, mind, and senses felt in moments of religious*

> *ecstasy, and it can be known in ordinary life lived with reverence and responsibility, Paradise is not a place free from suffering or conflict, but it is a place in which Spirit is present and love is possible.* p. 409

The disciple Peter, taught that God raised Jesus from the dead, the Jesus whom they had crucified, and declared that "the stone that had been rejected by the builders had become the cornerstone."

"The Kingdom of our God is become, the Kingdom of this world, and of his Christ," as it proclaims in "The Messiah" by Handel.

The Realm of God is in our midst coming into being.

JESUS' LIFE, DEATH, AND RESURRECTION BELONG TOGETHER

When we read about the end of Jesus life, it is important to remember and embrace his life, how wise his teaching, how deep his healing, how profound his love, and how much he relied on those who followed him to continue his ministry in the power of the Spirit.

The theologian George S. Hendry points out that Jesus' life and death are to be seen together. God comes to us in the fullness of the incarnation.

> *The truth that is being increasingly recognized is that the death of Christ may not be separated from his life. His life and his death are all of a piece, and neither of them can be properly understood apart from the other. What Christ accomplished in his death is nothing other than he had done throughout his life; in it he finished the work that had been given him to do.* pp. 145 and 141 (The Gospel of the Incarnation)

In Christian churches, we celebrate the 40 days before Jesus' death as Lent, following which comes Maundy Thursday, Good Friday, and Easter. After forty days of Easter comes what we call "ordinary time."

In the liturgical year, we begin Lent quite soon after we have celebrated Christmas. That does not give us much time to think about Jesus' life. But ordinary time matters. We must not forget the things Jesus taught, his life between Christmas and Easter.

Thinking about this, and frankly quite annoyed by how quickly Lent follows Christmas in the liturgical year, I wrote the following.

It seems like I just put away the Christmas things.
The place that held the baby Jesus is fresh with birth,
When I am asked to turn palms of celebration
Into ashes and wear them on my forehead
In remembrance of my mortality.
In just two months, Jesus has grown up and died.
Liturgical time violates my need to hold on to his life.
And yet they say his birth and death go together,
like gold, frankincense, and myrrh,
And bread and wine.
Micah has told us what is required of us.
To act justly, to love kindness, to walk humbly with God.
No sacrifice, no burnt offerings, just lifetimes
Of trying between birth and death to choose blessing.
The matter is not simple, human sin is complex,
Our wrong is often hidden while our pain is transparent.
The cross does indeed come too soon after Christ's birth,
But not too soon for assurance of our salvation.
God bore our murderous rage, our shame and blame.
Jesus has descended with us to the inner depths of hell.
To bring us back from the tears of unfulfillment
To daybreak, and the light of love
In ordinary time in extraordinary ways. PBK

The witness of Scripture is that God is present with humanity as one of us: as a baby in a manger, as a great teacher and healer, and as an innocent human being who, at the hands of religious and political authorities, and a mob, suffered and died on a cross and rose from the ashes of death to proclaim the power of life, the power of love, and the deep connection between the Holy and the Human.

COMMUNION AND THE CROSS

It is in the Sacrament of Communion that churches around the world remember Jesus' death and resurrection.

In communion whenever we take the elements of bread (body) and wine (blood), we hear the clergy say, "the body of Christ," or the "blood of Christ." Some Christians believe that the elements are indeed the body and blood of Christ, others see them as representing these elements. However, we see it, the Lord's Supper, or Communion, is a central sacrament of the church.

In Communion we are meant to come together as the body of Christ, each one participating is the making whole Christ's body once broken on a cross, proclaiming his resurrection and presence in our midst, holding open the doors between heaven and earth, celebrating with the saints who have gone before.

In taking communion we are meant to declare ourselves one with Christ and one another. We embrace the mutuality of serving one another as each is able. Communion is both personal and corporate. Too often theological doctrines about communion prevent our truly coming together in the name of Jesus Christ, but we are meant to move beyond doctrines to sacrament.

In the Communion service we remember the last supper that Jesus celebrated with his disciples, probably a Passover meal. We celebrate around the joyful table set for us in God's Eternal Realm. In communion we connect with the holy.

Sharing Communion, we remember. Around our Christian tables as we celebrate, many Christians do not believe that God is only with us in the church, or only with Christians. The salvation story is for everyone.

God is present at many tables, in our homes and around our world. God is with a friend who in worship remains seated during communion because she is not a believing Christian. God is with those who never enter the doors of a church or any other religious building. God is with those who worship in other ways. God calls us all to the communion table to celebrate on behalf of all humanity. God in self-giving love is calling us to community, to mutual caring and giving. Each one takes a piece of bread that makes them part of the Bread of Life, each one recognizing their connection to every other one and to the new life of resurrection.

The cup, the blood of suffering, is shed to end sacrifice, and becomes a cup of blessing and freedom, a crossing over from death to life, the blood accompanying new birth.

DIVINE POWER AND REIGN: THE ASCENDED JESUS

Ultimately, after reflection and meditation, we stand before the mystery of the cross and declare with the Apostle Paul, "Christ is the power of God and the wisdom of God."

There is little connection between the power of God and our human concept of power. As we see in the crucifixion of Jesus, human power can be blind and motivated by greed and jealousy and self-interest. It can be ominous and deadly. That kind of power cannot support life or bring about resurrection. In the life, death, and resurrection of Jesus Christ, God's true power is revealed.

God's power which brings to life cannot be defined in human terms. The god whose power was in conquering through war and violence never lived in Jesus. In Jesus, God suffers with humanity, rejoices with humanity, and raises humanity to new life. God redefines what human beings call power.

Jesus was not, is not, King as perceived by human beings. That was confusing to people then and is still confusing today. Jesus' power, God's power, is so beyond, so other than the powers in this world that it is often hard to comprehend. Divine power promises life beyond all earthly understanding. God's power suffers with humanity, and in love offers hope in this world and yet, is also mystery.

We can only catch glimpses of God's power. It is power that gives light and sustains life. It is the power of pure love. God's light refracts light like crystals and diamonds. It is the power of righteousness and understanding which, when embraced, is power for new life, for life renewed, of second chances of tragedy overcome, of heaven and earth meeting, of resurrection.

But what of the risen and ascended Christ? Does he become a traditional King then, King of all the world, sitting on the right hand of God on a throne? Ruling, conquering? The imagery is misleading.

It is a human temptation to make of Christ in heaven the kind of King he refused to be on earth. Three hours on the cross in exchange for eternity on a throne, a throne rejected by Jesus when he walked the earth.

Jesus can be "King of Kings" in the sense that he is above all earthly power. But, in an age when we live beyond monarchy, Jesus' "Lordship" requires a redefinition and new metaphors.

It is easy for us human beings, hooked on human power, to see the risen Christ as triumphantly militant as God was once perceived to be, and some of us still wish God to be. It is easy to want God to align with some nation, tribe, or religion. While most Christians have stopped singing, "Onward Christian soldiers, going as to war..." there are still those who want to sing it.

It is human to want God to have power to grant our every need, take away all our human pain, and deal masterfully with our enemies.

God's power as revealed in Jesus Christ is alive in the world around us and present in the physical and moral ordering of life; God's power is in the love that stands by us when we need strength, heals spirits and bodies, casts rainbows from divine light on ordinary walls, empties tombs, and turns mourning into the promise of a new day. It empowers us to love more fully and compassionately. God's power is in the Spirit who accompanies and guides us through life, connects us with each other in surprising ways, reveals the ways of peace, and leads us toward holy wisdom.

God's power does not align with any earthly powers except as they are agents of justice and mercy and only then when they are willing to love the enemy, not dehumanize the opposition.

The cross exposes both humanity's love of power and the depth of its ability to destroy goodness and life. It also reveals God as one who suffers with humanity, unmasks the pathos of raw human power and self-serving systems, and turns humanity toward life.

God in Jesus, God in the power of the Spirit, becomes one with us and calls us to live beyond fear of death, and opens hearts to hope. When death comes, as it inevitably must, it declares love to be stronger than death.

We praise God's name not because God meets our standards of power but because God transcends all power and is the giver of grace.

The image of Jesus on a throne, judging the nations, having power over all creation is a compelling image. But it is hard to connect the life of Jesus with a despotic god-king. It is on the cross that nations and all human powers, including religious powers are judged.

Wrestling with and frustrated by the need to believe in a God who is all powerful King by human definitions, and God as revealed in Jesus who refused to be the monarch people were expecting, I wrote the following:

Two headed God
Father- Son
Powerful Lord-Suffering Servant
I am amazed that you survive
The faith's distortions of your revelation
Our interpretations of your visitation
The power and glory of gore mixed with love
In the blood of Jesus paying the price
Required for our redemption.
My only hope is
That you are One,
At peace with yourself
That you live beyond the divided selves
Of our psyches and social systems
That you are sane, sound, source
Of abundant life.
Help us see through
Our own obsessions
With sacrifice and superiority

To your merciful, giving love
And final judgment.
We are all guilty and forgiven.
I am grateful for the truths
About the warrior you are not
Please speak to us again of who you are
In the quieting voice of your Spirit. PBK

God comes to us today in the assuring voice of the Spirit, still calling us to reform the societal idolatries and injustices that are connected to our worship of wealth and power. In pursuit of these idolatries, we become numb to sacrificing the lives of others who labor without just reward, who die in war, who are killed on city streets, and the list goes on. Human sacrifice is meant to end as we move into God's new creation in a new era and live as people empowered by God's Spirit in mutual service to one another.

The power of the Spirit is set free as the Christ living in humanity, who rather than being enthroned, becomes the universal Christ, the historical Jesus transformed by resurrection, touching our troubled world with healing hearts.

The tomb was empty when Jesus rose. Some recognized him, some did not. By some accounts he was able to break bread, cook fish, show his wounds. And yet, he appeared through walls. Those who loved him experienced him in diverse ways after the resurrection. After he left this world, he ascended, he was in the "beyond human comprehension space," beyond our time and place.

It was his Spirit, the Holy Spirit who was and is alive in the world. The living Christ, the Holy Spirit, was and is present in and with those who come after him, to carry his vision and continue his teaching and healing ministry. In them and those who will follow there is always the possibility of God's ongoing revelation and ongoing creating. God's law is being written in human hearts and lived out as the Realm of God unfolds. This is not a Utopian dream; it is the pragmatic key to survival.

And, just maybe, in the cross we are experiencing God's final judgment. Guilty and forgiven. Set free from the fear of death, free to live in the light of resurrection.

THE UNIVERSAL CHRIST

Over time, religious communities began to identify Jesus as the universal Christ. Jesus Christ comes into clearer focus. Seeing through the eyes of faith, people begin to see themselves and all humanity in Jesus: being all colors, all ethnicities, all abilities, all identities that make us who we are.

The fish is a symbol of Jesus and the Church

Kelly Brown Douglas, in her book, "The Black Christ," says (p. 116), "My grandmother's Christ was one she could talk to about the daily struggles of being poor, Black, and female. So, it is in this regard that I continue to learn from my grandmother's faith. Her faith in Christ's empowering presence suggests, at the very least, a womanish Black Christ.

We love Christ where we live as who we are. The image of Christ is actualized in us whatever cultural and genetic identities we carry.

On Christmas cards, sometimes the Madonna and Child are Black or Asian, or European, or Middle Eastern, or mixed. We can identify with baby Jesus from the vantage point of our own origins.

One Sunday before Christmas when I was worshipping in the Korean Presbyterian Church of Boston this came to me.

Praying in a Korean Church
I am surrounded by unfamiliar sounds
And since Christmas is approaching
I see the Christ child cradled In Asian arms
Almost immediately an African Jesus strolls across my mind
Followed by a child with pale skin like my own.
The original Jesus clearly looked like
His Middle Eastern parents.
With appreciation for them and history
We still dare to color him in every shade
Of our own desiring
Wanting ourselves and our own
To be recognizably his kin.
We want the holy baby for our own dear brother,
To be assured that our shared Mother/Father God
Welcomes us into the household of Love
Revealing to us the secrets of life
Casting out crippling fears
Opening our hearts to joy. PBK

There is a universal, ancient light by many names which is Love and Good, that shines in and for all creation, breaking through the shadows of brokenness and life's tragedies to the light of each returning day.

Jesus belongs to the world. There is a Muslim Jesus. There is a group in Hinduism who worship him. Books are written about the Buddha and the Christ. And there is that of God's love that is alive in every religion even when not expressly known as Christ.

There is the Spirit of Christ that leads us to see the Light in other religions.

We cannot contain the universal Christ. However, we can maintain that for us as Christians, Christ not be separated from Jesus, the Jew from Nazareth: what we have of his teachings, his healing presence, his vision of the Realm of God, what we make of his crucifixion, and how we experience his resurrection.

Without ruling out our or any other's experiences of Jesus Christ, we also need to heed his warning that many false prophets would come in his name. That is why we need to be grounded in the historical Jesus even as we embrace the risen universal Christ. It helps us be clearer about how we see God.

IN THE IMAGE OF JESUS: SIBLINGS WITH HIM

Jesus was and is both divine and human in the eyes of Christians. As Divine, he is one with God. As Human, Jesus is one of us, our brother. If Jesus is our brother, we are offspring of God, heirs with Jesus, his siblings. We are in God's image and the fullness of God can dwell in us,

Jesus looked out at the crowd one day and said, "These are my mother, my sisters and brothers." In saying this, he did not reject his own flesh and blood, he extended his human family to include his listeners, and by implication, all of humanity.

As children of God with Christ, though fully human, we carry the holy in us. We are part of Jesus' family, imperfections and all, prodigal or faithful though we be.

As heirs with Christ, we are called to see and nurture good in humanity, good in ourselves, and act for the common good. We are called to honor the sanctity of all creation, even as we confront the powers of unjust systems that continue to tear us apart, rain death, and harm creation. We are called to be creators and explorers. Sometimes we are true to this calling and sometimes we fall short or fail. Then we begin again.

Jesus was not born into a fair world. No one is. We all have obstacles to overcome, some more than others. All human beings are born with the capacity for sin, and all can be sinned against.

Jesus was also born into a world in which human beings share in the goodness of creation. We are born into a world where God is present whose judgment is just, merciful, and gracious and where the Spirit is alive as a healing, transforming, and empowering presence.

Ordinary people engage in life-giving activities every day as siblings of Jesus Christ, as human beings in the image of God. Even though life can be hard, we can be instruments of peace and hope. We can engage in daily work and relationships in ways that enhance life and nourish it. We can align with the creative energy of God and Divine wisdom. We are called upon to name and resist evil.

In the process of all reform, aligning with Divine Wisdom, resisting evil and trying to live faithful lives, there are debates about the means and methods that are right to use in achieving our goals. These discussions are not just about what works and what does not, but are about the ethics of means, the ways in which methods and goals are intertwined. Good ends can be pursued by destructive or deadly means. From the very beginning in his ministry we find Jesus rejecting means of deceit and power to achieve success and acclaim in his ministry.

So many people before and after Jesus, who called on God's name and those who did not declare faith followed in the path of holiness, participated as Jesus did, in both goals and means that contribute to bringing about a renewed creation.

There have been others who, intending to achieve worthy ends, tried to impose a Christian way of life by force or other unethical means.

As we move deep into the Twenty First Century, and into a new era, many leaders will face challenges as yet unimagined. The means they use to meet those challenges will matter, we need people with new insight and vision to keep creation spinning into the light, who try to understand the means that lead to peace.

At the heart of creation is a wholeness and well-being, a humility and strength, a wisdom and vision, that is waiting to blossom. God's image is stamped on humanity, it lies deep within. We can carry it into the world as heirs with Jesus, the Spirit of Holiness. But only if we are prepared to face our most serious temptations as he did.

The life of Jesus, as it opens our eyes to more of who God is, can also open our eyes to the more that we as human beings can be. Even though, to be human is to be limited and affected by all manner of social, emotional, and genetic realities, the seeds of God's Order have been sown among us and we can tend them. Love is at work in human hearts.

Believing in the humanity of Jesus, the Son of God, and the divinity of humanity, we find ourselves to be heirs with Jesus Christ. And we live in the amazing presence of the Spirit.

To close this chapter, I quote Howard Thurman's closing paragraph in his book, "Jesus and the Disinherited." He writes about Jesus:

> *His answer becomes humanity's answer and his life the common claim. In him the miracle of the working paper is writ large, for what he did all people may do. Thus interpreted, he belongs to no age, no race, no creed. When people look into his face, they see etched the glory of their own possibilities and their hearts whisper, "Thank you and thank God!*

In gratitude he becomes the man most worthy of action. To some he is the Eternal Presence hovering over all the myriad needs of humanity, yielding healing for the sick of body and soul, giving a lift to those whom weariness has overtaken in the long march, and calling out hidden purposes of destiny which are the common heritage. To some he is more than a Presence, he is the God-Fact, the Divine Moment in human sin and human misery. To still others he is a man who found the answer to life's riddle, and out of a profound gratitude he becomes the one most worthy of honor and praise.

CHAPTER 4
THE HOLY SPIRIT

You will receive power when the Holy Spirit comes upon you; and you will be my witnesses in Jerusalem, in all Judea, in Samaria, and to the ends of the earth. Acts 1:8

In the Twenty-First Century, our lives are crying out for the Holy Spirit to move among us in new ways, to empower us, to give us wisdom.

The Spirit is the Word of God, the Wisdom of God, the Breath of God; God communicating with and moving in and through humanity. The Spirit is God conveying God's ongoing revelation through time.

THE HOLY SPIRIT IN SCRIPTURE

The Holy Spirit is present in both the Hebrew Bible and the New Testament.

In Hebrew Scripture, the Holy Spirit is seen as God acting in the world in dynamic, often surprising ways. In Genesis, the Spirit is present brooding over creation. The Holy Spirit is alive in the living Law given to Moses and in the establishment of a covenantal people. It is there in the anointing of kings and thundering voice of prophets, alive in their words and work. It is there in the wisdom literature and poetry in Scripture. It is God at loose in the world.

In the New Testament, the Holy Spirit is with Elizabeth and Zechariah as they conceive John the Baptist, and with Mary as she becomes pregnant with Jesus, and with Joseph as he takes Mary for his wife. It is with the prophets in the Temple who declare that their Messiah is coming in Jesus. The Spirit is with John the Baptist as he preaches repentance and prepares the way for Jesus. It is the Holy Spirit who descends on Jesus like a dove at his baptism. The Spirit lives in him in all that he does and is.

Jesus promised his disciples that he would not leave them bereft. He would send the Spirit, a "Comforter," a "Helper." the Paraclete. And so it was.

The Spirit was a silent presence with Jesus' disciples and followers when they were still mourning his death and trying to absorb the fact of his resurrection. They wanted to move on, to continue his ministry but they were immobilized. And then the Spirit came to them with power and moved them forward in faith and action. It moved them beyond grief to not only accept resurrection, but to live in its strength.

It was the Spirit who enlivened and strengthened Jesus' followers both before and after his resurrection. The Spirit gave power to the emerging Christian church. The Spirit came to rest on the early followers of Jesus after his death, resurrection, and ascension. It enlivened and empowered them to be heralds of the good news of God's love. It was with them as they conducted Jesus' ministry in the world and emboldened them as they faced obstacles as believers.

THE SPIRIT AND THE EARLY CHURCH

The Spirit is very present in the early church and is spoken of often in the books of the New Testament written by the Apostle Paul and other leaders to new churches. The Spirit is alive and active. Empowering. It is their breath of life.

The book of Acts describes the coming of that Spirit to the gathered faithful on what has become known as Pentecost. The disciples and "devout Jews from every nation under heaven living in Jerusalem" were gathered.

> *And suddenly there came a sound like the rush of a violent wind and it filled the house where they were sitting. Divided tongues, as of fire, appeared among them, and a tongue rested on each of them. All of them were filled with the Holy Spirit.* (Acts 2)

At that time, though the disciples were speaking in different languages, all present understood them in their own language. The Spirit had come in a breath and a blaze to unite the faithful in a common ministry.

What happened on Pentecost is the exact opposite of what happened in Genesis 11. Genesis describes a time when everyone on earth spoke the same language. Until one day, people, living in a great city, wanting to make a name for themselves and reach God, built a high tower, the tower of Babel, that reached into the heavens,

As the story goes, God said, "Look, they are all one people, and they all speak one language; and this is only the beginning of what they will do; nothing they propose will be impossible for them to do. Come let us go down and confuse their language...." The story goes on. God came down and scattered those people to the ends of the earth where they all developed their own languages.

The coming of the Spirit on the day of Pentecost, instead of scattering people, enabled people to come together and understand each other even with their different languages. They were inspired, not to reach the heavens and become powerful like God, but to bring heaven to earth, God's love to the world. Jesus Christ's message and life would live on.

The Holy Spirit, known in the thundering words of prophets, lived in Jesus Christ and became Christ among us after his ascension. Just as it enlivened and empowered the early church, it can revive the church today. We need the Holy Spirit in religious communities and in society today as never before.

The Holy Spirit can give us the wisdom we need to face the challenges of our fast-changing and often confusing modern world. We need the Spirit's guidance and courage to make choices that will lead to humanity's survival and thriving and the survival of the natural world.

In the Reformed tradition, we have tended to focus on the first two persons of the Trinity, God the Creating, Parenting Presence, and Jesus Christ, the Saving and Redeeming One. The Holy Spirit is their energy and love at loose in the world. It is time for us to seek and trust ourselves to its presence among us in the new era we are entering.

THE SPIRIT'S MOVEMENT

"Ruach," wind or breath, is the word for Spirit in Hebrew. In the New Testament the word for Spirit is "Pneuma," also breath, "Sophia", wisdom in Greek. The Spirit is also seen in the "Logos," the Word of God made manifest in Jesus. The Spirit is the life-giving breath of God; God's vitality, God's presence, empowering, enlightening, correcting, encouraging, enveloping, embracing, revealing God to beloved creation. Moving creation into the future.

The Spirit fosters life-giving connections between people, between humanity and the rest of creation, and between humanity and our creating Source of life, our God. It is the presence of the living Christ in humanity.

The Holy Spirit is God. The most amazing thing about God as Spirit is that though invisible and mysterious, it becomes visible in the world as it is embodied in the flesh, in human beings and human communities. It is God incarnate in the world from age to age.

Just as God was in the world in Jesus Christ, God is still among us in the Spirit. It/she/he is alive in all creation. The Spirit moves to open our hearts and engages our lives in all that sustains and enhances life. It helps us discern that which destroys life and that which enables us to walk in the ways of peace.

The Holy Spirit opens our senses to beauty and moves us toward God's creating power. The Spirit is in our midst whether or not we recognize it. It is the force of holiness, reminding us of the sacredness of life. Human beings can feel, and experience its presence, embody its presence, in ways both profound and ordinary.

Like a gentle, yet powerful energy, the Spirit gives and restores life, in matters great and small. It can infuse even the mundane aspects of life with meaning and depth, with pleasure and persistence, in our places of shelter, in homes, in workplaces, in communities of faith. It confers wisdom and blesses our bodies. It works through people to turn the tides of history toward wholeness and liberation. Even in desperate times when God seems absent, it is there. It counters evil.

Dr. Paul Beran, a Professor and Consultant in the field of Middle Eastern studies, sees the Spirit as "an innovative, revolutionary understanding of God."

We need such an innovative and revolutionary understanding of God in today's world as an age is turning and we enter a new era in human history. Material innovations and political challenges are coming faster than we can manage. The earth, our home, is in danger.

Worn out traditions and doctrines often obstruct our view of God. Unholy mergers of religious and political institutions come together to undermine the fabric of faith. Propaganda corrupts truth. Misinformation can play havoc with our minds. War brings only death. It has no winners. The Holy Spirit's light can clear our sight to use modern technology for the well-being of society while resisting its dangers.

In a changing world, as the Spirit moves us toward the future, it reminds us that we do not need to give up all that we have treasured from the past and the people of faith, courage, and vision who have gone before us. The Spirit moves in all times and connects all times. It is recognized in almost all religions in various ways.

God in the Spirit who brooded over emerging creation guides us toward a renewed creation, opening our eyes to see the demons and graces of the past.

Significant changes come over the course of centuries. The Spirit works in all times and seasons and its flame is never extinguished, even in the most tragic of times.

Each generation builds on the good works and wisdom of their forebears and learns from their failures, and dangerous ideologies. Each generation is called to add its own sacred vision and guard against unholy pitfalls. Every age needs to give up ideas about God that could become idolatrous and socially dangerous and listen for the guiding voice of the Spirit.

God's Spirit as a dynamic, living Presence cannot be contained or destroyed but it can be ignored. The Spirit carries the revelation of God into the future and can comes into the world in surprising ways. As oriented toward the future as the Spirit is, it exists beyond time, carries the past on its wings, and lives in the present.

Jesus did not throw away his tradition. He knew it well and was grounded in it. He transformed it and revealed more of God's will in the fullness of time. While he opened the door for the birth of the church, he never abandoned his own people. While there was tension between the Jewish leaders and the emerging church in its early days, the Spirit never departed from Judaism though the New Testament goes on to tell the story of the Spirit's movement in the developing church. The Spirit cannot be confined to any one religious expression.

God, whose revelation is ongoing in the Spirit, opens doors to the future, sanctifies the present and tries to reconcile us with the past. The Spirit loves us into being, into our tomorrows. We do not know what surprises await, what wounds will be healed, what new doors will open. God is not static and locked in time: God's Spirit moves us toward the Realm of God on earth.

This we know. The Spirit is for us and all of creation. It is a manifestation of God. We can open our hearts to receive it or not. We can trust that it is with us or not. Sometimes we will only recognize its activity in our lives and world in retrospect. The Spirit often functions beneath consciousness, touching the depths of being.

The Spirit is at work where people care deeply for one another, where people can understand each other across differences, nourish one another across cultural barriers, embracing diversity in one world. The Spirit works in the world to enable us to open our eyes to one another's suffering without leaving us in despair. In the most tragic of times, when God seems absent, the Spirit can still breath life. It can lead toward active hope toward confession, justice and peace. It is the Energy of sacred goodness.

The Spirit can inspire us and allow creativity to flourish. It inspires people to use their gifts and talents in service of a better world. The Spirit is with us in community when our hearts and minds are open to its breath of life. We connect with the Spirit as individuals and the Spirit connects us to one another, and we need its power and presence in ever widening circles of connection.

We can experience the Spirit through music and other forms of art. It comes to us in meditation. It is in our play as well as our work. It is with us in our deepest loving and longing

The Spirit comes to us in nature through the song of a bird or the sound of rain. And it can be there in the stillness of the night or the bustle of daylight hours. The gifts of the Spirit come through grace. They are freely given and help us appreciate simple things and unravel complex puzzles. They call us back to the ways of life that honor the moral bones of the universe. They draw us toward people of goodwill and are shared across all human boundaries.

The Spirit can be in a mighty wind or in a still small voice, in a whisper or in silence. It can be present in Pentecostal worship or in the quiet of a Quaker Meeting, in the liturgy of a Catholic Mass, in the music of a Protestant choir, or in Orthodox icons. However it comes, it unveils the connection between the holy and the human and lifts it up.

The Spirit is in the movements of every act that affirms life and defies violence, prejudice, and war. And yet it is profoundly with those who suffer.

The Spirit who moves in human beings, in all cultures and across cultures. It has no specific cultural identity. The Spirit is free. In that freedom, the Spirit can free us from bondage to cultural norms and prejudices. We share our belonging to the human race with each other.

Just as we all need air to survive in our physical bodies, we need the breath of the Holy Spirit to connect with our very human spirits that lie at the heart of being. Like the air we breathe, it is there whether we are aware of it or not. It is the Soul of Life.

On a personal level, when our human spirits are broken, or confused, or suffering abuse, or lost in addictions, or subverted by idolatry and seduced by false prophets, a Spirit greater than our own is an Advocate for us and wills our healing. Even when life leaves us in despair or fear, in grief and loss, the Spirit is a silent companion reminding us that life must go on.

As abstract as the Spirit sounds, it is embodied in the very practical realities of life. It is down to earth, it is present in feelings, intuitions, senses. It is rooted in the realities of creation and of human nature and human society. It calls upon us to use our common sense as it grounds us in reality.

The Spirit can give us wisdom to negotiate the world and expand our understanding of ourselves. The Spirit who led prophets in paths of wisdom and righteousness through the ages, moves among us still. The Spirit is the word of God calling to the prophets of old and speaking saving words of life in every time.

THE LIVING WORD OF GOD

The Bible is a closed cannon, known to Christians as the Word of God. It provides us with a foundation for our lives. It is, as we have noted, the only record we have of the historical Jesus. It is the written Word. We also know Jesus Christ as the living Word, alive in the Holy Spirit.

We live in a time that the people of Biblical times could not even imagine. Spiritual and ethical issues arise that the Bible simply does not address. Just think of all the technological changes that have happened since Biblical times.

Consider the fact that the Bible was written in a time when poverty, slavery, and war were taken for granted, even sometimes seen as God's will. While in the Bible we find the seeds of justice to challenge these systemic evils, it was only over time that those seeds came to fruition and society began to work for an end to systemic slavery, poverty, war, and discrimination.

We need the Holy Spirit to breathe life and new wisdom into us and our ever-evolving world. The Spirit not only helps us to understand Scripture in our time, but it is also the carrier of God's ongoing revelation in changing times.

The Spirit speaks to individuals, communities, and institutions in ways that are hard to describe. And those who pray for the revelation of the Spirit and claim to have felt its presence and heard its voice must be tested by time and by others who have also felt inspired by the Spirit.

Church traditions and doctrines emerge as leaders and communicants in church institutions ponder and pray for God's guidance in each age. They can be a source of insight into God's ongoing activity in the world through the Spirit. But they must be tested by other voices and the movement of history. The Spirit is in the writing of inspired reflection on faith and action and in the judgment of its claim to be of God.

The process of discerning God's will and listening for the Spirit can be messy. The Spirit is with us as we ponder the will of Holiness. It can help us ask questions, voice doubts, declare certainties, and work our way through the mazes of written and lived religious doctrine and theology. And especially our own experiences. The Spirit brings the past into the present and leads into the future.

God's revelation did not end with the Bible. God is alive in today's world. The Spirit of God is alive and free as the world turns and continues to speak God's word in each generation. The Spirit meets us in the midst of our reality.

The Spirit sometimes moves to disquiet us and to awaken us to forces that destroy or diminish life until we take notice and act to address them. Through the wisdom and power of the Spirit. Human beings are called to be the living word of God in the world. Human as we are, we carry the divine within us and it lives through us.

While life in Biblical times was very different than it is now, there are things about being human that have not changed. Human beings are created in God's image. There is beauty in humanity and hope. Yet, sin persists and is a root cause of much pain and suffering. We can often turn to the pages of Scripture to see ourselves in our forebears. In their stories of stumbling, of redemption, of apostasy and reform, there is hope for the world and new challenges as each new age unfolds.

In a Sojourner's email it tells of a symbolic bird In Ghana named "Sankofa" which means "go back and get it." It is represented by a symbolic bird, Adinkra. This bird is looking backward while moving forward. In a way, the symbolic dove that represents the Holy Spirit calls us to look backward while moving forward, discerning the lessons of the past as they guide us into the future.

Jesus left it up to his disciples and followers to move his message into the future and into the world. He said he would send the Spirit to empower and guide them and they would do greater things than he had done.

THE PROPHETIC VOICE OF THE SPIRIT

The Holy Spirit spoke and continues to speak through prophetic voices. In the Bible prophets are not people who foretell the future. They do make clear what effect the beliefs, practices, and attitudes of the people of God in the present will have on the future. They are truth tellers and heralds of the ways that lead to life or destruction.

It was with the prophetic voice of the Spirit that the Prophets in Hebrew Scripture warned against the dangers of godlessness, of amassing wealth while ignoring the poor, of trusting in false gods, of striking out in violence, of bending reality, of forsaking all that is sacred for self-serving ends. The Prophets called their own religious community to reform even when in exile. And they speak these things to us today.

The prophets saw God's anger as judging evil and showing the way to righteousness. We still need prophets to remind us that evil, ignorance, violence, and prejudice lead to suffering and destruction. These forces can rain down consequences on the just and unjust until the cycles of sin are interrupted.

The voice of the Spirit, of the living Christ, speaks through today's prophets as a voice of judgment and vision, of discernment and hope. It leads into the future. The Spirit is both about nurturing, empowering, and loving individuals and about enabling people in community to be agents of God's ongoing creative power for the common good. The Spirit is with humanity for saving and enhancing life and unmasking evil. It is about social healing and reaching for the justice and peace inherent in loving.

The Spirit can work in individual lives for their salvation, not only after death, but in this world. Individual salvation for Christians is not only or even for some, primarily about life after death. Helping us discern God's direction for our lives and listen carefully for Jesus' ongoing way and finding the courage to follow it, is the ongoing work of his Spirit. Sometimes it is only as we look back on life that we know the Spirit has been at work in our lives. Every person has a part to play in addressing the overwhelming needs of the world. Everyone brings their own gifts and trusts in and supports the gifts of others as they can. That is their prophetic mission.

As human beings, we can be distracted, confused, or depressed by the many conflicts swirling around us, by the unending needs, and by our own limitations. Daily living itself can for some be hard at times. If we are to be agents of change in the world, we need to address our own needs and listen to our own hearts. We need to care about one another. The Spirit is our advocate and support and source of persistence and courage. The prophetic voice of the Spirit which affirms life. Knows us as we are and accepts us. It affirms us and calls us from despair when we need it most.

Sometimes it is in meditation or in nature that we experience a peace that is of the Spirit. When we return to ordinary life, the Spirit is with us even if we are not conscious of it. It connects with our human spirits, our bodies, our minds, our whole being.

The prophetic work of the Spirit brings wisdom and courage to those open to its insights and we carry its prophetic voice amid all the mundane realities, joys and sorrows and challenges of daily living.

At times movements develop in Christianity and other faith communities that lead back to ideologies that defy justice and peace. They lead back and lead forward toward authoritarianism and violence, and to the idolatries of wealth and power, and self-interest that yield to prejudice, to behaviors that destroy body and soul. They claim to be of God, but their fruits betray them. They breed hatred and distrust. They spread disinformation and lies. They promise greatness and dominance. And they threaten harm to those who unmask their dangers. It is against these forces that the prophetic voice of the Spirit cries out.

In the Spirit we are called to mature emotionally, socially, and ethically as surely as we mature physically. We are inspired to grow up into the image of God and all that we are meant to be. We can experience the depths of love, mutual justice, and the renewal of play and sabbath. We can be resilient in the face of adversity. We are forgiven for our own sins, and we are called to engage in the process of forgiving. We are never called to accept threats to life. The Spirit calls us all to be a light in the world, imperfect as we are. But we need the Spirit's presence and one another to claim that legacy.

In Hebrew "tikkun olam," repairing the world, can be seen as summarizes the prophetic work of the Spirit. Repairing the world and our lives is the active work of love in which we engage in the power of the Spirit.

However complex the process of repairing the world is, we are called to that task. And more than that, we are called to prevent those forces which lead to brokenness and great tragedy from taking over and taking hold in the first place where we can. We are called to not only repair the world but build God's new creation.

Addressing oppressive forces and suffering of all kinds, supporting life in all ways possible, requires change. The Spirit cannot protect us from the conflicts that accompany change or from the perpetrators of evil who resist change. The Spirit can be an ally, can give courage and offer comfort to all who truly seek goodness and life. But it is up to those who face change to embrace it in faith.

The Holy Spirit is not a personal or social fixer. The Spirit works to enable people of goodwill to make the world a better place, to name and confront evil, heal the wounds that afflict humanity, and sing the angel song of deliverance.

Human beings in each new generation are called to share a new vision of life together on this planet, a vision of God's new creation, a vision of justice, mercy, and peace. A vision of a world, not without conflict, but with the ability to deal with differences creatively. A world where art and beauty are treasured, where lines between religious and secular are blurred in the service of creation.

Sometimes we fail miserably. But we are always called back. The vision is the path to life.

THE SPIRIT, DISCERNMENT AND CONFLICT

Sometimes, the authentic prophetic voice of God's Spirit is clear but at other times, it only becomes clear after a period of discernment, debate, and discussion. Conflict has almost always accompanied the search for the Spirit's guidance as contemporary issues emerge in each age…or old issues reemerge that have lain unresolved. No one can claim absolute knowledge of the leading of the Spirit even if they think they can. In trying to discern the Spirit's movement and direction, many people, coming from a variety of orientations, are needed to uncover the path that leads into life and light.

During discernment, as we listen for the Spirit's voice in others and to the Spirit's voice within, we open ourselves to the Holy's challenging entrenched human perceptions and prejudices, fears, and histories. In the midst of this, we have the right and responsibility to stand for what we believe and open ourselves to change as the Spirit guides us.

In the Twentieth Century, the church has faced internal conflicts over many ethical, social, and theological issues including some as basic as the ordination of women, the acceptance of and ordination of members of the LGBTQA family and their right to marry, women's right to abortion, racial, ethnic and religious discrimination, saving the environment, rejection of war, denial of an epidemic, to name some of them.

Churches have been divided over political allegiances and differing attitudes about God and country. There has been disagreement on what it means for a nation to be "great" and "first" in today's world, and what to do about it. How to view China's rise to power and the importance of the military might of nations. In some cases, the direction of the Spirit becomes clear over time. In some emerging issues, ethical questions are hard to clarify.

As a given, Christians look back on Jesus' life and teachings for direction and the Spirit's guidance. Jesus was concerned with what was in people's hearts. There is a goodness, a desire for healing, empathy, compassion, love for others that precedes all outward expression of behavior. Sometimes, outward engagement in just causes and encounters with others can lead to internal transformation. In any event, Jesus taught that loving others as self summarized the law.

As people of faith look forward, we pray to find ways to be true ourselves and respectful of others as we seek God's will in controversial matters. We seek the wisdom of the Spirit as we engage in the moral quandaries of emerging issues and the conflicts that accompany them, In the process of discernment, everyone must act on their conscience, which can change. And act boldly when they are convinced that they are on the side of justice and life.

As I am writing, moral issues surrounding ex-President Donald Trump emerge daily, some reaching the level of legal action. Some Christians continued to support him. Attitudes about him set family members against family members, friends against friends, states against states, and churches against churches. Society is deeply divided.

As Christians we need the Spirit's guidance on how to understand the ethical issues before us and we need help in healing the chasms between factions in the United States. No matter how divided, sure of ourselves or confused we are, we must continue to search for means that serve justice and love.

The Spirit of Life is not only active in the moral positions we take and the life objectives we have, but the Spirit is also in the process of how we manage conflict. If, as the popular saying goes, "the devil is in the details," the Spirit is also in the process. Non-violence was the way Jesus embraced. Whatever else is true, we can assume that his Spirit continues to call us to this way of life.

The early church, though inspired and set on fire by the Spirit at Pentecost, faced its own struggles as it moved forward in the real world to build communities of faith made up of very diverse members: Jews wanting to be true to their faith and pagan Gentiles trying to find new footing as followers of Jesus.

How could Jews and Gentiles ever live, work and worship together in the same faith community? Trying to be loving communities meant dealing with simple matters like the fair sharing of food at communion, and resolving personal loyalties to leaders, and larger issues like negotiating differences over circumcision, and deciding whether and how to keep Jewish purity laws, and what pagan practices needed to be left behind and which observed.

Individually and in community they prayed for discernment, direction, and strength from the Spirit. In the face of life-threatening forces inside and outside of the church, they sought the Spirit's wisdom, who was the source of inner strength.

Conflict in not new in the church. Where there are individual differences and conflicting loyalties, and multiple opinions at work, they are to be expected. The Spirit moves through them toward justice and peace.

There are times when what is right is clear amid conflict but only a few see it. There are times when what is right is seen by some who are challenged by the powers that be. There are times when church and society are tilting toward justice.

But where is the Spirit when conflict between people of faith turns ugly, or the actions of the faithful turn deadly? There are times when the worst instincts of people of faith take over and the ways of the world prevail and alienation, even violence erupts, and people of faith take wrong turns. The church has at times prosecuted and killed those thought to be heretics who turned out to be prophets. Amid such times, the Spirit speaks through often lonely people of faith, spirit filled prophets who seek both the reform and peace of the church.

There are also times when churches are persecuted and in conflict with secular authorities. There were conflicts between Christians and the religious and secular cultures around them in the First and Second

Centuries. Some churches are persecuted or strictly controlled by the state in modern society.

The Rev. Dr, Martin Luther King, Jr, said, "But I know somehow, that only when it is dark enough that you can see the stars, that the light of the Spirit shines through."

The Spirit continues to be our light and strength as we face conflicts within and without today. We have to pray for grace to stand up to evil without demonizing each other. I lift up a person who did just that.

A PERSON FILLED WITH THE SPIRIT

I lift up a person in whom the Spirit was at work in our time as an example of what it means to stand up to evil and demonstrate faith in action in the middle of conflict and take responsibility for the process of healing when there is light at the end of the tunnel.

Archbishop Desmond Tutu was a person guided by and empowered by the Spirit as he worked tirelessly and courageously, because of his faith, for an end to Apartheid in South Africa. After its end, he led the Truth and Reconciliation process.

He did not stop there. He wrote books and preached around the world bearing witness to his faith and continuing to work to bring God's Kingdom on earth.

Toward the end of his life, Tutu called attention to apartheid in Israel as it is practiced against Palestinians. He called attention to injustices wherever they are practiced. He offered hope for an end to suffering and believed in humanity's capacity for love through the working of the Spirit. He saw the potential for good in humanity and promoted healing though the process of repentance, forgiveness, and reconciliation.

Tutu took seriously Jesus expanding of love to include even one's enemies.

He, like Jesus, was aware that sometimes those perceived as enemies are those who turn out to be righteous. To the Jews in Jesus' day, the

Samaritans were enemies, and yet, in some of Jesus' parables, they turn out to be the ones who exhibit goodness.

Over time, there can be a fluid line between oppressor and oppressed and how we see one another and ourselves and how power is distributed. As time moves on victims can become victimizers. Being a victim does not mean that one is without sin. No one is without sin. No one is beyond salvation. And there are by-standers who are drawn into the violence of oppression by their silence. There are also by-standers who help and act to stand with victim.

THE SPIRIT BRINGS HEART AND MIND TOGETHER

Bishop John Shelby Spong in his autobiography, "Here I Stand," has a whole chapter entitled, "The Heart Cannot Worship What the Mind Rejects." He is dealing with reconciling faith and science and experience. For instance, as he is advocating for the liturgy of worship to be revised to speak justly to the lives and needs of contemporary society, he is seeking to bring heart and mind together.

For many women in the church, bringing mind and heart together meant leaving behind entrenched and frankly, comfortable concepts of the roles they were "supposed" to fill as women. Those roles once accepted without any conscious thought, were seen by many as part of God's ordering of creation. But the Spirit was leading beyond those assumptions. Betty Friedan wrote her book, "The Feminine Mystique." As we in the United States responded to her writing and that of others, we had to struggle to bring heart and mind together.

Sometimes it was men who were breaking out of stereotypes and women who were holding on to them.

In conflicts arising out of the Israeli occupation of Palestinian territory, the Presbyterian Church was often divided. Congregations were trying to establish good relationships with their neighbors in Jewish synagogues. Criticizing the government policies of the Israeli State was often not taken well. It was mistakenly called antisemitism.

Keeping the peace seemed more important than working for peace with justice. Eventually, at several General Assembly, the church found its voice and the courage to be true to its own conscience. It called for an end to Apartheid in Israel and joined with Jewish voices who also stood against any kind of racism. Longing for peace between two faiths connected by their origins, bringing heart and mind together meant working for peace with justice.

This all sounds so serious and difficult, this seeking spiritual guidance for living. What is to keep us from being overwhelmed by all the ethical discernment and conflict going on around and just withdrawing in a feeling of helplessness and weariness? The answer is nothing, not even the Spirit.

There are times when we need a break. Human beings must have space to live their lives as well as take on global issues. If we take on worldwide concerns, we also need to find time for living. We need the Spirit as both Comforter and Advocate as well as Prodder and Prophet. We must, however, through it all, never let go of compassion.

Remembering that attitudes matter as well as action, and eventually lead to the actions we take, we need time for silence and prayer to figure out where we stand. We need to know that where we stand matters and what we think matters even when we are not in a position to act. "They also serve who wait and pray." Even when thinking seems like too much and we just need time to rest and renew, the world is waiting at our door.

The Spirit cannot protect us from the anxiety within ourselves that conflicts in the world create. The Spirit can give us courage and, when we need it, new breath and rest, and retore our ability to move against evil as each is enabled to do.

All of us, whatever the time in which we live, can pray with the Rev. Longfellow who wrote the following hymn.

Holy Spirit, Truth Divine,
Dawn upon this soul of mine,
Word of God, and inward Light,
Wake my spirit, clear my sight.

Rev. Samuel Longfellow, 1864

The world in which the Spirit is present, our world, is clearly finite and broken and so are we. Evil is real. Good is also real. The Spirit cannot eliminate all pain and suffering. It is with us as a guide, a comforter, a hope, a strength. The Spirit honors us, gives us courage, and reminds us that we can participate in the transforming power of resurrection now.

And there is more than meets the eye.

There will be times when justice is rising, when love is prevailing, when God seems very much present. And there will be times when God seems silent. There will be in-between times when nothing seems clear, and life seems like a roller coaster. Sometimes life seems as if it is shattering and sometimes life seems good. And times when it is all happening at the same time.

The Spirit of God, invisible but tangible in human beings, leads toward abundant life and loving relationships. It leads toward the justice and righteousness that are part of the Holy's very being.

THE SPIRIT CONNECTS WITH OUR HUMAN EMBODIED SPIRITS

The Spirit moving to deepen our understanding of God also moves to deepen our understanding of ourselves and brings out the best in us, it connects with our human spirit. In the physical world, the spirit and body are inseparable. We are each a self, a being, an "I." All of us, unique people that we are, share a common humanity. We are part of the human race.

As human beings, we need one another. It is only in death that the human spirit, the essence of self, is set free from physical reality and we must let go of physical life or of the physical life of those dearly loved. The world goes on. God's Holy Spirit envelops us is in this world, it is present like the air we breathe. It is there in our becoming. It accepts our finitude and multiplies our gifts. It moves in the world for the good of creation. It is with us in all of life's seasons. It enables us to continue beyond the death of those we love.

The Spirit can laugh with us and open our eyes to beauty and fill us with awe. It rejoices in our loving and in our sharing of talents. The Spirit can weep with us and knows well our human weaknesses. The Spirit can open doors that meet our needs. And it is through us that the Spirit is at work in the world.

Life can be unfair, and cruel. Whether because of sin or tragedy, we lose a grip on hope, God's Spirit does not abandon us. Life can be hard and heart breaking for many varied reasons: accidents, health crisis, natural disasters, economic fluctuations, death. evil.

The Spirit is with us through it all, reaching out to us, willing healing, wellbeing, and hope, and peace at the end. The Spirit cannot eliminate all pain and suffering on this side of heaven, but it can be with us as a comforter, a strength, a giver of gifts and it can empower us to receive gifts that are passed on.

I remember when my siblings and I were standing by the bedside of our mother on the night before she was to undergo dangerous, experimental heart surgery. She was going into the unknown. We were all very worried and trying hard to put on brave faces for her.

She told us that she was not afraid. She knew she was not alone. God was with her. Whatever happened, she was at peace. The Spirit was with her, and with us as we waited, albeit anxiously for the surgery to be over. We continued to worry, but we did not fall apart. We could be there for her. Her faith helped us. She lived through that surgery and her faith was with us until the day she died.

Not all life is made up of challenges. Life can also be wonderful, enriching, inspiring, fulfilling. The Spirit is with us in good times as well as hard times and all the in-between times.

Love, grace, pleasure, beauty are also real in the world. The Spirit rejoices with us in times of celebration and joins with us when we are at play. Movement toward "The Realm of God" and individual wholeness/salvation, is always in process, and somewhere the Divine Spirit is connecting with the divine in humanity.

The human enfleshed spirit can rise, soar, seek goodness, defy evil, grieve, overcome tragedy, just keep on putting one foot in front of the other. The Holy Spirit accompanies us, speaks truth to us, and miraculously works through us.

As human beings we are creators, artists, and fashioners of human communities and institutions. We can create a world that supports life and enhances our lives, that nurtures and heals, that preserves the good earth, or we can destroy each other and our habitat. The Holy Spirit is on the side of life and our human spirits can be on the side of life too.

The Spirit moves us toward seeing ourselves and each other as sacred, toward seeing ourselves through God's eyes, eyes of love and understanding even when we are hard to love.

In the end, a realistic, yet gentle and loving attitude toward ourselves is essential to loving others. Accepting who we are with our limitations leads to compassion for others. We cannot know all the forces that affect each one of us. We can know that the Spirit who moves in this world is also in the world beyond our knowing.

Human beings are meant to be God's body on earth. The holy dwells in us though we are sometimes fragile earthen vessels. God's Spirit is our wisdom, our breath of life, our indwelling Christ. And lest we forget, the Spirit's work can be in the human hearts and hands of those who do not profess God but who seek the salvation of this beloved and vulnerable world and those in it.

The Spirit's presence in human beings can seem to be drowned out by the sounds and temptations and afflictions of the world. There are times when the lives of people are tragically affected by war, inhumanity, natural disasters. Tines when we weep and the Spirit weeps. Times to ask how we can stop the pain and ease the suffering. Even when it seems the human spirit has become evil, the Holy Spirit cannot be defeated. It can rise. Humanity is entrusted with creation; the Spirit calls and gives us wisdom to fulfill that awesome trust if only we would listen.

Barak Obama said, "We are reminded that in the fleeting time we have on this earth, what matters is not wealth, or status, or power, or fame, but how well we have loved and what small part we have played in making the lives of others better."

Remember "the Tree" left standing in the garden of Eden in the Creation Story, the Tree of Life? We are encouraged to eat its fruit and share it. Jesus entrusted his work to the disciples in the presence and power of the Spirit. The tree of knowledge of good and evil that became the tree of death when evil prevailed, is becoming the tree of life.

THE SPIRIT AND HEALING

In the chapter about Jesus, we discussed his healing ministry. That ministry was passed on to his disciples after his resurrection. They healed in his name in the power of the Spirit.

The third chapter of the book of Acts tells the story of the disciples, Peter and John, healing a man who had been unable to walk from birth. Every day people would bring him into the temple where he could ask for alms. As Peter and John are entering the temple, he begs for money from them. Peter says, "I have no silver or gold, but what I have, I give you; I the name of Jesus of Nazareth, stand up and walk." v.6. Peter takes his hand, and he gains strength to walk and all around are praising God.

Peter goes on to say that it is not by his own power that the man has been healed. It is in the name of Jesus, the Author of Life, the one you rejected, and God raised from the dead, that this man has been healed. This healing and those that would follow are to attest to the fact that Jesus was the Messiah whom God raised from the dead.

Peter and John preach and teach after this healing and they raise the ire of the priests, the captain of the temple, and the Sadducees. What follows is an extraordinary struggle between the disciples who saw Jesus as the Messiah and who preached resurrection, and the old guard.

The Spirit was at work through the disciples and their transforming and healing power was an integral part of their witness as they continued the work begun by Jesus. Today, the Spirit's healing power is a part of the overall healing power of God in our midst.

In the modern world, we are far from the context in which Jesus' disciples lived. We know much more about healing, and it is the work of many professionals in the medical world. They are healers, doctors, nurses, therapists of all kinds. Healing takes place, not in the context of disciples trying to convince people in their own faith community of the Messiahship of Jesus as was often the case in Scripture. Healing takes place for the sake of those who are sick and in need. It is in that context that healing professionals practice their calling.

The place of faith in healing is different today than it was right after Jesus' resurrection and yet, faith can have an impact on healing. God's Spirit wills life to be restored where that is possible and brings comfort and peace where it cannot. Believing that healing can take place matters.

In an opinion piece by Tyler VanderWeele, a Professor of Public Health at Harvard in an article entitled "Why public health should address the spiritual side of life, he cites study after study to prove his contention that in looking at health outcomes, religion is a positive factor to be considered.

So many factors and professions go into healing. Scientists can be healers too. They discover new medications, vaccines, and treatments for diseases of all kinds. There are those who care for the dying, hospice workers and family members who are healers. There are clergy in local churches who are healers as they provide pastoral care. The Spirit works through all of them.

There are some people who also have a special gift for spiritual healing. There are also some who claim to have that gift from the Spirit who are charlatans. One way to discern the true healers is to ask a simple question: Are they doing this work to glorify God or are they seeking fame and power for themselves along with financial gain.

Jesus was a charismatic leader who attracted large crowds as he went about teaching and healing. He clearly rejected the temptations to benefit personally from healing others. The disciples who came after him were healing in his name and were not seeking fame or fortune for themselves. In fact, they were often persecuted for what they were doing.

A person who is endowed with healing gifts does claim to heal all illnesses. They do not use mass media as a tool to attract those who will do anything for health, including giving away their money. They do not prey on the vulnerable in their time of need.

Prayer and participating in community are a part of healing. We can all bring healing in multiple ways. There are times when psychological and spiritual healing is what matters most.

The Spirit is with the healers who need strength and courage themselves as they seek to help others. It is there like air in the atmosphere.

There are times when healing is not only needed on a personal level, but also on a societal level. When great harm has been done to a whole people through discrimination, crime, war, neglect, or natural disaster. The Spirit can be in the process of identifying social and physical injustice and trauma leading toward the restoration of life. the Spirit is in the process of healing through confession, forgiveness, and reconciliation, in the process of ministering to those who mourn and those who are wounded.

The Spirit is on the side of individuals or social groups in need of healing. Sometimes having the strength or hope of faith to want healing is hard. Sometimes sickness can be used as a shield against the world. Sometimes sickness itself leads to despair or hopelessness. The Spirit can be at work in those for whom simply living, let alone having responsibility for others, takes courage.

According to William Sloan Coffin, Pastor and University Chaplain, the will to be well is a virtue and takes courage.

"The courage to be well is a crucial virtue. With the currents of history threatening to carry before them everything we have loved, trusted, looked to for pleasure and support, we are called to live with enormous insecurities. The churches (and I would add individuals could become centers of creative and courageous thinking. They could also become sanctuaries for frightened Americans, recruiting grounds for authoritarian figures and movements, some of which already bear the earmarks of an emerging fascism. p.15 in "The Courage to Love."

The Spirit calls us to live with courage amid insecurity and change and seek adaptive wellbeing. Otherwise, as Coffin says, we can succumb to the lure of authoritarian figures who offer security in our search for stability. He suggests, the struggle to be whole is hard. The Spirit calls us from retreating into ourselves to live in the light of God's salvation.

Every new generation of people of faith will have to discern the healing gifts of the Spirit in their own time and in their own lives. There is a Divine energy surrounding us that can have healing power in our lives and live through us to bring healing to others.

The Spirit has multiple healing powers. One of those healing powers is the power of resurrection. Some diseases are still incurable. Some addictions are hard to address. Suicide is a reality. And eventually, we all die. The healing of the Spirit lives beyond death and is there for those who mourn.

Perhaps, all who love are touched by the healing power of the Spirit and can pass that power on.

THE UNIVERSAL SPIRIT

God's presence is not only there for Christians and Jewish communities of faith, but the Holy Spirit has also been and is with all people of good will through all time, it is present in all religions as they reach out for the Holy, each in their own way. The Spirit of God is with each of us in ways that we may or may not even recognize, supporting and guiding us by its presence.

The entire world is the Spirit's playground in all eras and cultures. Its activity cannot be confined or its wisdom the sole possession of any generation.

Often, Christians have seemed to have an extremely focused and linear view of the Holy Spirit: first, there is God the Creator/Father/Parent, then follows the Son, then the Holy Spirit. After the Ascension of Jesus, the Spirit comes with tongues of fire to empower and live in the emerging church.

There are problems with limiting the Holy Spirit with linear thinking. The Spirit spirals through space and time. The Spirit calls to us to a liberated and liberating view of its presence and activity in the world. It does not follow a simplistic Christian timeline.

The Spirit as the Breath or Word is existing, creating, and connecting with the world from the beginning of time, though all time, and beyond time. Like the air we breathe, it surrounds the world and gives life.

Of course, both linear and nonlinear perceptions of God's Spirit can be simultaneously true. From one way of seeing, Jesus came into being at Christmas when he was born to Mary and Joseph. Yet, in another sense, Jesus was one with God from the beginning, returned to God, and is present in the world today. So, it is with the Spirit who is and was and will always be.

What matters is that Christians recognize that the Spirit cannot be claimed as solely our own. She who was in Christ and with the Hebrew people, was with those who came before them. While we attest to and detect the Spirit's activity in religions born in the Middle East, the entire world is alive with the energy of the Spirit wherever life is being loved into the fulness of being. The Spirit is like the light that falls on human beings like the sun during the day, or the moon at night. The Spirit is consciousness rising and love coming to life.

Every faith has its special revelation that is essential to its existence and grounding for people in that tradition. Calling on the Spirit carries us into the world of all creation, of other cultures, of the universality of being human, of the Holy beyond naming.

In the modern world, we are becoming increasingly aware that we are all part of one world, a tiny world at that, set amid an unimaginably vast universe. What people do in one part of the world affects every other part. We need to find our way to common values that protect life. We need to be committed to the preservation of each other and our planet, respectful of the other, and committed to compassion.

The Spirit is a universal expression of the Divine with many names and no name who calls us to support life. As we practice our own faith and respect the faith of others, we are called to reject the violence and extremism that has caused so much death and destruction in the name of religion.

In an interfaith world. We are all responsible for the reform, renewal, faithfulness, witness, peacefulness of our own traditions. The presence of the Spirit does not mean an absence of conflict. It does guide the way conflict is dealt with. The Spirit is not constrained by any institutional or cultural expression of faith nor is it hostile to them. It can use them.

Through the centuries, religions have often strayed from the Spirit of holiness that is meant to reside in them and have fallen into prejudice, war, and violations against both their own people and others.

The Spirit calls us back from destruction and despair at such times and moves us toward the right to survival of all humanity, and to the peace that protects survival.

In Christianity, the Spirit of God is and always has been alive in the priestly tradition of nurturing faith, in the prophetic tradition of calling us back to our senses when we lose our way and is there to empower us and strengthen us for our living in the present so that we have a future.

ONE SPIRIT BILLIONS OF PEOPLE

To claim that the Spirit is universal, a force for social change, and able to touch individual people's lives, and move through whole communities is simply hard to imagine. It is hard to imagine a creating God, or a risen Christ or a Holy Spirit who can connect with the billions of people who live in the world, a Spirit who hears each one's prayers in a personal way and accompanies individuals throughout life.

How can the Spirit of God address the diverse needs and conditions in the world and relate to individuals personally? Christianity says that we can have a personal relationship with God or Jesus or the Spirit. We pray as if God hears us, specifically us. But how can God, God's Spirit, hear all of us?

I drive down the crowded highway from Boston into New York City and as I approach the city, I glimpse the massive apartment buildings that line the parkway. There are so many of us, so many people living in those buildings. Each one, each family has its own sorrows and joys, its own needs, and dreams. There are So many of us humans that it seems like we are like ants, or bees in hives, or grains of sand on the beach. How can each one of us think we are important enough to feel the touch of the Spirit? Multiply us by billions.

Here on the outskirts of New York City, I thought of my Kenyan son in Nairobi and my Cameroonian and Ethiopian dear ones, my close friends from China and Korea, my colleague and friend in Germany, my theologian colleague in Argentina, and friends here at home scattered across the United States. We are part of a global village. All breathing the Spirit's breath. The Spirit is there for all of us and can connect with our human spirits. That is the mystery of One beyond my comprehension. An invisible force is with us like sunlight, energy, or air. Not just in an impersonal way, but in a way that empowers the good.

Perhaps it was the Spirit who led me to The Rev. Dr. Grace Ji-Sun Kim who gave me a way of imagining what I was having trouble imagining. In the Asian tradition there is the concept of Chi. She says:

> *Chi is translated as wind, energy, spirit, and breath which is similar to the Old Testament ruach and the New Testament Pneuma.* p. 76
>
> *Chi reinforces the notion of Spirit as breath, lifegiving and helper in all things. The Spirit is key and important in our ways of thinking and being. We need to be aware of Chi in our lives and see how we can move forward with this concept of life. Furthermore, Chi is an embodied understanding of the Spirit in contrast to the predominately philosophical way of viewing the Spirit in White western Patriarchal theology. ...Chi is in our bodies and flows throughout our bodies, much the same as blood does. Chi is also all around us in the universe and it is what gives us life and sustains it.* p. 80 from Spirit Life.

A force for good, the Spirit of God, breathing on the world, breathing on individuals all over the world, brings human spirits to life. Different as we are, separated as we are, we are connected by forces outside of and within ourselves. Beyond all powers on earth, and within the powers on earth, we are connected by life itself, by the creating power and energy of Holiness, of God.

Professor Ji-Sun Kim then goes on to speak of the Spirit of God as Spirit-Chi.

It is toward healing, compassion, kindness, comfort, and hope that the Holy Spirit calls us in all times as it lives in us and surrounds us. The Spirit-Chi reminds us that we live in this world together and life is better when we respect and learn from one another, each in our particular identity. When a loving human being reaches out to another human being in kindness, the Spirit of life, of God is there.

The Spirit is there even in times of oppression and war. It is there when the Covid Pandemic affects the world. It is there when the unthinkable happens and bombs fall on children in Gaza, or lives are lost in mass shootings. It is there grieving with those directly affected by all forms of hatred, violence, and sickness, and weeps with world in the midst of tragedy. It is there to comfort those who mourn and restore them to life. It is with those who risk their own lives to help and those who cry out against carnage. It is there with those who endure to live another day. And it calls those who inflict pain and disaster to confess, repent, and be restored to life.

The Spirit is with the peacemakers, with the healers, with those who pursue righteousness. The Spirit is in the world in all times and places as a force for life that unmasks evil and ultimately overcomes it.

The Holy Spirit is a force for good that lives world-wide as an invisible life giving and life affirming creative power, a Presence that takes root in the embodied spirits of human beings leading and leaning toward wisdom. It is a vital force, an energy able to touch each person at their core as it lives and moves around the globe, speaking prophetic words.

The Spirit reveals the deep connection between heaven and earth. It brings us back to the image of God in us and leads toward reclaiming that image.

The Spirit moves humanity toward the love that gives life. It does not coerce, it invites, encourages, comforts, and empowers. It is with the world in all seasons, in life altering times and in very ordinary times. It calls us to treasure one another.

As human beings, we tend to attribute human form to God, to anthropomorphize God. We know Jesus as the man who lived among us and as the risen Christ. We can feel the invisible life that comes to us as Spirit-Chi. The Spirit lives for and in us. It is a Holy life force whether we are aware of it or not. It brings the Realm of God, beyond our understanding and the physical realm of our existence, closer together, it bridges the chasm between them.

WISDOM AS THE SPIRIT OF GOD

Another word used for Spirit in the Hebrew Scriptures is Chokmah, the Wisdom of God. It is the same word, Hikmah in Arabic. Wisdom is universal and connected to many religions in the Ancient Near East and beyond.

Wisdom in the Hebrew Bible and the Apocrypha is personified as being with God from before time. There is a tradition of blending the Holy Spirit and Wisdom as the Breath of God, the Word of God, active in the world.

The book of Wisdom, being in the Apocrypha and of late origin, between the Hebrew Bible and New Testament, shows signs of Greek and Hebrew influences combined.

Wisdom is described in the Book of Wisdom, Chapter 7.

A hymn to wisdom.

> *There is in her a spirit that is intelligent, holy, unique, manifold, subtle, mobile, clear, unpolluted, distinct, invulnerable, loving the good, keen, irresistible, beneficent, humane, steadfast, sure, free from anxiety, all powerful, overseeing all, and penetrating through all spirits that are intelligent, pure, and altogether subtle. For wisdom is more mobile than any motion; because of her pureness she pervades and penetrates all things. For she is a breath of the power of God, and a pure emanation of the glory of the Almighty; therefore, nothing defiled gains entrance into her. For she is a reflection of eternal life, a spotless mirror of the working of God, and an image of his goodness. Although*

> *she is but one, she can do all things, and while remaining in herself, she renews all things; in every generation she passes into holy souls and makes them friends of God, and prophets; for God loves nothing so much as the person who lives with wisdom. She is more beautiful than the sun and excels in every constellation of the stars. Compared with the light she is found to be superior, for it is succeeded by the night, but against wisdom, evil does not prevail. She reaches mightily from one end of the earth to the other, and she order all things well.* Wisdom 7:22-8:1

With these amazing, descriptive words, the author defines and extols Wisdom. Wisdom and insight as envisioned in this passage may be essential to realizing the true meaning of life and finding a path to life affirming relationships and societal harmony.

We are not likely, in today's world, to personify Wisdom. We can, however, merge Wisdom and the Spirit of God and seek it out in our innermost being. And we can see Wisdom, like Word, as the living Christ Jesus in our ever-creating God.

Like most Protestant clergy, I seldom preached on Wisdom. Then, years into my ministry, I discovered the books of Wisdom, often personified as She. At first it seemed strange and then it seemed like an antidote for all the male language for God that was part of my faith. Today, what seems more important to me than the gender of Wisdom, is while Wisdom is identified as She and most often, God as He, neither has a gender and they are both, like Jesus Christ, Holy Mystery alive in the world, alive among us and alive within us, whatever our identity or state in this world.

Going through some of my old papers, I came across a sermon preached at an ordination with these words:

> *Wisdom is not another God. She is manifest in many ways as with God, as one with God. She is a creating and saving force, breath of life.*

> *This Breath of Life that was with God and is God, was in the beginning. She becomes manifest in the Word, in Jesus Christ, and dwells among us. She was incarnate in the Ten Commandments, the Ten Words. She lived in the prophets and all the faithful in Israel, she rested like a dove on Jesus at his baptism and was indwelling in him. After his ascent to heaven, she descended on those who were to assume Jesus' mission. She is with you today as you begin this new ministry. She is the Holy Spirit.*

That sermon was long forgotten. Now, as I write, I feel a need to reach out for Wisdom again as a much-needed expression of the Holy whose time has come in our new era.

The thing that seems important about Wisdom is that it addresses matters of daily life and daily relationships. The Spirit is with us in our homes as well as with us in the wider world.

Over time, so much of faith has come to do with life's big moments, birth and death and resurrection and salvation, and eternity. Faith has addressed global issues, mega social ethics, and God's coming Order, and the end of the world. We live in the in -between- times.

Yes, the Spirit is a voice of prophecy as we have discussed, and through human beings speaks truth to power on religious and political stages at critical times. But it is also a breath of life that sustains us in everyday living and ordinary times.

The simple issues in life can turn out to be quite important. Words spoken in relationships. The repetition of doing daily tasks is essential to staying alive like cooking, doing dishes, washing clothes, cleaning, paying bills, and creating a little artfulness around us. And yes, raising children. My father-in-law, Raymond Kepler's advice to my husband and me when we were married was to remember that "in marriage as in life, it is the little things that matter."

Wisdom connects with our common sense and everyday living. Making ethical decisions in our homes and following through on them is spiritual work and extends into public spaces. Whole faith communities along with secular societies have often ignored household ethics.

We can find the beauty and the fulness of the sacred in ordinary things when we reach out for the Spirit of Wisdom. We can find an approach to God that satisfies our longing for reason and stability as well as mystery and the unknowable.

The Spirit as an empowering, creative energy, is a resource for daily living and a guide in revising worldviews and systems that begin at home and from there, influence our view of the world. The Spirit accompanies us and upholds us, using our talents, healing old wounds and crippling loss, reviving dead bones, guiding us to love in our relationships. opening ever widening connections, correcting us, and using even our challenges and failures for our good, cutting off evil at the knees.

In many ways, Jesus embodied wisdom and dealt with ordinary life as well as with issues of ultimate concern. He is not known for doing daily chores during the years of his ministry. But before his ministry began at age 30 or so, he was said to be hands-on, a carpenter and was always part of a family and network of friends.

In his ministry, Jesus dealt with relationships between people and the ethics of living, dealing with taxes and feeding people. He brought about individual healing, changed personal attitudes, and addressed morality in lived life. He talked with and worked among common people: shepherds, housekeepers, laborers, tax collectors, fishers, soldiers, fathers, and mothers. The truth is that we have no record of Jesus' personal life, but we do know that his family was important to him, and his mother appears often in the telling of his ministry.

As Jesus was dying on the cross, he thought about his mother and who would take care of her when he was gone. He said, to his disciple and mother, "John, behold your mother." "Mother, behold your son."

There is no way that we can maneuver our way through the complexities of our changing world and its challenging ethical issues with stability and sensibility without Wisdom to guide us. The Spirit is with us in wisdom in all seasons of life, whether we recognize it or not, hear its voice or not, and its revelation is ongoing.

Early Christianity focused on God's coming Realm (Kingdom) and God's present indwelling in the world. They believed that that which is coming is already in process, is already here. Some thought the end was imminent. Life in this world and eternity are joined. The God who cares about life on a grand scale also cares about life as we live it day-to-day.

The Word made flesh is meant to come alive in all aspects of life. The Holy Spirit/Wisdom pervades the world and is active in individuals. It is essential to all things and is the breath of life itself.

We may not call Wisdom by name, but one day, we may wake up and realize that it has been a guiding force in our lives and a supporting presence. Through it, we draw close to and are drawn into the beauty and mystery of God.

In the Spirit, Jesus is living again, and our nurturing-parenting God continues to create and nurture life. God is present with the world. The Spirit is the energy of God at loose becoming incarnate in the world in human beings and alive in all creation.

The Spirit of Holiness calls us to live into hope. We are never alone. The Spirit is still brooding over creation as it did in the beginning and is with us in ordinary times, through tragic times, and in times of joy. The Spirit may well be the most important expression of the Trinity as we move into the new era in an increasingly small and connected world.

John Adams, a musician, and Director of Music at Clarendon Hill Presbyterian Church wrote the music for the following simple words about the Spirit. I was honored to be able to collaborate with him and thankful for his spiritual and musical gifts. I wrote the lyrics realizing that the Spirit has been with me throughout my life, loving, guiding, and surprising me and I am beyond grateful.

In our hearts, Spirit sings,
Peace on earth Spirit brings,
Calling us from crippling strife,
Leading us to joyful life.
Walk sure in Spirit's grace,

Spirit shine on your face,
Gifting you with Word and Light,
Guiding you both day and night.
Refrain
On the earth Spirit falls
To the deep Spirit calls
Resting now in you and me
Co-creators we will be.

Spirit Song
Rev. Patricia Budd Kepler
John Adams
On the earth Spi - rit falls. To the deep Spi - rit
calls. Rest-ing now in you and me, co - cre - a - tors we will
be. In our hearts Spi-rit sings. Peace on earth Spi-rit
Walk sure in Spi-rit's grace. Spi-rit shine on your
brings. Call-ing us from crippling strife, lead-ing us to joy-ful life.
face. Gift-ing you with Word and Light, guid-ing you both day and night.

Spirit Song

CHAPTER 5

THE BIBLE

BIBLE BASICS

Speaking about God, Jesus, and the Spirit, we have often referred to the testimony found in the Bible. It is to the Scriptures that we now turn our attention. What follows will be basic information.

Knowing basic things about the Bible, whatever one's faith perspective, is essential to understanding Christianity. The Hebrew Bible has been a resource through the ages for Judaism and both the Hebrew Bible (Old Testament) and New Testament are foundational resources for Christianity.

Protestants include 27 Books in their New Testament Canon with the Roman Catholic and Orthodox Churches including the Apocrypha, 14 Books of Intertestamental writings. The Old Testament has 39 Books.

The Bible is a collection of books that have been both revered and interpreted and reinterpreted by Christians through the centuries. It has been a source of revelation, information, personal devotion, and ethical guidance. Scripture, also called, the written Word of God, is at the heart of Christian worship and a resource for living.

In its pages, the Bible contains various forms of literature from poetry to prophetic writing, from allegory and myth to historical narrative, letters, and elements of biography. When approaching Scripture, an appreciation of its many literary forms adds to understanding its messages and meanings.

There is no other compilation of books that has been studied with such interest and intensity in the Western and Middle Eastern world, and increasingly around the globe.

The Hebrew Bible takes place over the course of thousands of years. The New Testament, being about Jesus' life, death, and resurrection, and the birth of the early church, takes place over the course of about one hundred years.

Since the Hebrew Bible was written over a large expanse of time, it is reasonable to expect people's understanding of their relationship with God to change with changing circumstances. In the New Testament, which is written over a brief period of time, one is not dealing with faith through centuries and yet, there are major shifts in the development of faith in its pages.

As they write, the authors of Scripture tell us about how they and their people see and experience God in the context of their cultural and political realities. Many of their writings were handed down from oral traditions.

Some Biblical writings emerge out of worship, and contain songs of praise and lament, prayers, and instructions for ritual observances. Some of the writings in the Bible resonate with other religious writings of their time.

Dobbs Allsopp, an Old Testament Scholar, says that "much of Biblical poetry is dominantly oral, earmarked by pauses and inflections that are meant to be spoken. The language they use is language of the tongue and voice, and that presents an oral orientation." This material is then adapted to a written medium.

Horace Allen, professor of Worship and Liturgy at Boston University Theological School, taught his students that the Bible when used in worship, is to be listened to rather than read because of its oral orientation. In its earliest form, it was read aloud to a public unable to read its text. It was not until the invention of the printing press that that changed. But more of that later.

God is revealed in Scripture through many minds and hearts across ages and cultures and is read and listened to by many minds and hearts across time and geography.

Churches have believed that the Spirit of God, the Holy Spirit, was at work as people wrote the Bible, at work in those who selected the cannon, and with those who translated it and interpret it, and is with those who read it. This is true even though there has been much debate about what the Spirit is saying through the Bible.

Through the years, many people have become Christians by simply reading or hearing Scripture. Others who were born into faith traditions have found a deepening of faith through studying and meditating on it. Still others never relied on Scripture as a foundation for faith but relied on tradition. All Christians who are part of a religious community encounter the Bible in corporate worship.

For some, the Bible can be an almost mystical/magical book. For some a sacred resource. For others, it is simply literature.

Evangelical Christians believe, as reflected in the Statement of Faith once used by Gordon Conwell Seminary, "That the sixty-six books of the Bible as originally written were inspired of God, hence free from error. They represent the only infallible guide to faith."

When I was a child, I was taught that one was never to put any other book on top of the Bible. Carrying it around was a statement of faith and a testimony to the world. It was in the same category as the American flag. There were rules about how to treat and honor it.

As an adult, I have moved away from the Bible as sacred symbol approach, and I do not want to flaunt my faith by visibly carrying it around. But I think I respect it more than I did as a child and use it more in ways that increase, inform, and enhance my faith. The word "infallible" has no meaning for me as I reflect on the writings in Scripture over changing eras.

As a Minister, I have preached more than 11,100 sermons from the Bible. And in preparation for those sermons, I have studied it in many ways as all clergy do. I have also given speeches and lectures about theology and pastoral care based on its teachings. And I have meditated on its contents and tried through the years to seek out its many meanings for my personal life and engagement in the world. I found joy and inspiration in it, and comfort and even gotten a few laughs. It has been the source of my commitment to social justice and peace.

HOW THE BIBLE CAME TO US: INTRIGUE AND STRUGGLE

The history of how the Bible came to us is filled with intrigue and conflict. That history is a complex and sometimes violent story that can only be hinted at here.

A long and arduous journey took the Bible from its original texts in Hebrew, Aramaic, and Greek, to today's translations. The whole Bible has been translated into 704 languages and the New Testament into an additional 1,551 languages according to Wikipedia in 2023.

In early centuries, judgments had to be made about which writings were going to be codified into Canon, a collection of authoritative books, Scripture. It fell to religious councils and authorities to decide which writings they thought should be in one book that would be handed down from generation to generation as Holy Writ. The work of deciding which books belonged in the Bible was critical because the Canon was to be a closed collection.

As important as deciding which books were to be in the Bible is the translation of those books. Only fragments of the original early manuscripts existed by the time the Canon was formed. All that was left in addition to those fragments were copies of the originals, many of which differed from one another. Scholars had to decide which manuscripts to use as they gathered them together. That work was arduous and time consuming and many unsung scribes and scholars dedicated their lives to that tedious work.

One early version of the Hebrew Bible was a Greek translation, "The Septuagint." The early church also had the Bible translated into Latin, "The Vulgate." Interestingly, none of these languages, including the original Hebrew, was a language most people could read.

One early version is the Syriac Peshitta Bible. The Rev. Dr. Donald Walter and his colleagues are translating much of its text into English even as I write. I treasure my inscribed copy of his translations of the books with women's names.

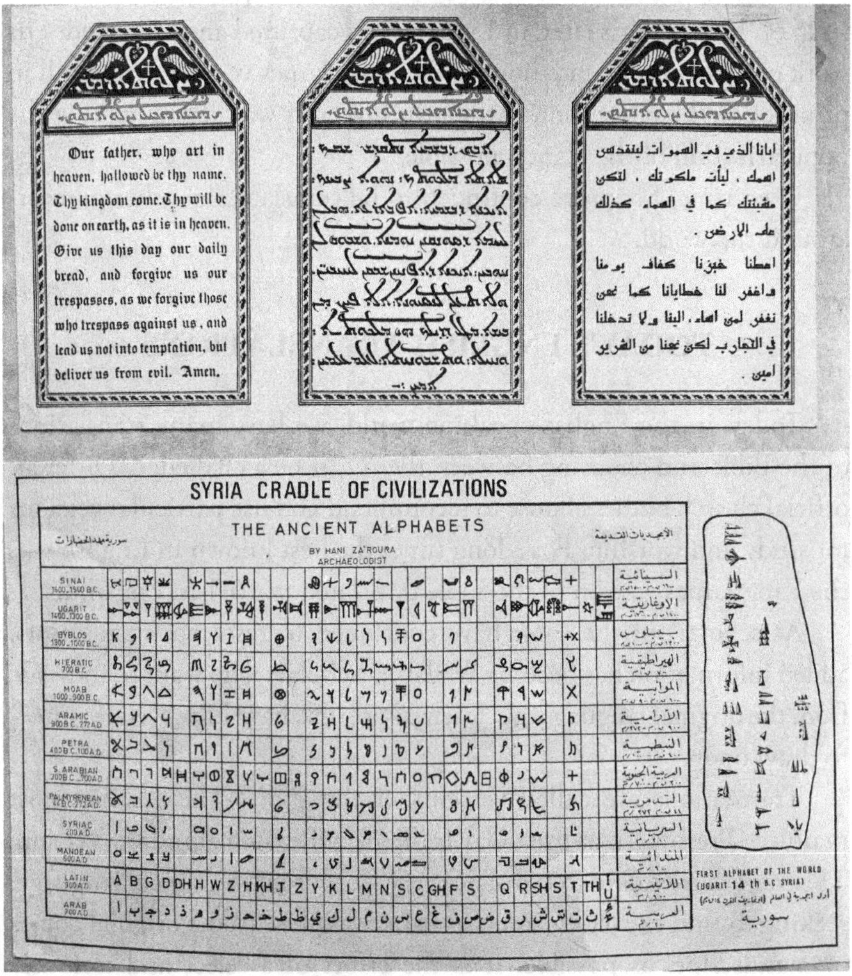

The Lord's Prayer in English, Syriac, and Arabic.

Reading his translation with Aramaic and English side by side and reading from what we would call back to front, I could appreciate the intense and discerning process that is involved in making an original manuscript come to life in one's vernacular.

Some of the first people to translate the Bible into the common language of the people lost their lives in the process. William Tyndale was the first person to be executed for heresy for translating the Scriptures into English. Knowing his life was at stake, Tyndale escaped from England to Germany to do his work and completed his translation in 1524. Eleven years later, in 1536, he was captured and martyred. His work provided the foundation for the King James version that is still in print today. The invention of the printing press was key to making the popularization of the Canon possible.

Over time, Scripture continued to be translated by other pioneers around the world.

TODAY'S ENGLISH TRANSLATIONS

Today, in the English-speaking world, we have many translations of the Bible and choosing between them can be a challenge. Different official church bodies choose to recommend and use particular versions for study and worship. For a long time, the best known in English was the King James version of the Bible translated in 1611 in England.

As scholars of the Bible have continued to research manuscripts, added information has become available. Scholars who want to translate from the original languages as closely as possible have improved resources to draw upon.

Translations are called versions of the Bible. The version most mainline Presbyterians use today is the New Revised Standard Version. This version tries hard to translate every word from its original language, seeking to find the oldest sources that are as close to the original copies of manuscripts as possible. It is the effort of a select and uniquely qualified group of scholars. The Roman Catholic Church uses "The New American Bible," also carefully researched by scholars. These versions do not use old English.

There are versions of the Bible that rather than translate word for word try to put the Bible in more colloquial language. While these versions can tilt toward existing beliefs or cultural settings, they can be helpful. The New English Bible and The Messenger are examples of colloquial translations.

In 1984, the National Council of Churches published Inclusive Language Lectionaries of Scriptural texts for each of its three years (A, B and C). These translations were based on the Revised Standard Version but were so controversial in using nonsexist language for humanity and God that some who worked on it received death threats: reminiscent of the threat to the lives of those early pioneers who translated Scripture into vernaculars. In 2009 a group of Roman Catholic priests published "The Inclusive Bible."

In some cases, these versions corrected translators who had translated generic language in the original tests, into male language. For instance, where the Greek indicated "people" and the translators wrote "men," they returned to "people." In other instances where "men" was used to include women, they rejected the idea that women are the invisible gender and used men only when the text meant men. They wanted to represent the basic principle of God's impartiality toward human beings and the equality of women and men. In replacing the primary exclusive reference to God as male with a more inclusive approach, they were affirming God's being as ultimately indefinable and God's Being as Spirit as well as present in Jesus Christ and humankind.

Inclusive language was being recognized and used in other institutions in society, in education, the media and business. Awareness of the problems of patriarchal language in both church and society led to a new translation of Scripture.

Whatever version of the Bible one uses, there are a multitude of resources available for Bible study.

AIDS TO BIBLE STUDY

Clergy, religious educators, and laity, who teach and preach from the Bible use commentaries as aids in their Biblical study. They investigate the meaning of words and the context of the times in which they were written. For most people who read the Bible, study Bibles are available that provide basic information about Biblical books, their authors, the dates when they were written, and the circumstances surrounding the writing. There may be cross references to other similar texts along with helpful footnotes.

A Concordance is another aid for studying the Bible. It is made up of words that appear in the Bible. Following alphabetical ordering, it gives information about where these words are found in Scripture. A Bible Dictionary contains information about people, places, and concepts in Scripture.

The Lectionary has common readings for every day of the week and is used in corporate worship on Sundays. Through the Lectionary, we move through much of the Bible, using texts from the Hebrew Bible, from the Psalms, the Gospels, and the Epistles as already noted. Many denominations use lectionary texts in their worship services.

However, many times the Bible is read or heard spoken aloud without reference to any other Scriptural aides. Most churches believe that the Holy Spirit alone can inspire those reading Scripture and open doors to meanings and understandings that meet their spiritual needs without the help of scholarship. Where scholarship is available, information about context, the interpretation of specific words, and connections to other texts are among the things that can be helpful.

As we read the Bible, we are listening for the testimony of those who have gone before and asking how its message applies to our own lives. As we do, differing faith traditions will come into play as will the multiple different identities of readers, preachers, and scholars.

Individually, people who know the Bible well have their favorite books or texts that they quote often. We are all prone to pulling out a favorite verse or two that we especially like or have heard quoted frequently that resonates with what we already believe or that gives us new insight.

When we take a text out of context and use it to support a particular theological or ethical position, that is called "proof texting." All of us who read the Bible do that sometimes. It is all right to find texts that speak to us but bending the text to fit what we want it to say is not. Being aware of how we are actually using the Bible is important.

THE BIBLE IN COMMUNITY AND IN WORSHIP

The Bible is a book meant to inspire and inform us in our personal lives and is used in communities of faith where people of diverse backgrounds and ages come together as the church, to worship, share insights, support one another, find direction and meaning for life, and companionship for living faithfully in the world.

The church gathers in many different settings to study the Bible, to find insight, comfort, inspiration, and guidance. People gather to read and study the Bible, alone or in community, from prisons to nursing homes, from Sunday School rooms to universities, from human made sanctuaries to nature's sanctuaries.

The Bible as used in weekly Worship and periodic rituals is a living document meant to come alive in every new age. In worship it tells the story of God and humanity's relationship through time. In worship we recount the dramatic story of ongoing creation and salvation in poetry and narrative.

Scripture provides the foundation for the observance of the sacraments and rites of the church: in communion, baptism, marriage, ordination, anointings, rites of reconciliation, funerals and celebrations of seasons, its symbols and words combine to communicate the mysteries and realities of life passages.

In the Reformed tradition, the Bible and preaching are central to worship, the Bible is read and interpreted by lectors and Ministers, and its message is reflected in hymns, music, and art.

Many people have come to love the stories and poetry of the Bible through art, as they are set to music, as they are danced, and as they are encountered in dramatic readings and portrayed in stained glass windows. Art can carry the meaning and tell the story of God with us in ways that words alone cannot. From Christmas Carols to the Alleluias of Easter, the Bible can come alive in music in ways that touch our hearts and bind us together.

It would be a mistake, though, to ignore the words and concepts that are transmitted in hymns and art. They matter. As times and places change along with social reality so do the symbols and theologies communicating the religious message. Hymns sometimes repeat Scripture but more often, interpret it. Over generations we can track the developments of faith in hymnody.

The Bible is not just literature or history when used in worship. It is a guide for faith. In as far as we can, we want to be open to the truths it speaks to us and the ways in which it draws us closer to God in the dynamic movement of faith.

In addition to studying books of the Bible or specific texts, the overall direction and message of the whole Bible matters. Each Scriptural passage can be studied for itself and for its place in the whole movement of time and revelation.

THE BIBLE AND CHURCH TRADITION AND DOCTRINE

Branches of the church have their own theologies, liturgies, and worship styles. These evolve over time and become deeply rooted in faith communities. The traditions of faith communities become authorities alongside Scripture, officially and unofficially.

In the Roman Catholic Church which has a strong central authority amid its diversity, church Tradition stands alongside of the Bible as a guide and authority for faithful living. In the Protestant Church, with central church structures that do not carry ultimate authority, the Bible stands as the primary authority for faith and life, though tradition is unofficially a strong influence on theology and practice.

The Orthodox Church believes that Church Tradition and the Bible are inseparable, and the Bible is embedded in Tradition. The following quote speaks to their position:

> *It is from the church that the Bible ultimately derives its authority, for it was the church which originally decided which books form part of the Holy Scripture; and it is the Church alone which can interpret Holy Scripture.* Bishop

Kalliaston Ware, from Holy Tradition on the Source of the Orthodox Faith.

Some evangelical churches believe that all Scripture is to be taken literally and is the clear and direct word of God to the world.

Church Doctrine in Tradition and Scripture are each authorities to be taken seriously. Clearly it was the church that decided over time, which books belong in the Bible. The Synod of Regus in North Africa in 393 accepted the Canon in its present form. The Council of Carthage in 397 recognized the twenty-seven books now accepted in the New Testament Canon.

The Jewish tradition had its own process for deciding which books belong in their Hebrew Bible, the Tanakh. The Christian Church accepted their Canon but arranged the books in a slightly new form and often referred to it as the Old Testament.

With the Canon set, it is up to religious communities, religious leaders, as well as individual readers to interpret the Bible for their own time and decide which versions of the Bible to use.

It is up to scholars to study the original languages and contexts of the Bible and continue to provide resources to enrich its study. The choosing of which manuscripts to use was and continues to be the work of scholars and often took place in monasteries in the early days of Biblical translation.

Ultimately, as we read Scripture, we each decide what authority to assign to it as we search for a glimpse of God's being, relationship with the world, and presence in Jesus' life, death, and resurrection as recorded through the witness of people of faith who, each in their own way, bear witness to the Holy in the pages of Scripture.

Some insights in Scripture transcend time and place and their universal significance is clear. Other passages need to be taken in their context and interpreted considering current history. Discerning which is which is vitally important.

APPROACHES TO SCRIPTURE AND THEIR SOCIAL IMPLICATIONS

Different churches, groups of people, or individuals approach Scripture differently and see different things in Scripture and that affects how they see the world. It contributes to their positions on social and political matters. Diverse ways of approaching Scripture are one way in which Christians differ significantly from each other.

These diverse ways of approaching the Bible can lead Christians to come to very differing conclusions about God and humanity and come to very differing ethical and missional positions.

Speaker of the House, Representative Mike Johnson, was asked in 2023 what his view was on several current issues. He replied that if anyone wanted to know what his worldview was, just read the Bible.

Of course, many people who have read the Bible do not share Mr. Johnson's view of the world.

Fundamentalists have believed and believe that God somehow dictated every word that is in Scripture through the person or persons who recorded the words. And they believe we are to follow the Bible to its letter.

If you really put a literal interpretation of the Bible to the test, it turns out that it would be impossible to follow Scripture literally. Not only are many of its writings not meant to be taken literally on some matters, but there are also differing viewpoints within the pages of the Bible and following those different perspectives would be impossible.

In his humorous book, "A Year of Living Biblically," A. J. Jacobs writes about his experiences of trying to, well, live Biblically. While it was an interesting adventure into growing a beard, wearing the right clothing, parenting Biblical style, tithing and on and on, he proves the absurdity of taking the Bible word-for-word.

Actually, it is impossible to live the Bible literally or interpret it literally. Nonetheless, Biblical literalists continue to assert that God wrote the Bible through its human authors and intends us to do just that. It is a fact that everyone comes to the Bible with some preconceived notions that may have been someone's reading of the Bible at some point. These preconceived notions are rarely articulated.

Another way of approaching the Bible is to believe that the people who authored its many books were inspired by God: they were in communion with God, experienced God, and that led to insights and interpretations of life which they put down in writing in the context of the times in which they lived. With this approach it is possible to see that some parts of the Bible were addressing faith in particular contexts, while other writing is meant to be more general and universal. Of course, this calls for judgment on the part of the reader, and Christians would say, the inspiration of the Spirit.

There are also those who value Scripture for its insights but do not see a revelatory Divine influence at work in its pages.

People have always taken different approaches to Scripture. Those approaches have led to religious conflicts throughout history, some violent, pitting Christians against each other, and leading to conflicting positions on social actions in the world.

When clergy, deacons, elders, are ordained today in the Presbyterian Church, one of the questions they must answer is:

> *Do you accept the Scriptures of the Old and New Testament, to be, by the Holy Spirit, the unique and authoritative witness to Jesus Christ in the Church universal, and God's Word to you?*
> Book of Order 2017-19, p.104 (W-404)

That sums up a universal moderate Protestant approach to Scripture. It explains why Scripture has figured so critically in our search for understanding Jesus Christ and why it has authority as God's written word to us through the testimony of its authors. It also clarifies the fact that Scripture is open to interpretation through the Spirit.

We can hold the paradox of changelessness and change together. The Bible speaks of the foundations of faith while tracing faith changes. The Bible shines light on the constant interplay between the Divine and human and opens doors to the future of spiritual relationships and ethics.

In a new era, the Holy Spirit is the carrier of new revelation that is grounded in Scripture and Tradition, aware of the deep faith of generations and their faithful commitments while recognizing that life evolves in ways thar Biblical authors could not have imagined.

MODERN CULTURAL BIASES AND BIBLICAL UNDERSTANDING

Anyone who picks up a Bible can see that it is a complex collection of books. Some books can be puzzling, some boring, while still others can be highly meaningful. Everyone will bring their own personal perspectives and experiences to their reading of Scripture.

Everyone comes, at some point in their lives, with preconceived notions about God and humanity that can get in the way of uncovering the meaning of texts. Whole communities of faith and institutional church bodies inevitably come to Scripture with biases. We can find what we want to see there or have been taught to see there.

One challenge everyone faces throughout time is to let Scripture speak its truths and try to let its revelations emerge. That is not easy. People become very invested in what Scripture says to them and sometimes hear things that reinforce their already held beliefs, or beliefs of some teacher or scholar they admire. It is a challenge for Christians to try to come to Scripture with open minds and be willing to listen to those who see quite different things in the Bible than they do.

Sometimes, approaches to Scripture can say more about who believers and institutions want the Divine to be than about who God is. The hope always is that Scripture will shine light on God, Jesus Christ, and the Holy Spirit amid and through our human conditions, limitations, and preconceptions. It is not easy to read Scripture with humility and an open heart. So much seems to be riding on what we see.

Even given different approaches to Scripture, Scripture provides a foundation for faith and living faithfully. We must wrestle with one another about its meanings. We should never lose track of the fact that people lost their lives trying to make the Bible accessible to the public, not just to those in power. The Bible is now the people's book. We can expect different interpretations given our diverse cultures and situations.

Clergy and Biblical academics and other students of Scripture can help us understand it. We educate clergy so we can benefit from their deep study of the Bible and theology just as we educate doctors and lawyers in their fields. But ultimately, everyone seeks to find meaning for themselves in Scripture as the Spirit and life experiences guide them.

Sue Monk Kidd describes how she finds new layers of meaning as she reads a text.

"I select one verse, one sentence, or one word. After I read it, I close my eyes and "free fall" into the different levels of meaning that lie within it. *What is God saying to me right now in this piece of Scripture? What does it mean?*" p. 181 God's Joyful Surprise

Most churches believe that when people read the Bible with an open mind and heart it can draw them closer to God and Jesus Christ and lead to insights about how to live faithfully in the world.

Despite this belief, the controversies in today's world over what the Bible says about social issues proves that people of faith can come to opposite conclusions about what the Bible says, and what it means to be Christian now. Working through these controversies also shows how we can be changed and change our minds in the process.

Some see in Scripture a call to building a world where all are equal while others see creation ordered to empower some whom others are meant to serve. Some see a God who favors some nations above others, and some see a God who is impartial. And when it comes to power, some believe in a powerful militant God and Christ while others are more focused on a God of non-violence and peace.

In the chapter on the Holy Spirit, we discussed the ways in which conflict can sometimes be a road to discerning God's will and way.

The Bible is such a rich collection of writings and stories about God's relationship with human beings that every individual who reads it can discover new insights every time they read it, even in the same passages. Sometimes they feel their faith and beliefs confirmed.

I am always amazed when I see something new in a passage I have read, studied, and preached on for years.

The following discussion about the Bible and Patriarchy is one example of how people in churches can read Scripture differently. It is also an example of how I discovered new things in Scripture.

MOVING BEYOND BIBLICAL PATRIARCHY

The Bible was written in a time when Patriarchy was taken for granted as a system given by God by which to organize and understand society. It was the context in which the Bible was written, translated, and interpreted until the Twentieth Century, except for a few forays before that time into challenging a social system in which positions of dominance and privilege are primarily held by men of an entitled class.

There were women in Hebrew history who rose above the stereotypes of their time. And in the New Testament we find Jesus challenging many of the norms of society. Women were among his followers in ways that defied religious and social convention.

Jesus treated women as whole human beings. It is important to recognize that his teachings and actions challenged the times in which he lived and sometimes the religious traditions of his faith. Jesus' treatment of women set a precedent for the future that is even today only partially realized.

For the most part, communities of faith still read the Bible and sing hymns written in a patriarchal milieu, even though patriarchal social systems in society at large are being challenged and language usage is becoming more inclusive.

We have already addressed this as it relates to our understand of God. Here we look at the issue of language as it relates to Scripture.

Facing and addressing the patriarchal context of Scripture has implications for how we think about God and humanity. The language we use for God and "mankind" reflects a way of ordering life that belongs to an era that is passing, however slowly. Some believe this is the moving of the Spirit.

Christians, like other people of faith, are invested in the language to which we are accustomed and to the language of the saints who have gone before. For centuries we have used male language for God without thinking about it.

Patriarchal language and its resulting assumptions and view of the world are embedded in most religious devotions and worship. Old words are familiar and beautiful to the ear and live in the heart's memory. Many still have vital meaning.

The question that needs to be answered today, however, is whether Patriarchy and all related hierarchical systems is in humanity's best interest for the future and imaginable as God's loving will. In Scripture, we are called by the Prophets and Christ to move toward a new creation where all are equally respected, all are made whole (saved) and are guided by the Spirit toward abundant life.

Changing patriarchal language in religion, especially in liturgies based in Scripture, is frankly, demanding work and people can be faithful Christians without making that effort. They can challenge discriminatory practices in other ways. However, it is an issue that cannot be ignored in the future. The symbolic nature of language has great power.

We have mentioned the Inclusive Language Lectionary, and the Inclusive Language Bible in our discussion of English translations. They were both reviled and more popular when they were first published than they are today. Attention to patriarchal culture waxes and wanes.

It was not until the last half of the Nineteenth and the Twentieth Century that systemic patriarchy was challenged in the United States on a wide scale as a problematic form of social organization and one instituted by God. It was not until 1920 that women won the vote in the United States of America and then only after a lengthy struggle. It was not until 1957 that women could be ordained as clergy in the Presbyterian Church and there are churches worldwide that still do not ordain women as clergy. including the Roman Catholic and Orthodox Church.

While some people of faith began to believe that God's Spirit was leading humanity away from Patriarchy toward a new era in which human beings would be equal whatever their gender or sexual preference or orientation, others were defending Patriarchal practices.

While it could be clear that more inclusive language would better reflect the belief that "God is Spirit and those who worship God will worship in spirit and in truth," it remains an emotionally charged challenge not only for those who believe every word in the Bible literally but for those who have come to love traditional language and embrace it without worrying about its social consequences.

On a rational level, God is not male or endowed with so called human "masculine" traits. However, these concepts were implanted in people's very being and in their sacred texts. Liberating our images of God is not easy though many of us feel God's Spirit is leading in that direction.

Those who want to make Scripture more inclusive are translating into the vernacular of our day. Those who originally translated Scripture into vernaculars were condemned for doing so. Those who are translating Scripture today and using more inclusive language are not changing the meaning or movement of Scripture. They want to follow where Scripture itself leads them, toward a God who is inclusive and impartial whose impartiality was lived out in Jesus Christ.

As for using inclusive language for human beings, it clarifies Scripture. Where men means men, it says so. When men means people it coveys that. When brothers means brothers, it translates it that way, but when it means sisters and brothers, all siblings, it translates it that way. It is simply a more accurate translation of the original text. Sexism both crept into former translations and was inherent in much of the writing.

The Bible is not just a historic document or great literature. When used in worship, the Bible is a living document used to speak about faith, the faith of our forebears, faith for now and for new generations. As a living testimony to God, it can be translated for contemporary worship to clarify what it means about God and humanity as creation evolves. It would be easy to just leave it alone but the religious cost of doing so violates the testimony of Scripture that God is a living God in every generation.

We do harm to God's name if we leave "Him" in the dust of Patriarchy while the Creating Power of the Holy is trying to move us on.

Many who are committed to everyone's right to the fulness of being and respect, as a matter of religious integrity and conscience, will continue trying to free themselves and religious practice from old harmful stereotypes and divisions, uncomfortable as that may be.

Even before the Inclusive Lectionary and Bible came out, Elizabeth Cady Staunton and a group of women and men confronting sexism in religions had developed "The Women's Bible," and after them, a Unitarian Minister, Brackenbury Crook in 1964 published, "Women in Religion."

Even though the Bible was written in a patriarchal context there are ways to be true to its texts while moving beyond its time bound limitations.

The Rev. Dr. Paul Hanson, writing in "The Ecumenical Review," in 1975 says this:

> *The dominance of the male metaphor in designations of the deity is no mere historical accident of indifference to the discussion of sex discrimination in Biblical religion. It is the product, not of a society that could freely choose the gender of its primary metaphors, but of a society driven to choose male metaphors predicated on sexual inequality. Moreover, these male metaphors have been taken up – in what must seem to be a conspiracy spanning three millennia – by contemporary males, of another systemic discrimination of women deeply rooted in societal structures.*

Since Paul Hanson wrote this, we have learned that women as well as men can be loyal to patriarchy. Patriarchy may have seemed like a conspiracy of men. It was an entire world view of which men and women were a part. And there were economic and social reasons for its success as an overarching way of organizing and perceiving a way of social ordering.

Now, a universal social evolution is in motion whose time has come that will benefit everyone. But, in social evolutions, decisions are made that affect the future. For those for whom religion is a life foundation, we must listen carefully for the voice of the Spirit leading us into the fulness of God's being and humanity's wholeness. We listen for as much of the truth that we can hear, bear, or understand.

Gender identity, roles, relationships, and justice are foundational for all societies. This leads us to ongoing revelation.

ONGOING REVELATION

When you read the Bible, what is of first importance is that you are reading it. It can have something important to say to you as it has for so many before you. Because it is a compilation of sixty-six different books (counted from a Protestant perspective), written over vastly different historical times, some parts will make more sense than others to each reader.

If we can, we try to take the whole sweep of Scripture into account as we read from various books.

When we are using the Bible in worship, the community around us hears the text with us and we are called together to act as people of faith. A big question we have not yet asked is whether we can have new written revelations of God that are as important as those in the Bible.

Here is a fact, we cannot add to the Bible. It is a finished book. God, however, is a living God and the Spirit moves in every time. Some believe traditions, interpretations, and positions of the churches constitute ongoing revelation. In fact, if pressed, most Christians believe that God is active through time in the positions churches take which must be tested through time.

The fact that Scripture is finished does not mean that God does not continue to interact with individuals and communities. That would limit God to the past. The Spirit works in science, government, art, and in the evolution of social ordering. The Spirit can help us decipher new meaning in ancient admonitions and enable us to act with God in the process of ongoing creation. We spoke of this in the chapter on the spirit.

God has been perceived as omnipotent, omniscient, and omnipresent in the world as defined in Tradition. And God's love is central to God's being. But our human understanding of what this means changes. It affects how we relate to one another in families and in society. It affects which leaders we trust.

As our social situations change and new spiritual and ethical challenges emerge, how do we know in any given time what God's will for us is? We have the Bible as a guide. Its principles stand. And yet, new questions about faithful living emerge that could not have been conceived two thousand plus years ago. We must be willing and able to interpret transcendent Biblical truths to specific situations in each time.

THE WRITTEN WORD AND GOD THE LIVING WORD

One God, in Jesus Christ and the Holy Spirit is the living Word. The Bible is the written Word. The living Word continues to speak through time. That enables us to try to free our perceptions of God from any cultural prejudices that limit our perceptions of God and our understanding of human beings created in God's image and living in a world where evil is a reality.

The fact is that we can only know when we have been true to our living, moving God in retrospect. We want to free ourselves to live in God's light but our ability to do so is always partial because we are part of a greater whole. Other people are also seeking God's will. And as human beings we are limited by our time and place and though we have luminous moments, we can only be sure of their veracity over time. Ongoing revelation needs to be tested by time.

Humanity is in a transitional time in the Twenty-first Century at the opening of a new era. We innovate as we live between times and listen for the guidance of the Spirit, and Jesus Christ, the living Word.

The first commandment, accepted by Jews and Christians alike, makes clear that we are not to make any idols to represent or replace God. Each generation must know what their idols might be and find ways to ensure that they are not making God into an idol. Or worshipping God in idolatrous form. No material reality, no nation, no individual, no ideology is deserving of our ultimate loyalty. Idolatry is an ongoing temptation.

Prophets emerge whose writings and actions give guidance and wisdom in each age. There may well be a prophetic potential in all of us. How we see and experience God in each "now" matters along with our honoring the God of our forebears as recorded in Scripture and history.

We need to be humble. Religion has caused harm as well as good throughout history and the Bible itself has been used for inhumane ends. So has church tradition. We want, as far as we are able, to be on the side of life not death and destruction. That takes discernment, the acknowledgment that we are not always right and, at the same time, the courage to stand for what we believe is right.

In the New Testament we read about how the early church had to wrestle with emerging ethical questions. Then as now, Christians did not always agree on the faithful way forward when facing current issues. People of good faith had to listen to one another, be in dialogue, and prayer as they tried to discern God's will. Eventually each person and communities of people had to take a stand. God's will emerges in time and must be evaluated through time. In the meantime, Christians stood for what they believed until the way became clear.

Mainstream churches took a stand against racism during the Civil Rights Movement. Black churches led the Movement and members of other churches joined in solidarity, all certain that that was God's will. Though racism continues, time has shown its elimination to be of the Spirit.

The issue of whether to ordain women or practicing gay people as clergy was a hot issue in the twentieth century. People on both sides of the issue used texts from the Bible to support their position. In most Protestant Churches, the answer was yes to women and in some denominations, it was yes to practicing gay people. In other denominations the answer was no to both women and practicing gay people. The debate continues. Ordination of women and practicing gay people was to those who supported it, in keeping with the principle of God's impartial love and the equality of people in the service of God.

There was a time when a similar debate took place over slavery. Though today there are still white supremacists, the Christian consensus is that slavery was not God's will or the right ordering of creation even though it was taken for granted in Biblical times and there are admonitions in Paul's letters in the New Testament for slaves to honor their masters.

Eventually most Mainline Churches began to practice what they believed: God is a God who embraces all people as equals. That means all, truly all. These decisions were reached after spending years discerning where the Spirit is leading and where the overall thrust of Scripture is guiding.

Another issue that Christians have debated over time is the issue of war. Mainline churches tended to support a theory of Just War and went on to describe what constituted a Just War.

Some Christians have always taken a prophetic stand for peace, rejecting all war. The Quakers and the Mennonites were pacifists long before other Christians began to grapple with the ethical implications of engaging in war. Their members were conscientious objectors when it came to the draft. There were Christians in other denominations as well who were conscientious objectors. Slowly other Christian groups are recognizing the right of members to be conscientious objectors. The discussion about war continues. With the advent of modern warfare, the conditions of a Just War cannot be met. And yet, while many Christian institutions advocate for peace, not many have taken an absolute stand against war.

Becoming aware that climate change is threatening the future of the earth as we know it brings our human stewardship of creation into focus as spoken of in the Genesis creation narratives.

New ethical issues are emerging that arise out of our ubiquitous use of the internet and the complex issues surrounding it: consumerism, pornography, informational and propogandist issues, individual privacy, what constitutes "reality," the effect of the internet on children, etc. Having access to the internet is a crucial ethical issue as well as how it is being used. Are we building a society built on a new dimension of class, those with internet access and those without? The Bible never imagines the internet.

Of course, the Bible is not solely about ethical issues. In ways that are embedded in its pages, it deals with the nature of God and humankind. In the section on God and Jesus Christ we dealt with some emerging theological issues. While these are not as all-consuming in the present era, they are of critical importance and arise as we discuss ethical issues.

We need to use Scripture with great care not only as we seek ethical and spiritual guidance on critical matters in our time, but also as we ask theological questions about who God is and we are in relation to God. Ongoing revelation. We pray for insight from the Holy Spirit.

As we seek guidance on modern matters, we know that people can see in Scripture what they want to see. One of the favorite idolatries Jewish, Christian, and Muslim communities have seen in their Scripture is Divine sanctioning of nationalism and the favoritism, imperialism, and discrimination on God's part that that implies. Scripture points beyond these as ultimate loyalties. But, if we are not discerning, we can get lost in God's favoritism, merging of religious and political entities, or confusing or substituting political passion or national loyalty for religious commitment.

THE BIBLE AND NEW GENERATIONS

As we live our lives personally and in community, the Bible as God's word can be used in many ways by each generation: as a witness to God and Jesus Christ and a people's faith through time. It can be an invitation to faith, a doorway to God, to Jesus Christ and the Jewish people and to the faith of the early church which is prelude to churches that follow and prelude to faiths that follow such as Islam.

Scripture can be used in personal devotion, personal and communal study, worship, and as a resource for ethical insight and guidance. It can also be used to foster the personal agenda of national or religious leaders.

The Bible connects new generations with the faith of those who have gone before and, in many ways, it traces the evolution of faith in the context of changing history and ongoing Divine creation and revelation.

Over time, the importance of the Bible will be different for different people. For some it will remain important to life and faith. For some, tradition and the Bible will be equally important. For others, it will just gather dust on a shelf, if it is present at all in a home. And others will dismiss it and consign it to history and a testimony to the outdated faith of prior generations.

For Christians, it is the only early written testimony we have to the life, death, and resurrection of Jesus and the beginnings of the church. We need its witness, and we continue its message in each new generation. Christians are not united it what it says to us. If we want to continue to honor the Bible in our changing environment, we need to be in dialogue with one another. Sometimes we must recognize irreconcilable differences as they exist in any given moment in time.

Every generation learns from those who have gone before. No matter what changes are believed to be needed in new generations, respect for generations who have gone before is essential, imperfect as they were, every new generation is equally imperfect. The faith of generations who have gone before have faults to be corrected and deep resources to share.

Through all time, first of all we pray that coming generations will pay attention to Scripture. we pray for the light of Scripture that led the way for saints who have gone before, to light our way and shine for us and shine for generations to come. And we pray that when that light shines, we will be open to it and embrace its testimony with hearts open to the Holy Spirit.

CHAPTER 6

COMMUNITIES OF FAITH: THE CHURCH AND CHURCHES

The worship of God, the study of Scripture and theology, offering prayer and engaging in personal meditation, providing pastoral services, and healing, marking life's passages, the pursuit of ethics, serving the needs of the world, and engaging in art in sanctuary and music, these are the work of religious communities.

Christian religious communities, churches, have continued the Christian faith through the centuries since the time of Jesus and will continue to do so for generations to come around the world.

This they do whether or not the dominant political system accepts people in its midst who believe in God and want to gather in community.

Today, churches are organized at the local level, as well as at the state, national, and international level. They are an influence on culture and history wherever they gather.

In this chapter, we recognize community based and national/ international institutional expressions of faith. With an eye to what purposes they each serve; we are concerned with what the future holds. But before we get to the future, let us look at the past and the beginnings of the church.

THE BEGINNING OF THE CHURCH

The beginnings of the early church, is recorded in the book of Acts, whose writer also wrote the Gospel of Luke, and in the Letters to young churches found in the New Testament.

Followers of Jesus, already a community of faith, continued to meet and pray together after his death and resurrection. His brothers and some women, including Mary his mother were together with them. Jesus had promised that the Holy Spirit would be with them. Then one day, the Spirit descended on them. That day is marked as the time the church was born, Pentecost.

The Holy Spirit, embodied in Jesus, was present in those who came after him. Those who had mourned his crucifixion now experienced his living presence and passed on their excitement to those around them as they went about teaching and healing in his name and formed worshipping communities.

The early church was originally part of Judaism. It began in Jerusalem and spread throughout the Mediterranean. We are told in Acts that the early converts, "Devoted themselves to the apostles' teaching and fellowship, to the breaking of bread, and to the prayers." 2:42. And that, "All who believed were together and had all things in common: they would sell their possessions and goods and distribute the proceeds to all, as any had need." 2:43

These early Christians soon raised the ire of the high priests because of their great popularity with the people, and their message that Jesus, who had been crucified, was the Messiah. There were attempts on the lives of the leaders of the Jesus movement.

It is a miracle that the early church survived. As believers went about their ministry, they faced opposition from both secular and religious authorities. And they experienced internal conflicts. Yet, they preached and taught with boldness in the face of opposition and challenges. The book of Acts records how one of them, Stephen, was stoned to death for his faith. Among those present at Stephen's death was Saul, known for persecuting the followers of Jesus. Saul was an upright religious Pharisee with a zealous, vengeful, and self-righteous spirit.

One day, Saul, as he was walking on the Road to Damascus, experienced a blinding light and the voice of the risen Christ came to him, calling his name. Blinded and confused, he retreated for a while to a home in Syria, after which he became a prime mover in the emerging church. His name changed from Saul to Paul.

Paul opened his Jewish faith to the Gentile world and became a missionary and a prolific writer of letters known as the "Pauline Epistles" in the New Testament.

Before Paul began his outreach to the Gentile, outreach to them was hotly debated in Jerusalem by the Disciples. The tide turned when their leader, the disciple Peter, was convinced that they should open their community to Gentiles. It happened this way:

> *Peter was approached by the emissaries of Cornelius, an Italian Cohort who had been told in a vision to send for Peter. Cornelius was a Roman and a Gentile who according to Jewish purity laws was unclean. Before his emissaries arrived, Peter had a dream in which it came to him that "What God has made clean, you must not call profane.* Acts 10:15.

Following the dream, Peter and other believers went to visit Cornelius and proclaimed, "I truly understand that God shows no partiality, but in any nation, anyone who fears him and does what is right, is acceptable to him." Acts 10:34 And so the outreach to the Gentile world began.

Paul's missionary work was blessed by the Apostles as he began his ministry. Communities of both Jews and Gentiles began to come together, and it was in Antioch that the disciples were first known as Christians. (Acts 11:26)

As people in the emerging church began to gather in communities of faith, they proclaimed the good news of God's love for the world in Jesus Christ, Son of God, and Son of Humanity. They preached about a God who was calling them to be harbingers of a new creation based on love and the justice and the peace to which it leads. They felt transformed and empowered by the Spirit.

However, the coming together of Jews and Gentiles in the church was not easy. It was a marriage of diverse cultures and religions that had often been at odds with one another. Forming viable ongoing communities of faith was a challenge.

There were bound to be issues to work through in these new congregations. Keeping the history and covenant of Jewish Christians with God was a given, so was worshipping in congregations like synagogues. Keeping the Ten Commandments was assumed as central and was accompanied by grace and translated into love. But keeping the multiple purity and ritual laws of Judaism became controversial.

One heated debate early on, was whether Gentiles should be circumcised as the Jews were as a sign of belonging in the emerging church. Eventually, circumcision continued as a rite for Jewish Christians but was not required of Gentiles.

People of different nationalities and cultures became part of the community by believing in God and that Jesus Christ was of God and that the way of life he preached was God's will. Faith replaced ethnicity and birth and as a sign of communal belonging and baptism a rite of passage. The Gentile Christians gave up worshipping other gods and some leaders as god for the One God of Judaism.

The rift between the Judaism that did not believe in Jesus as the Messiah and the Judaism that did, deepened over time. The Apostle Paul made clear after his conversion that his people, the Jews, were still God's people despite this alienation. But that did not resolve the matter. Conflict continued.

Christians also faced increasing hostility from secular authorities. Paul and other leaders were thrown into jail several times, James was killed. Still, the formation of Christian communities continued. They were sustained by their living faith and the Spirit, by faith in the resurrection of Jesus and the triumph of life over sin and death through which they found a living hope.

The Spirit of God which had always brooded over the face of the earth, and was powerfully alive in Jesus, was alive in his followers in life changing ways. The Holy Spirit energized the life of the early church as it spread throughout the Mediterranean.

The church was called the "body of Christ" by the Apostle Paul. As we think about Christ being embodied in gathered communities of believers that evolve over time, we can recognize how hard it was for the first followers of Jesus to open their doors to Gentiles and be grateful that they did. Being guided by God and filled with the Spirit is what made this possible.

That opening of their faith reminds us that God is not confined by any group of believers but is active in all of creation: a creating energy, a Spirit breathing life, love, and hope into all creation. The whole world can be seen as God's body. The church from the beginning was called to be inclusive.

CENTURIES OF HISTORY

From the beginnings of the church until now, lie two thousand years of complex history. And before the beginning of the church, thousands of years of other worshipping communities. All of that is beyond the scope of this book except for noting a historic moment in its evolution that changed everything.

A sea change in the history of the church occurred in 325 CE when the church went from being an often-persecuted minority to being the accepted faith of the Roman empire under Constantine. Before that, the Church had been officially accepted in Armenia by its Emperor.

As their position in the world changed churches faced new and different challenges and opportunities, the most important of which was remaining true to the teachings of Jesus once it was embraced by Empires.

Christians eventually had to define their faith in theological terms. Creeds were developed by Councils and with that, heresies were named. Those called heretics were often prosecuted amid theological disputes and sometimes put to death.

The New Testament church, attested to in Scripture, developed institutional form as it spread throughout its part of the world. Today there are two billion four hundred thousand people known as Christians in innumerable institutional manifestations.

The church was and is constantly challenged to contemplate and remember who Jesus was and what he taught as it interacts with political powers in the world. The challenge is to be open to God's living Spirit and its guidance amid social, political, industrial, and technological influences and change.

Christian communities, through time, were carriers of beliefs and ethics, rituals, and worship, practiced in a variety of forms in differing contexts.

People gathered in local communities of faith, leaders emerged, and churches developed more complex organizational structures that became the keepers of Scripture, the creators of Christian tradition, the developers of theological positions and the carriers of their religion in society.

As faith institutions formed, and re-formed, three of today's major traditions came into being. The Roman Catholic Church was the first to take shape, then came Orthodox Churches, and eventually Protestant Churches around 1500 AD, Protestant churches emerged in a variety of manifestations.

As in the early church, there was the building of community, the development of faith, the defining of beliefs and ethical positions and always, worship. Through the years struggles within and between religious institutions continued. Through the centuries churches were affected by the culture and times in which they were set. They established national affiliations and loyalties that affected churches along with the culture and times in which they were set.

Throughout this book, we have talked about some basic beliefs that were held in common that identified these differing believers as Christian even when within the basics there were strong disagreements. Each institution tended to believe themselves to either be the "one true church" or carriers of "the true faith."

Religious institutions along with other social institutions are made up of human beings who live in an imperfect world and have the capacity to do great good and harm. Religion is a part of public life and reality.

As church institutions interacted with governments through time, they sometimes merged with them, sometimes stood alongside them. Some enjoyed political privilege while others were discriminated against and persecuted.

Even as Christian institutions developed differing relationships with political powers, Christian congregations continued in local communities to serve the needs of their congregants: the worship of God, rituals of passage, education in faith, and trying to carry the teachings and life of Jesus Christ in the wider society.

Clergy were the professionals who gave leadership to the church. Religious bodies engaged in preparing their clergy for Ministry in its many forms. Eventually, graduate Theological Schools emerged that became essential to the evolution of the church and an educated clergy.

While diverse religious bodies had different requirements for clergy, clergy took their place among other professionals, doctors, lawyers, and teachers.

In the Romand Catholic Church, monasteries and nunneries were early educators in faith and keepers of Scripture and tradition.

Theological Schools and some Catholic Orders became scholars of the academic disciplines necessary for leadership in communities of faith such as Biblical Studies and languages, Church History, Theology, Ethics, Pastoral Disciplines, Religious Education.

Even before theological education developed, Christianity had missionaries and mission enterprises.

CHRISTIAN MISSIONS

From its beginning, Christianity was a merger of cultures. Being a Christian was not an ethnic identity, it was a faith identity. Much of the New Testament is about the missionary journeys of the Apostle

Paul and other religious leaders of the time as they traveled to spread the faith. The New Testament contains letters to the new churches they established.

Over time, Christianity spread from the Middle East and became well established in the Western world. This led to a desire to spread the good news of the Gospel throughout the world and new missionary enterprises were born. These missions were much like the early outreach movements of the early church, except that now missions were often coming from churches in nations with power.

The influence of the church on world-wide cultures was mixed. Missionary movements brought educational and medical resources and outreach to the poor and marginalized in Jesus' name wherever they went, as they sought to spread his message of love and hope in the world.

Sometimes, however, missionary movements coming from colonial powers, also brought the imposition of the values of Western cultures on other civilizations around the world in questionable ways.

Institutions can fail on some fronts while on others they have a liberating and life-giving influence in society.

As Christian communities formed throughout the world and populations developed Christian congregations and networks of their own, missionary enterprises and churches began to serve one another across national lines.

In the modern world, mission work is increasingly becoming a cooperative venture between many cultures and Christianity now has native expressions throughout the world. Churches in South America, Africa, and parts of Asia are strong and growing in size and influence. In 2023, the National Church of Kenya had so much influence in society that it was nominated for the Nobel Peace prize.

However, in some regions, the issue was not so much the influence of outside powers. Some churches were co-opted by dictators and tied to nationalisms. Some local Christian leaders and some missionaries with ties to nationalism, preached a fundamentalist Christianity with an inclination to authoritarianism. Both colonialism and nationalism remain a threat to the integrity of Christianity and other religions well into the Twenty-first Century. All religion can be coopted to serve political ends.

RELIGION AND CULTURE

The basic message of Christianity as it comes to us from Jesus is a message of inclusion and breaking down cultural barriers of status whatever they are since God is an impartial lover of all creation who calls us to love one another.

And yet, Christianity through the years is itself set in time and space and limited by the era in which it exists.

In the beginning of Christianity, God's love could be expressed in individual relationships and in the life of Christians communities in the world. However, Christianity and Judaism from which it came were embedded in patriarchal, militaristic cultures, in which slavery was taken for granted. These elements of culture were givens in the worldviews of the times.

In Galatians 3:28 we find these words:

> *There is no longer Jew or Greek, there is no longer slave or free, there is no longer male or female, for all of you are one in Christ Jesus.*

At that point in time, what was true "in Christ" was systemically unthinkable in the larger society. Some discriminations were givens in that era.

Over time, some Christians had a vision that that which was true in Christ, could become true in society as a whole. After all, God's righteousness and love called for justice and love in all the created order. They saw following Jesus' example of ministering to everyone as individuals beyond cultural discriminations and religious taboos as applicable to all society.

If we skip to recent centuries, we have begun to see cracks in systems of injustice taken for granted for thousands of years. Theologies of liberation emerge as essential to God's new creation. The seeds of reform in Jesus' teachings and in the teachings of other prophetic leaders speaking out for justice and peace are beginning to bear fruit in social systems. But there was and is resistance to systemic change.

Some faith communities still see patriarchy and militarism as part of God's given order, and colonialism and authoritarianism as legitimate ways to achieve God's desired ends. After all, that is how it was in Biblical times.

On the brink of a new era, churches are seen as keepers of tradition. They exist through time and provide foundational beliefs for people. These cannot and should not be changed lightly. But God in the Spirit is dynamic and with wisdom leads toward faithfulness in every new age. The Spirit works were transcendent truth meets real life.

We are at a crossroads.

As we have noted, social discrimination was embedded in Scripture and is embedded in law and culture. Social discrimination was buttressed by ideals about God's order that helped support unjust practices and ideologies. Changing ideals is serious business that can shake people's foundation.

Christian communities are always struggling with ethical change and continuity. The changes that bring us and our world closer to protecting the sanctity of all living life are key to finding paths to survival. The call to peace rings out with new urgency in a world still living with wars and the threat of a Third World War and competition for power run amok.

It is not surprising that Christian communities often had to, and still must, deal with conflicts within the church and in the greater society as they seek to discern where the Spirit is leading. Churches are made up of people from many backgrounds, of many ages, and many opinions who are just plain human. Change is hard. The early church found that out.

We have come through a time in the United States when both religion and society are facing injustices and trying to come to terms with them. We mention them again: sexism, racism, homophobia, poverty, militarism, ableism, and threats to the environment. It has been a time of d progress, of advancing, regressing, and trying to advance again. Spiraling, hopefully toward that which is life giving. And of course, as we are addressing current ethical issues, new ones arise.

PRESENT CHURCH TRENDS

A piece in the Jessica Gross newsletter for readers of The New York Times is entitled, "The Largest and Fastest Religious Shift in America is Well Underway." (June 21, 2023) She is writing about the decline in membership in communities of faith. For instance, she points to a statistic in the book "The Great Dechurching: Who's Leaving, Why Are They Going, and What Will it Take to Bring Them Back?", by Jim Davis and Michael Graham with Ryan Burge.

Fifteen percent of Christians have dropped out of church in the last 25 years. That means that eighty-five percent are still there. That eighty five percent may continue to decline or remain stable. Aging members will eventually die, and new members will join. This will happen as other changes are taking place in culture.

In other Faiths there are also pockets of decline and growth as our nation becomes increasingly multifaith.

While churches are losing members, the "nones" have increased. They are not necessarily people with no faith. They are people with no religious affiliation. They have always existed but now their numbers are growing, and they have a name. At the same time, Humanists and other atheists have become more vocal in claiming a place in society.

Speaking of atheists, China as a world power is coming into its own. Communist China, by the nature of its political ideology, is atheist though the religions that existed in China's past continue to have an influence. Communist Russia as another communist countries continue to exert influence with an Orthodox Church in its midst.

Even looking at these realities, I do not see much point in focusing on whether church membership will decline or increase in the future even though this issue has economic and organizational implications. The issue for Christinas through the ages, though often ignored, is meant to be faithfulness to the gospel of Jesus Christ regardless of numbers. The challenge has been to resist being coopted or absorbed by national politics.

What we need now and in the future are Christian communities ready to meet the needs of members and friends, and willing to wrestle with translating Jesus' teaching into action, and embracing worldviews that offer a foundation, a grounding for human wellbeing and survival. We need congregations who find strength in faith and who pray and work for a world that embraces the sacredness of life in the modern era.

These are transitional times when old systems are breaking down and going out with a vengeance and new systems are in formation. Churches can be part of the creating, waiting, birthing process but there is bound to be some attrition.

As I write, the backlash against change is harsh. Divisions in our nation and the world are deep. Violence is increasing and authoritarian regimes are gaining some traction. The radical Christian Right and religious nationalisms of all kinds are vociferous. Even some moderate Christians are drawn into militarism that accompanies nationalism and believe in control by raw power. But there are signs that amid it all, there is the opening of new possibilities for progressive religious communities to come to life, even tired religious communities weary from fighting the numbers battle and revisiting human rights issues again and again.

In the mist of transition and chaos, the affirmation of human rights and human worth, and the will to meet human needs, can be a unifying factor for Christians and other people of faith who are in tune with the Spirit's guidance. These are the religious communities waiting at the door of the future. Numbers are not the point

Despite differences, mainstream Christians at their best have held in common an appreciation of familial love in all its forms, a commitment to truth and civility, a will to reach out in kindness to strangers, a desire to be good stewards in creation, and enactors of peace with justice. They have known that means matter as much as goals and paid attention to how people do things in addition to what they are doing. They have provided a place in their sanctuaries for the expression of art, music, and beauty, and acknowledged our human need for Sabbath.

Acting with courage in times of national and world crisis and speaking truth to power is part of religious faithfulness. So is just plain living every day with integrity, resilience, and hope. At the heart of Christian community, indeed all religious communities as they are meant to be, is a search for faithfulness to a Divine Reality and Holiness alive in us and all around us that is committed to humanity's common good.

Of course, religious communities like the human beings who make them up are imperfect. Not only must they resist the temptation to court power and pander to wealth, and conform to unjust social norms and laws, they must resist the temptation to engage in internal power struggles and petty disagreements that have been known to alienate people from religious communities.

There is no denying that religious communities have at times provided platforms for the elevation of leaders, both clergy and laity, whose egos have become more important than their service to God and people. These leaders have, rather than being in awe of the Holy elevated themselves as semi-divine. Followers too have succumbed to the worship of human power or popularity.

Of course, all social institutions, whether committed to politics, education, medicine, science, commerce, or art, have given in to corrupt or egotistical leadership even though they claim to have the interests of society at their center.

In the present and future, as we critique the failures of faith and the mistaken merger of God with personal or national interests, it is equally important to acknowledge the times when religious communities have spoken prophetic words and born faithful witness for the healing of the world. And it is important to be critical of forces and institutions outside of the church that are capable of misguiding and destroying human life. Leaving religious community does not save us from failures of other institutions.

Society continues to benefit from religious communities and their leaders who continue to minister to the ongoing needs of members and strangers, who provide a place for worship for those who seek a spiritual expression for their lives, and those who want an outlet for pursuing justice and peace with others of like mind. Society needs communities who offer love and hope and even a place to mourn in times of transition.

And in an era when patriarchy, militarism, racism, and classism need to end, society needs religious and secular communities with the creativity and wisdom to build a new order beyond these forces whose continuance threatens the future survival of the world.

Religious communities already cross national borders. We need international political systems that are effective and more powerful than the economic forces that now exist. Religious communities can build on international ties in the future to contribute to a world already functioning beyond nationalisms as nationalisms engage in battle.

COMMUNITIES OF FAITH AND A CHANGING WORLD

Christians in the United States in my generation and those that follow, have seen and continue to see, changes accelerating in religious communities and growing divisions among them. We are witnessing a sea change that is important to notice.

I have been an eyewitness to change. In the following pages, I have chosen to tell my story as one way of looking at that change. By telling my story, I share what I have seen as an entry point to looking at the modern history of the church. I speak as an older White woman and a Minister in the Presbyterian church. My perspective is colored by those realities but is not totally determined by them as colleagues and friends from other backgrounds and life situations have deeply affected my perspectives. I will begin at the beginning of my adventure in church to set the stage. Where we come from effects our testimony.

While we are looking at changes in church life, we want to affirm the fact that the Spirit is at work in people in other religions and outside of them in secular organizations. God's Spirit is alive in all creation.

TRACKING CHURCH CHANGE FROM A PERSONAL PERSPECTIVE

My Early Years in the Church

To begin, I grew up in the Protestant church, specifically in the Presbyterian Church (USA) which is its current official name. I am what we call, a "Teaching Elder" (Minister) in that denomination.

I was ordained to the Ministry shortly after it became possible for women to be ordained in our denomination. People often ask me what possessed me to go into Ministry at such a time. I could simply say that it was the work of the Spirit or that I was called. But the Spirit does not work in a vacuum. Context counts.

In fact, it was not my relationship with God alone that initially led me into ministry, it was my experiences in and love for the church and the people who made up my neighborhood church, St. Paul Presbyterian Church in West Philadelphia that moved me toward Ministry. They contributed to my deciding to pursue a graduate degree in theology when, in my senior year at Drexel Institute of Technology, now Drexel University, I was struggling to discern my professional direction in the Fifties. My father had always assumed I would get a professional degree. He had law in mind. The Korean War ended in 1953. I was aware of it but not directly involved.

I began my journey in St. Paul Church because two young people knocked on my door one day and invited me and my sister, Mary, to come to their youth group when we were teenagers in their neighborhood. We took them up on their offer and stayed to become part of their community. Eventually, our parents joined in. I am incredibly grateful for that visit!

There are many ways that people find faith communities. Some just see church signs and drop in. In my case, I can attest to the fact that the church dropped in on me and it worked.

Before we moved to that neighborhood in West Philadelphia, we lived about six blocks away and had gone to another Presbyterian Church that was much more conservative. I went to Sunday School and mid-week classes regularly and was scared into faith and being good by my Sunday School teachers. Here is a verse that sums up my motivation then. This verse is speaking of being taken to heaven after the Second Coming of Jesus: "Then two will be in the field and one taken, and one will be left. Two women will be grinding meal together, one will be taken and one left. Keep awake therefore, for you do not know on what day your Lord is coming," Matt: 24:40-42.

I was young when I attended that church, and I did not want to be the one left on earth and in hell. I could either be good or hang out with really bad people so I would be the one chosen. I did not know any people I considered really bad, so I chose to be good. The fear is gone now but that verse is engraved in my mind.

My Sunday School teacher would teach with the aid of a flannel board. She seemed attached to naming the sins that would end us up in hell. I remember an image of a great green giant whose name was jealousy. I must agree with her, now that I am an adult, Jealousy, that great green giant is a human problem.

Then she told us the story of a young girl being kidnapped right out of her bed. She had a Bible by her bedside table and grabbed it as she was being whisked away. When she got to the place where her captors were holding her, she began to read the Bible aloud to them. They were so moved that they took her back home. The fear of intruders at night lingers maybe because I do not always have a Bible by my bed.

That was before St. Paul Church. I was not very conscious of it, but I was experiencing two quite different kinds of Christianity. One scared me into goodness which has its benefits. The other, as it turned out, helped me find myself. I later learned that the first church believed in Millennial/end days Christianity.

Yet another influence helped me appreciate the aesthetics and significance of the church. At home, growing up, I discovered how universal and diverse Christianity is. I came to appreciate Roman Catholicism through my beloved grandmother, Marie Dick, who lived with us, and my first cousin, Rosemary who also lived with us while she attended college. When she graduated, she became a Sister of Mercy and took on the name, Sister Mary Thadeous. Later she began using her own given name, Sister Rosemary Budd. There was a radical, far reaching unsung revolution in Catholic Orders of Nuns that occurred after Vatican II, 1962-65.

I learned from my maternal grandmother, Marie Dick, a German immigrant, how important the church could be for an immigrant. The Roman Catholic Church grounded her. She went to Mass every morning. As a newcomer to the United States at the age of fifty who didn't speak English, the church was her lifeline, a place where she felt at home across the ocean in a place where she did not speak the language. It was as familiar in the States as in Germany. And back then, the Mass was in Latin, unfamiliar in both places. She knew change and with it, continuity through the church.

Today as I write, the Mass is in vernacular and has been for many years, but there are many immigrant churches where the language of the homeland is spoken offering a lifeline for many as it did for my grandmother.

It was through my grandmother that I learned to appreciate the Roman Catholic Church. I loved lighting the prayer candles (real candles in those days.) I appreciated the beauty of the sanctuary, its size and yet, the intimacy of sacred space and the anonymity, if chosen, of being able to worship there in solitude and peace.

My mother, Theresa Budd, who became Protestant when she married my father, carried her Catholic background in her bones. It had instilled in her the value and importance of the church in her life. She would have to be completely bedridden to ever skip church on a Sunday morning. And for her, attending church, rather than interrupting her Sunday, was a gift, a foundation, a comfort, an essential beginning for the week ahead.

When she was in hospice care at the end of her long life, three different Ministers came to offer her communion as she lay dying. Even on her death bed it gave her a chuckle that three different clergy showed up. And that did not count me. I was there too, but as a daughter.

But on to my experience of church in my preteen and teen years.

Thriving Church Years: The Late Forties to Early Sixties

In my adolescent years, St. Paul Presbyterian Church, was a thriving urban church with an amazing, active youth group and significant social network. The youth group was affiliated with Westminster Fellowship, a national Christian Education program for youth. It was in that group that my faith was formed, and life-long friendships were established. My faith shifted from fear of the second coming of Jesus to gratitude for the first coming of Jesus.

Our youth group was both a religious and social group for us. It was in that group where my sister, Mary, met her husband, Bill, and other couples met their spouses too.

The youth group was a place where young people could develop leadership skills and continue their Christian education. I became a leader in our youth group: planning meetings, leading worship, and meeting people from other youth groups around the city and suburbs of Philadelphia. I was invited to visit and speak in other churches and that opened the door for me to expand my church experience. It was the late Forties.

I became familiar with the connectional nature of the church at various levels of institutional life: every part connected to every other part for governance and programs, from the local church to the Presbytery, to the Synod, to the General Assembly (the national church.) Most mainline churches have some kind of connectional system and a national presence in society.

As with many young people, I was influenced and supported by the adults in the church, several of them were influential women lay leaders with families and professions of their own which was not the norm in those days. A lawyer, Caroline Kennedy, was especially supportive of me.

Many people learned the basics of Christianity in our local churches: the joy of worship, the significance of the liturgical year, and the security and nurturance of an intergenerational faith community. There we developed a growing faith in God and Jesus Christ and a commitment to wider community involvement as Christians.

Our parents, Harold, and Theresa Budd were fully supportive of my sister Mary's and my participation in church and our much younger brother Harold and sister Theresa were baptized there. My father became a church Trustee and taught an adult Bible Class. My mother never missed Sunday worship and hosted many church events at our home. It was a family affair.

The church was a social hub. We had many parties in our finished basement. The Halloween parties were the best. One year a man dressed as a bum came to the party and sat silently in a corner. (That was in the days when no one was scared by someone doing that.) The rest of us, in costumes too, tried to figure out who it was to no avail. Turns out it was our Pastor. If an unrecognized bum showed up at a teen party today, that would end the party!

Looking back, I realize that the church, along with my family, provided a grounding for my whole life. They were, each in their own way, a center for love, fellowship, faith, and identity formation during my adolescent years.

Our youth group was so important in all our lives that as adults, we celebrated the 50th Anniversary of our founding with a gathering that included a visit to our old church, which by then was a thriving African American Methodist Episcopal Church. A sign of religious and sociological change.

In the 50 years since we were young, changes had taken place in our city and in West Philadelphia: among them, the suburban exodus of white families at the end of World War II, and the incoming of African American families into the city. My parents were part of the exodus to the suburbs.

St. Paul, with a dwindling membership and an inability to appeal to the changing community, eventually had to close and was glad to have another church buy the building. Theirs was the story of many urban churches. Some were able to pivot and change, but they were the exceptions. Another wave of church closings was to come later.

As it happened, my husband and I were the Supply Pastors at St. Paul Presbyterian Church when it closed, and we facilitated that process. It was the second Pastoral position for each of us after graduating from

Seminary. Before the church closed, we had an active youth group of mostly African Americans. Our sons were usually the only White members. In the congregation were a core of faithful older White members who had stayed in the neighborhood along with a few African Americans who had recently moved in.

Churches provided a place where people could worship and be in community. Pastoral care was provided, and significant rituals were observed. Music was at the heart of church life. Some found opportunities for leadership, and some could use talents they could not use in other settings. The church responded as it could to the needs of the surrounding neighborhood. This was true for our Presbyterian Church, and it would be true for the AME Church that took its place.

Of course, I know that not everyone's experience of church was as positive as mine even in the heyday of churches. Churches can also be places where people act out unresolved personality and relational issues. Churches can be and unfortunately many were, as society was, racist, sexist, and homophobic. Churches are made up of people who are just plain human and live in social contexts. The Fifties were the days of oblivion to many social issues in predominately white churches. But even though social change was not yet universal, churches of all kinds did reach out to individual people in need and supported mission work in other countries with educational, nutritional, and medical work there and in the States.

Education in a World Waking up to Liberation

Church was clearly not the whole of my or anyone else's life. Outside of my involvement as a young person in church, there was my educational journey. I attended Lea School in West Philadelphia through eighth grade. There, at least half of the student body was Jewish, and I took quite for granted an interfaith society. Then I went on to Philadelphia High School for girls from 9th through 12th grade. Girls High was a magnet high school in the city. My sister and I and two other neighborhood girls, Marjorie and Charlotte Morgan, took two buses and the elevated train every day to get there. We got a wonderful education at Girls' High and were able to engage in many extracurricular activities, among them was the Peace Club where I met Betty Lin who would become a lifelong friend. The teacher who met with us was a Quaker who was well ahead of her time in environmental consciousness. We were all well aware of her non-leather shoes.

After High School, I earned a BS at Drexel where my father taught law. In addition to my academic work, and sports and drama, I participated occasionally in Intervarsity Christian Fellowship. Intervarsity was more conservative than my church, but in those days, I did not know the difference and frankly, it didn't matter then.

From Drexel I went on to Seminary. When I became a student at Princeton Theological Seminary where I was admitted on a probationary basis into the BD (now the MDiv) program. It turns out my BS in Business Administration was not deemed a proper preparatory degree for Ministry. I have since learned otherwise.

At Princeton, I fell in love with theology and discovered the breadth of disciplines essential to professional Ministry. I bonded easily with other students as we shared our educational journey toward Ministry. There were four women in the Ministerial track with other women in Princeton's special three-year Master's Degree Program in Christian Education.

In Seminary, I became aware of liberation theology in Latin America. Our President, The Rev. Dr. John Mackay, had been involved in South America and was an avid ecumenist. I was inspired to action at a Christian Student Movement conference, by the Rev. Dr. Richard Shaul, a missionary in Brazil and early liberation theologian.

One summer, several of us theological students heard him speak at a Student Volunteer Movement Conference. After hearing him speak, five of us were inspired to go on a pilgrimage to Mexico to visit with churches there, mutually share our faith, and learn from them.

Our group consisted of three people from Argentina, one person from Germany, one from Scotland, and two from the States: two Baptists, two Presbyterians, one Lutheran. We were two aspiring clergy, one aspiring professor, one aspiring missionary, one church musician, and one dedicated lay person. We were supported by our Presbyterian Board of Ecumenical Missions who provided us with a van for our journey and their blessing. We raised our own money for the trip.

In Mexico, we discovered and delighted in the universality of the church, the fellowship of our little group, the grace of Christian community in Mexico, and were overwhelmed by their hospitality. We also experienced poverty firsthand.

One day, I accompanied a missionary to a home in an isolated part of the countryside as she helped deliver a baby by candlelight and well water warmed by a wood fire on a large stone. My appreciation for the Christian church deepened and was enriched that night.

After the baby was born, the missionary handed this newborn bundle of life to me. I had to take her, but I was really uncomfortable. I thought everything around birth had to be antiseptic and there I was, full of germs holding a baby fresh from the womb! But all was well. The miracle of birth had happened before my eyes. The baby and mother were fine and grateful for the missionary mid-wife.

Princeton at that time in history had a liberal bent because of its leadership in ecumenism and respect for national diversity. Our President John A. Mackay was a leader in modernizing the concept of mission. And he stood up to McCarthyism for the danger it was to our democracy.

McCarthyism was our first introduction to the ability of ideological forces to raise irrational fears in the American public. In this case, those fears centered on communism. Sen. Joseph McCarthy was out of control accusing people of being communist whether they were or not, causing some to lose their jobs, imprisoning others. Mainline churches were an important voice speaking out against his excesses.

Many of us heard in the teachings of Jesus a message of love for all humanity and a call to justice with mercy and grace and truth. In some sectors of the population, those concerns for justice and for the poor were considered "left leaning."

In our Seminary context, some students were focused on personal salvation, "being saved by Jesus' blood," and taking Scripture literally. There was a divide between social gospel thinking and a focus on personal salvation. Even while engaged in my theological education and drawn to liberation theology, I was still theologically naïve though becoming more socially aware.

I suppose it was quite natural for me to fall in love with Thomas Fitch Kepler, a fellow student whose parents had been missionaries in China and their parents before them. He was smart, educated at Mount Hermon and Yale, had parents who had lived their faith in exciting ways, had crossed the ocean five times and changed schools twelve times before college. I was a pretty boring middle class American with a fascination for faraway places. Tom was cynical, which provided a balance for my kind of innocence and positivity. After we began dating, he went to Mexico with the Seminary Choir while we were on our mission trip.

One day, while in Mexico, we ran into each other in a huge department store in Mexico City, Sanborns. The odds of that happening must be off the charts. That sealed our relationship. It was destiny. More magic than predestination. Or was it providence?

I have mentioned the fact that when I entered Seminary, Ministry was a field closed to women. In our Senior year, the Presbyterian church approved the ordination of women. Oddly enough, I did not pay much attention to that. I was married and pregnant with our first child when I graduated. But it was a sea change for our church.

All of us who were among the first to be ordained would encounter resistance to our ordination. Even as our numbers increased, it was years before women would be called to leadership positions in the church and in theological education. It was years before the Episcopal Church ordained women and to this day, the Roman Catholic Church has refused to ordain women.

I encountered resistance in myself to being ordained as a married woman with children. Somehow, in spite of graduating from Theological School, I was fully acculturated to female roles though I had taken a path less traveled. Women could be ordained in my mind if they were not raising children.

Our first-born son, Thomas, was born before Tom was fully settled in his first church, the First Presbyterian Church of Englishtown. Son Tom was followed within four years by two other sons, James, and John.

Systemic Social Issues Take Hold in Church and Society

The church to which Tom, my husband, was called was in a small town near Princeton. I became a Pastor's wife. I was determined to fulfill that role happily. But it did not happen that way. After a few months, it became clear that some key lay women felt threatened by me. I was not enough in the background though I tried to be.

Local churches were run by male clergy and female lay leaders though men made up most of the official boards of the church. It was understandable that some women who were male clergy's right-hand people would resist female clergy at first. (Even though I was not in any way assuming that role, my professional training was known.)

As providence would have it, an African American Church which was being administered by my husband while they were between Pastors, was in desperate need of a preacher one Sunday. I seemed to be the only one available. They agreed to my coming… conditionally. I went to preach and ended up preaching to a congregation of two male elders who were late. I ended up becoming their Pastor and staying for eight years at Westminster Presbyterian Church in Manalapan where we developed a thriving children's and youth program and an active but small congregation. They accepted me fully.

Westminster Presbyterian Church, Manalapan, New Jersey

I loved the Ministry, but my husband was restless. As a missionary's son, he had moved so often in his early life that he was unfamiliar with local church life and a settled family life. I was at home with both.

Despite his questioning his vocation, he had a productive Ministry at First Presbyterian Church of Englishtown. He oversaw the building of a new educational wing of the church and celebrated one hundred years of the church's ministry. And became involved in civil rights. We both got our second theological degree, our ThM.

The Civil rights Movement was in full gear when we were in our first churches, and both Tom's predominately White church and my

Black church were involved. Members of the church I was serving were deeply affected by racism.

With help from the surrounding churches that were predominately White, we began a Head Start program that was integrated, both racially and economically, a tutoring program for youth, a large summer community Bible School. We advocated for our members in the public educational system where discrimination was rampant and hoped that these programs would enrich our children's lives.

One example of both racism and empowerment involved a teenage member of our church who would go on to become a Presbyterian Minister. Elenora Giddings was brilliant and admitted to a college prep program for High School. When admitted, she was told that she got in because was not like "her people." Deeply offended, she declined the college prep program and stayed with "her people." She eventually went on to college and graduate school. She documents her professional life in her book, 'World View from Elenora Giddings Ivory Tower: The Life and Times of a Religious Advocate."

Members of our church in Manalapan were instrumental in reaching out to White churches in our area to discuss issues of racial discrimination and integration. We had a traveling drama group and a basketball team. And several White churches, including Tom's church in Englishtown were involved with us and helped enable our work.

I could minister to the church with our growing family because our home became a meeting place. We often had meetings around our kitchen table. Our youngest came to church with me while our two older sons went with Tom. And we had competent babysitters.

And my gender role acculturation was changing. Most of the women in my church were working parents too so that began to feel like a quite natural lifestyle for me. In Tom's church, most of the mothers were not employed. I missed being able to join them for morning coffee get-togethers, but I loved my work.

Not all churches around us supported civil rights. A friend of ours, the Rev. Robert Beaman, lost his pulpit for his vocal stand against racism. He and his wife, JoAnne Neff Beaman, ended up working with the church I pastored, and when I left, he pastored, until the Presbytery closed the church and merged it with another Black church a half hour away.

Those years began a time when churches at all levels of organization, from local to national, became places where key social issues and the direction society was taking were discussed, debated, and acted on. While some churches were places where the status quo was doggedly supported, other churches became catalysts for a more just society.

Of course, Black churches and their leaders were taking the lead in the Civil Rights Movement and were deciding its course.

All Churches were in a position to ask how the new creation of which Jesus spoke was coming into being in society. What attitudes need to change for humanity and creation's survival and wellbeing? What laws needed to be implemented. How did hearts need to change?

In Jesus' life and teaching, people in the Civil Rights Movement saw a call for an end to racial discrimination that eventually included a call to end poverty and the Vietnam War. The traditional segregated order that had prevailed for centuries was not seen as God given or in keeping with God's will.

In 1963, President John F. Kennedy was assassinated, and the nation reeled. President Lyndon Johnson came into office and in 1964, The Civil Rights Act, which had been proposed under President Kennedy, was passed. It would take time for it to filter to local levels. But it was cause for celebration.

The trend in Mainline churches in the north was to be supportive of Civil Rights during the Movement era of the Fifties, Sixties, and Seventies. In those years, while some local churches divided over Civil Rights issues, the national church in all major denominations took strong stands in support of Civil Rights. And some Pastors put their lives and careers on the line.

The Rev. William Hervey and the church he pastored were examples of courage and action. Bill, with the support of his predominately white congregation in New Brunswick, New Jersey, and the blessing of his wife, even though they had eight children, joined in the bus trips to Mississippi to help with voter registration.

Bill made such fast friends with other activists on that trip that he was later asked to return to Mississippi to conduct the funeral of James Earl Cheyney, an African American who had been ambushed with two others, Andrew Goodman, and Michael Schwerner, killed by police and the Ku Klux Klan for their work for racial equality

During the Civil Rights years, Dr. Martin Luther King Jr. was the face of the Movement. Black leaders at the forefront of the movement and bearing the brunt of opposition, welcomed those Whites who wanted to stand with them. Clergy and laity of all denominations and faiths walked together in marches to end segregation, to end poverty, and to end the war in Vietnam. They often wore clergy collars or other forms of identification to show the presence of religious bodies.

After the Civil Rights Movement, the anti-Vietnam War Movement, the Feminist and Womanist Movements came into focus. The Gay Rights Movement would follow.

In the Movement days, I was employed as the staff person for the United Presbyterian Church's Task Force on Women. But that is getting ahead of the story.

Before that, both Tom's and my father had died while we were in Englishtown and the impact of those losses was significant for both of us. After ten years as Pastors, we took teaching jobs at the Vanguard School in Florida so Tom could explore teaching as a profession. My brother, a Treasurer at the School, helped us get those jobs.

Vanguard was a school for dyslexic children. There Tom found his calling while I was now the restless one. I wanted to continue my career in the Ministry. I enjoyed teaching but I missed church work.

After a year of teaching in Florida, we moved back to the Philadelphia area where he could continue teaching at a Vanguard School in the area and I had a better chance of finding a job in Ministry.

It was only after we got back to the Philadelphia area that our sons spoke of their experiences with racial segregation in Florida. Because we were teaching in a private school, we were unaware of the separate bathrooms, water fountains, and seating arrangements for Blacks and Whites in public schools. It had been very disturbing to our children.

The Women's Movement Comes into Focus

After we returned to the Philadelphia area, Tom continued his teaching I began a job search, and we served as Co-Stated Supplies at St. Paul Church. After a few months, I was called to be the Secretary for Women's Program for United Presbyterian Women at the Board of Christian Education of the Presbyterian Church. I can only credit my getting that job to the Holy Spirit and one woman, Eileen Gould, who was on the Board of Directors. I did not have much experience in women's work other than what I had done at Manalapan and Englishtown. I had certainly not "come up through the ranks" though I had demonstrated some leadership skills.

Shortly after I went to work for the Board, responsibility for following up on an early foray into sexism in the church fell into my lap. The Task Force on Women was formed and the Presbyterian Church, involved in addressing racism in society and conscientious objection to the Vietnam War added addressing sexism to its agenda. But not before one General Assembly had laughed and snickered at the idea. We were among the first Mainline churches to look at patriarchy in church and society and we certainly experienced some resistance. Over time, we found significant support.

A sea change was continuing to happen in church and society. We were well into the Movement years and a new culture of openness by 1968 when we began to address issues of patriarchy in earnest. The movement for women's ordination as elders and clergy had gone on for many years before then.

For some, the Movement years also included hippie culture, drugs, and more sexual freedom. It was a heady time. While some saw it as a time of liberation, others saw it as a time of cultural anarchy.

In the Presbyterian Church we worked to address sexism in the church. We had a dedicated group of women and men from across the country establishing our agenda which ranged from requiring that women, when being referred to in print, be known by their own first names and not by their husband's name (Mrs. John Smith), to supporting women's right to choose whether or not to have an abortion.

We collaborated with other church groups and secular women's organizations to address sexism. Wilma Scott Heide, past President of the National Organization of Women (NOW) and a feminist leader, became a friend and colleague. We built many bridges between secular and religious groups, and with Joyce Mitchell, another friend, established the first Task Force on Religion in NOW.

Many women and men in churches, contrary to popular opinion at the time, were at the heart of the women's movement. Protestant, Roman Catholic. and Jewish women were working for change within their own networks, and we were all working across religious and secular lines to reform the public sector.

Churches, as institutions in relation to secular institutions, can speak prophetic words to power, and participate creatively and cooperatively with other institutions supporting human needs and rights. There are times when the prophetic voice comes from secular to religious institutions.

Christian and Jewish groups were addressing issues of theology as well as issues of social justice, the nature of God was key among them. Over time, Muslim and Buddhist women added their voices. Some men were deeply involved from the beginning as advocates for women and as people who believed patriarchy was harmful to everyone, including themselves.

During those years there was a pushback against institutions that were working for social justice but then, they were a minority voice. Of course, not all institutions are the same, and they have many parts, some more concerned with human rights than others. At that point in time, religious institutions who were exercising their prophetic, life-giving voice were being heard. Even so, some anti-authoritarian voices saw all organized religion as part of the problem.

In 1968 the United States was shaken by the murder of the Rev. Dr. Martin Luther King, Jr. and a few months later, US Attorney General Robert F. Kennedy was also murdered. It was a difficult and sad time and a turning time for the Movement for racial justice in the church and world. It became the beginning of Black Power Movements.

At a General Assembly meeting in the late sixties, the meeting was interrupted by Mohammed Kenyatta who demanded reparations for Black Americans and the economic injustice they suffered. That confrontation let to the Redevelopment of People Program of the United Presbyterian Church and outreach to communities in need of help and reform. I was there.

The following year, we hired his wife, Mary Kenyatta and Gail Hinnand to lead our Women in Leadership Program established to foster women's leadership at the local level.

Institutional Church Life

I was fortunate to be able to see and participate in the working of a church institution from within. I gained profound respect for the church's democratic process and learned a few things about how things get done behind the scenes. I also learned how much potential there is for change at the local level when resources are provided, education and action are joined, and movement toward the Realm of God, heaven on earth is alive and encouraged to flourish.

As I traveled across the country and met with Presbyterian Women's Groups and Task Forces on Women, I was amazed by the energy, dedication, and creativity of women in all their diversity, working to end Patriarchy across our nation.

In 1974, we developed a bicentennial women's group, joining secular and religious groups across racial lines. The Women's Coalition for the Third Century was formed for our nation's celebration in 1976 of 200 years as a nation. We established the Coalition following several meetings of women leaders convened by the White House for the Bicentennial. The White House Commission saw women as gracious hostesses for Bicentennial events. We had other ideas

In addition to other actions, the Coalition produced the "Declaration of Interdependence," accompanied by a "Declaration of Imperatives:" The document on Interdependence articulated a commitment to our nation's Third Century and the interdependence of all people on one another and the earth, in harmony with Divine Reality. The Declaration of Imperatives was about women's rights as essential to the justice implied in interdependence.

The work of the Coalition was a model for how secular and religious groups can pursue common goals, resolve complex issues, and work together for the common good. They can do so with respect for one another's deeply held beliefs. The fact that we could agree together on "The Declaration" attests to our ability to cooperate across racial, religious, economic, and all other divisions.

Unfortunately, the Coalition, in spite of many press releases and journalists in our ranks, got no media attention. This was a lesson for all of us on how the media works and how limited it is by prevailing power structures and a tradition of reporting on violent and visibly very controversial events and people already deemed as icons.

While working at the Board of Christian Education and chairing the Women's Coalition for the Third Century, I was offered a job at Harvard Divinity School as Director of Ministerial Studies. The Presbyterian Church was reorganizing at the national level, and our offices were moving from Philadelphia to New York. It was a good time to make a change since our family would have to move anyway.

As we were preparing for change, I was aware that the impartial love that Jesus had practiced in his ministering with individuals had taken on a systemic form. Society was changing.

In the Heart of Theological Education and More Change

I was excited about my new position and able to suggest The Rev. Dr. William Yolton for the position of Field Education Director on our staff. Bill had been very active as a staff member of Church and Society working on peace and draft issues. His daughter, Beth had collaborated with us on women's issues, and I knew his wife, Kattie. After they divorced, he married Diane Engstrom whom we both met at a Synod Retreat.

At that point in time, the Movement days were beyond their peak, but the agendas and social issues they had addressed were in full swing and far from resolved in Academia or the Church. The Vietnam War was still going on with all the protests and controversy that surrounded it. Our youngest son had to take a stand on the draft and declared himself a conscientious objector.

A shift had occurred in the Presbyterian Church about conscientious objector status, once reserved for traditionally peace churches like the Society of Friends and the Mennonites. Any baptized Presbyterian could now claim this status.

The Presbyterian Church became a church supportive of those who chose to be conscientious objectors during the Vietnam War and had established a division to address Peace issues.

By the Seventies, it was time to implement the changes the Movement Years had brought about. The Sixties had been a time of anti-institutional sentiments. Churches were beginning to have to become advocates for their own existence and forms of governance. My attention, apart from my work with the Women's Coalition had to shift from feminist advocacy to supporting the education of clergy in a changing church.

Protestant churches were still thriving in some parts of the country, but they began losing members in major urban areas again and liberalism was in some decline. The moral majority was gaining force in the wings. Harvard Divinity School was increasing its focus on the preparation of clergy for Ministry in a hopeful and prophetic move.

The Dean of the Divinity School, the Rev. Dr. Krister Stendahl was committed to the church and to vital and learned clergy leadership. He felt that the church still had a critical role to play in people's lives and in society. And that is why I was at Harvard Divinity School.

South American liberation theology was continuing to be advanced by brilliant and involved theologians in South America and some of them were visiting scholars at Harvard. Interesting that this emphasis was vibrant at Princeton Theological School in my student days.

The Divinity School was closely related to the Center for World Religions. Interfaith issues were becoming vital to the educational core of Christian studies.

I was deeply involved in establishing a professional program for clergy that would add in-depth and pastoral competence to the academic excellence expected at Harvard. We needed to pursue an in-depth understanding of Ministry in the local church in its wider social and institutional context. We offered a wide range of Field Education Programs so students could explore the variety of professional positions open to clergy and educated lay leaders.

In our multi-denominational setting, we developed courses to prepare students for ordination in denominations. At least half of our students were Roman Catholic, and we had a counselor to minister to their professional needs. Professor Conrad Wright and I developed a course on "The Institutional Church" to introduce our creative student body to the reality of church life at all levels.

We were wrestling with the nature of Ministry as a Profession at a time when it was in transition. Theology had long ago lost its place as "The Queen of the Sciences." Clergy were no longer automatically seen as essential professionals. In theological schools we were becoming advocates for the profession itself as we looked toward its future.

Theology, the primary discipline of Ministry can provide insights essential into human being, survival and well-being that are not addressed by other disciplines. Theology can ask ethical questions essential to ordinary and changing times and provide a framework for worship and liturgy. It seemed more important than ever that we take it seriously and yet, there were increasing numbers of people who saw it as irrelevant.

Even with the challenges Theological Education was facing, we had confidence that our graduates would become leaders in their denominations and creative clergy in a variety of roles and be an asset to society. They had much to offer in the world. They did go on to fill creative and important leadership positions.

During the Harvard years, cross disciplinary work took place that signaled the importance of a dialogue between disciplines. We developed a program with the School of Education and a local school system to explore teaching values in public school. We developed a cooperative program with the Law School to address ethical issues in law and religion (The Committee on Religion and Law CORAL. We were in conversations with the Medical School on medical ethics. We were also in conversation with Eastern Pennsylvania Psychiatric Institute, in a desire to understand more about family therapy. It was a rich time of cross-disciplinary interaction.

In our Continuing Education Program, I had the opportunity to explore my longtime interest in Working Mothers and the church.

By 1980, almost half of the students in the MDiv program were women but the faculty was still predominately male. Harvard Divinity School was both a progressive and staid institution torn between being a Professional School and an extension of Arts and Sciences and preparing students for PhDs and teaching positions. It was, of course, both.

I was at Harvard for the five years of my contract after which time, I exchanged my academic position for a position as Pastor of a local church. The "Harvard years," 1973-78, were years of political turmoil at Harvard and in society. Finances were strained at the Divinity School and Dean Stendahl retired the year after I left. In society there was some unrest followed by a deceptive calm and shifts in our national direction.

Behind the scenes, a segment of Christianity which eventually became known as the "Christian Right" was in formation. The "Moral Majority" was founded in 1979. They consciously became a political force in reaction to the Movement years. The irony was that during those years, conservative Christians had quite self-righteously declared that religion has no place in politics. Christianity, already divided, was becoming an even more divided religion.

As the Christian right became more influential, the media began to equate the Right with Christianity itself. It was as if Christian liberalism, or progressive Christianity, whatever one calls it, was dead. And although, Christianity had never been a state religion, the United States being founded on the separation of church and state, the desire to merge Christianity with being American was in motion. Christian nationalism was very much part of very conservative Christian identity.

Aspects of Christian Nationalism would eventually merge with White Supremacy.

After Harvard, while I was evaluating my professional options, I served as Interim Minister at the Sudbury Presbyterian Church, an active suburban congregation with a social conscience. The time I was there was truly joyful and fulfilling. As I struggled to discern my professional future, I could see myself as Pastor of a local church. I could put into practice the things I had advocated at Harvard.

If I had continued in academia, I would have had to move out of the Boston area. My sons, now in their late teens, made it clear that they were going to stay in the Boston area. I wanted to be near them, so Boston it was. My husband was good with that. It was where he had finally put down roots. So I gave up my esteemed academic identity to become a Pastor.

A Local Face of the Liberal Church

After Sudbury and some contract work for our national Vocation Agency, I began my Ministry at Clarendon Hill Presbyterian Church in Somerville, Massachusetts, in 1979 as Co-Stated Supply with my husband on a part time basis (he was continuing his tent making ministry.)

President Carter was in office when we began our ministry at Clarendon Hill but did not get reelected in the wake of the Iran hostage situation though it was almost resolved before the election. President Reagan replaced him, and a more conservative national agenda that had been building began its rise.

As a pastor of a local church, and an activist during the Movement years, I remained on the liberal side of the ethical issues affecting our nation. I could see that the theological and social issues that had been resolved at the national level in favor of liberation were now having to be implemented at the local level. And that was not going to be easy. Especially since the political scene had turned conservative.

Clarendon Hill Presbyterian Church like many urban and ex-urban churches was in decline when we began our ministry there. It was on the verge of closing. We applied for and received a Redevelopment Grant from our denomination and by the congregation's hard work and my determination, and above all, the movement of the Spirit, we began to grow and change. New members, in addition to original members from Nova Scotia, and other Euro-Americans, included people from Palestine, Lebanon, Kenya, Cameroon, Ethiopia, China, and Korea.

We quickly became aware of Palestinian/Israeli issues. One of our members was marrying a Palestinian when her wedding had to be changed from a big celebration to a small family affair because of the massacre of Palestinians in Sabra and Shatila in southern Lebanon.

Another member and his family had lost their homes during a Zionist invasion of Palestinian villages in 1946, designed to rout people from their homes. It was a blessing for our church to play a leadership role in addressing the situation in Palestine/Israel. I needed much mentoring because I knew next to nothing about the history and issues involved. Like other Americans, all I could remember hearing when the State of Israel was formed was "A land without a people for a people without a land." I found out that it was not a land without a people. Some of the people whose forebears had been there for ages were in our congregation and in surrounding cities.

At Clarendon Hill, we were blessed to be near Tufts University with all the energy and diversity that affords. Students were part of our community. And Harvard Divinity School being close, we had the many blessings student interns brought us.

The congregation addressed inclusive language issues in worship and advocated for inclusive language in the Presbytery. Most of our members had a commitment to moving beyond patriarchal systems. For some in the community these were not pressing issues, but their faith was deep and their commitment to the church was strong, and they were invaluable members. Each one of us needed to be true to ourselves and give each other room to be who we are.

Of course, pastoral ministries were central in our church along with community building. Worship was at the heart of who we were. This foundation made inclusivity possible at all levels.

In our local community, we engaged in ecumenical cooperation. Amid political change, the Aids epidemic emerged. Bringing denominations together, we held healing services for people with Aids and their friends and families. We all knew that Aids was often deadly. It was a devastating epidemic. But we believed in the healing power of spiritual support and love and circles of presence for those affected, their lovers, and families.

Gay rights issues had been in the wings throughout the movement years. When gay rights issues and sexuality finally became issues in mainline denominations, we studied, discussed, and asked where our faith was leading in sexuality matters. Clarendon Hill became what Presbyterians call, a More Light Church, a community in which everyone is accepted whatever their sexual orientation, and able to serve in leadership positions.

Gay Rights continued to be hotly debated in ours and other denominations across churches. It was not until 2016 that the national Presbyterian Church affirmed the right to marry of LGBTQ+ couples. Massachusetts legalized gay marriage before the church approved it.

The day after it was legalized, I was privileged to preside at the marriage of two very dear friends who had already been partners for 20 years and were raising three nieces. It was an amazing, wonderful wedding and a real cause for celebration.

Most Mainline Churches finally approved gay ordination and marriage nationally. It was hard for conservative congregations to accept the national church's position. It also seemed hard for immigrant churches. Nationally, churches functioning in international decision-making systems, like the United Methodist Church, also had issues with Gay Rights. The United Methodist Church in the United States voted to ordain gay ordination in 2024 amid much celebration.

In our church, while all of this was going on, we found ourselves drawn into other international issues. Through our members we had ties to countries in Africa. Some of us took a trip to Kenya at the invitation of the choir of St. Andrews Presbyterian Church in Nairobi, the church of our dear friend, Dr. Francis Situma who worshipped with us while studying for his doctorate. He became an adopted member of our family. That visit led to our sponsoring Pastor Amos Kariuki to come to the States. In Kenya we experienced a vital growing church that spoke truth to power and was listened to.

Because of the influence of other members of our community from Cameroon, we had the great honor of meeting the head of the Presbyterian church in Cameroon. Emanuel Ekumah from Cameroon kept us posted on current events there. We were able to sponsor a young man from Ethiopia, Aboro Abebe, whose father was at Fletcher School of Law and Diplomacy at Tufts at the time when Ethiopia and Eritrea were at war.

In Somerville, we had a highly active Interfaith Peace Network as work for peace became a critical issue in our community and nation. The Mennonite Congregation of Boston met in our building and taught us much about pacifism.

We also formed an Interfaith Association that led to our celebrating Martin Luther King, Jr. Day together, holding joint worship services for Thanksgiving, and honoring one another's holidays. We developed a protocol for worshipping across faith lines and a statement of purpose that we could all affirm while being true to our own traditions. No small feat.

A Shift Away from the Religious Progressive Agenda

After years of cooperative activity, participation in our local ecumenical and peace organizations began to decline. It became clear that the climate for such work had shifted across the nation. At the time, Father Peter Casey and I were producing an interfaith Program on Somerville Community Cable Network called "Stories of Faith." That continued for ten years. But we lost our Interfaith Peace Network and our Interfaith group.

Churches who were expanding their racial, international, ecumenical, and international outreach and their commitment to peace and social justice were in decline numerically. They continued that work, but it was harder. The nation was experiencing backlash against the Movement years and a longing on the part of some to return to "the good old days" before human rights became an issue.

At the national level of our church, some changes did happen in the Eighties that were meant to heal old wounds. The merger of the Presbyterian Church in the north and south that had split during the Civil War took place. The reconciliation of churches that had divided during the Civil War was happening in other denominations as well and was a sign of hope for healing long overdue. But mergers required some compromises.

Those mergers, could not, as we were to find out, translate into political healing and reconciliation between conservative and liberal Christians. As voters scattered across the country, conservative or liberal religious beliefs translated into political leanings too.

By the turning of the Century in 2,000 CE, many Protestant and Roman Catholic Churches were still holding on to a prophetic voice regarding racism, gender issues, economic justice, and peace, though they were numerically in decline, especially in New England and parts of the West Coast. Attendance at church in the central and southern part of the country was not falling as quickly but it was slipping. Non-denominational Mega Churches had popped up along with TV evangelists.

President Bill Clinton saw our nation through the turning of the Century and there was still hope for a national agenda in support of human rights. And then his Presidency ended in a sexual scandal.

Mainline congregations and their faithful, dedicated, persevering members were about to become almost invisible in public discourse and the media as the door opened for the influence of the more radical right.

Modern Religious Extremism

When I retired from the full-time Pastorate after almost 20 years at Clarendon Hill, I went on to serve as Interim University Chaplain at Tufts University on two separate occasions. Through the Chaplaincy at Tufts, we ministered as an Interfaith clergy team across all our University Schools though our home base was at Goddard Chapel and the Interfaith Center in Medford.

I was University Chaplain when the attacks of 9/11, 2002 took place when President George W. Bush was in office. I was there again when the Marathon bombing shook Boston. As a nation, we had experienced our vulnerability to international violence.

Muslim militant extremists were responsible for both attacks. We had to both care for those traumatized and affected by the violence and help the community resist anti-Muslim feelings and actions and support our Muslim Chaplain. We were beginning to learn more about Islam and were revisiting the potential for religious extremism in all our faith communities. There were extremists in Christianity and Judaism as well as in Islam.

As a nation we began the first Iraq War and the War in Afghanistan which followed. It was our national response to terrorism. There were protests against those wars and statements against them by our churches, but nothing like the protests during the Vietnam War. For one thing, we did not have a Draft at the time of the later wars. I sensed a feeling of exhaustion and confusion on many people's part. There was remorse for how Vietnam veterans had been treated. And conservatives were in control in government. A vast number of people in the middle seemed disengaged.

Interfaith Cooperation and Complexity

As Chaplain at Tufts, on another front, I became aware of the growing strength of the Humanist Movement which was strong on the Harvard campus and proselytizing at Tufts. It was an atheist movement with a strong social conscience and an evangelistic bent. At least on our campus, their organizational structure followed that of religious communities with one exception.

One of the principles of the University Chaplaincy was that in our Interfaith context we agreed to respect one another's affiliations. It turned out that that was hard for some Humanists to do as they were militantly atheist and anti-religion in their early organizational days. Of course, some in our religious traditions had been anti other religions at some point in their history and some still were even if they did not talk about it. Eventually humanists and other religious groups would work together on campus and soften their approach.

While religious life on campus was thriving with Protestants having more trouble with numbers than Catholics, the Muslim worshipping community was holding its own, and Hillel, the Jewish community on campus was well funded and thriving. Buddhists and Hindu student groups were developing. While there were some signs that religions, which were deeply divided nationally, were having issues on campus, even as we developed a successful interfaith program.

On campus as in society, the number of people with no religious affiliation was growing. They became known as "nones." And though religion at Tufts was, like the University, progressive, there were divisions between students around social issues, particularly, issues of gay rights.

I found myself trying to distinguish between people's right to their beliefs while being clear that they could not act them out in the form of discrimination against other students. Beliefs themselves cannot be legislated against. No one can control what anyone believes. I am reminded of an old German song, "Die Gedanken Sind Frei," (Thoughts are Free.) But we must respond when thoughts and beliefs are acted on in ways that harm others, whatever side the actors are on.

Acts that harm others can come from people on all sides of the religious and secular spectrum. Ultimately, we pursued the importance of dialogue about beliefs and tried to be careful and respectful of each other when we disagreed, even intensely while affirming with clarity, the University's and Chaplaincy's anti-discriminatory stance. Conservative

Christians continued to struggle with how they saw God's will in matters of gay rights.

Long Standing Religious Institutions in Serious Decline

In the public realm, in the early Twenty-First Century, the religious right was gaining ever more momentum in the nation. And, in the midst of everything else, in 2002, the Sexual Abuse Scandal was exposed by the Boston Globe. Five Priests faced criminal prosecution and others after them. Eventually the scandal led to the closure of even thriving Romand Catholic churches and schools. In addition to the closings of churches, membership in all Catholic Churches was affected by the scandal and there was a growing shortage of clergy.

Locally, Protestant churches were struggling too for other reasons including sociological shifts in ethnic makeup. In Somerville alone, three mainline churches in our community closed. One sold their large building and moved to a storefront. Others were renting space to other organizations in the community to both serve the community and provide modest income for the church to survive. Ethnic churches were emerging, some growing, some also struggling.

In the big scheme of things, the development of the far right, the priest scandal, and the growth of independent mega churches along with the growing number of people who did not affiliate with any religion, influenced the Protestant and Roman Catholic Church at all levels. The growth of people without any religious affiliation was a sea change for churches, primarily moderate and liberal leaning churches.

In the Jewish Community there were slightly different issues. It was possible for people to be culturally but non-religiously Jewish. That was not an option in other faith groups in quite the same way. The majority of synagogues in the Jewish community had begun to associate advocacy for Israel with being Jewish. That advocacy was fierce, well-funded, and in public, uncritical of Israel. For some, the stance for justice for which the Jewish community had long stood as a given part of faith, was overshadowed by uncritical loyalty to Isarael which turned a blind eye to the treatment of Palestinians.

By the time I left the Chaplaincy at Tufts for the second time in 2014, the first African American President, Barak Obama, entered his second term as President. His election had been an occasion for celebration and hope that our nation was back on a path to a humanitarian agenda, attention to the middle class and disadvantaged after years of conservative politics.

During these years, environmental issues and global warming were becoming ever more urgent and recognition of their importance was to become another rift between the "right" and the "left."

The political scene was heating up and Donald Trump was in motion. He ran against Hilary Clinton for President and his election was a total surprise for many of us. Instead of electing our first woman President we had elected a white male authoritarian figure who pandered to the wealthy and had no interest in human rights and courted Christina nationalists.

Meanwhile, my husband and I went on to serve two churches as Interim Pastors. At the first church we served, the congregation was both Anglo and Cameroonian. It was the first church we knew of to combine two cultures and it was a rich experience.

In the second church we served, several transgender people were members, some in leadership positions. It was a place where LGBTQ+ people were accepted and in leadership. The church also had members who were physically challenged. The problem was that it was a small church with limited resources, and they finally had to close. Fortunately, a Taiwanese Presbyterian church moved in.

During our time there in Waltham, we formed close ties with the American Baptist and United Methodist Churches in town and their pastors. Ecumenical ties were still alive!

One issue that came up in several churches we served was the presence of an American flag at the front of a Christian sanctuary. Even in an open and affirming church, Christian nationalism was an unrecognized problem. It was hard to make the point that in Christian sanctuaries, worshippers are worshipping a God who is the God of all creation and not partial to any nation.

I am hardly aware of when it happened but before the turn of the century, our nation and much of the world entered the computer age, the age of electronic technology that signaled the beginning of a new era in human history.

Ordinary Life and Change in the Church

As I conclude this personal journey into changes in church life in the United States, it is clear that no matter what work we are engaged in or not engaged in for pay, and no matter what is going on in our communities and the world around us, we go on with our ordinary lives doing those things we need to do to survive in the context of family and friends. And it is in that context that we change. Over the years my family has taught me as much about our changing world and religious life than anything in my professional life did. As we were all going through our own developmental stages in our life together as a family, we were affecting each other.

When our family was negotiating life in the sixties and seventies and our sons were pre-teen and teens, life was exciting but not easy. I spent my first years at Harvard as a single parent until Tom moved to the Boston area. I got a taste of what it is like to be a single parent and my sons experienced life without their father, and it is hard.

Our family also lived through the early stages of the Second Feminist Movement. Early in our family life Tom and I were breaking from traditional gender roles in which the man in the house was the bread winner and the woman was housekeeper and parent. We were both engaged in all forms of work. It wasn't until I began my work with the national church that I had a name for it. I was a feminist.

Being a female in a household with four males, I knew early in my feminist days that men are not the enemy, and that feminism is bound to change men's lives as surely as women's, liberating both men and women from confining and unhealthy stereotypes and roles. But I was bucking the media message that feminism was an anti-male movement.

Through the years, every member of our family engaged in all the work living entails: housework, and nurturing work, earning and managing money, schoolwork, volunteer work, and pursuit of personal interests, as our personalities and life situations allowed or required. As it turns out, our sons are all good cooks and hands-on fathers.

More than anything else, my husband and sons taught me about love and how it remains constant through all of life's changes. It is love that gets us through and lasts a lifetime whatever else is going on in the world. I am very blessed by my family.

Of course, our family life was affected by the same dynamics that affected church and society on a wide scale. Each person in our small family constellation had to develop their own values and worldviews and cope with political, sociological, religious, economic, and ecological change.

In one way or another, our values and perspectives are influenced by the religious context in which we live. That, however, does not always translate into belonging to a religious community.

As I write, I am retired from paid work. Our family's lifestyle during our working years, with two parents employed outside of the home has become a common pattern for many families. Though I must note that for some it always was simply what life was like: for one of my grandmothers, a beloved aunt, and cousins and many parishioners in my African American Church women parenting and earning money were essential.

Today there are more recognized diverse family constellations: single parent households, two same sex parents, partners without children, other variations of gender identity.

All of these relational realities affect the now and future church.

LIFESTYLE CHANGES THAT EFFECT CHURCH BELONGING

On a very pragmatic and individual and relational level, lifestyle changes have affected church life. The Women's Movement has changed the traditional life roles open to women and men. This impacts family and church life very directly. Daily life is more complicated for more people now than it was in past generations. Non-binary expressions of gender have emerged that challenge traditional life roles as feminism does.

As Patriarchy is challenged, gender stereotypes and roles are changing, new family life-patterns are emerging. More people are juggling paid work and family life. People often live together before marrying. Add to this economic change and the spiraling costs of housing and education and more people than ever struggling to make ends meet. There are no laws regarding commerce on the Sabbath. New generations probably don't even know that any ever existed.

The old pattern of male clergy and female volunteers keeping the wheels of the church turning is no longer viable in most settings. Most women have less volunteer time than women before them. New ways for men and women to participate in and take leadership roles in the church need to be found that work in these changing times.

More women clergy serving as Pastors contributes to shifting gender work patterns in the church. New ways of organizing congregational life are on the horizon.

No matter how competent, wise, compassionate, prophetic, courageous, and educated religious leaders are, they are dependent on the laity for the existence and strength of the church. Churches are places where participants can explore what they believe, use gifts of leadership and art that they cannot use in other contexts. Churches are places where people can ask hard questions and agnostics are always welcome. But people have to be there in churches for these things to happen.

It is easy to see that many people do not feel that there is much time left in weekly schedules for religious belonging. Giving priority to participating in church and face-to-face connection takes conscious effort as does any semblance of honoring the Sabbath. Weekends are precious times for families and individuals to catch up on home responsibilities. What religious communities have to offer needs to be valued for people to make the effort to show up.

Changing Patriarchal patterns are accompanied by changing Patriarchal views. Traditional belief systems are being challenged, often indirectly. Some of these have been identified in previous chapters of this book including traditional images of God.

Religious communities have some facts to face and some catching up to do, and some changes to make in how congregations function as old gender patterns become obsolete and faith views are changing.

New generations simply live in a time when the centrality of assumed religious belonging has shifted. As ethical issues and strong convictions are coming into focus in this time of transition between eras, congregations are not necessarily seen as central to finding resolutions to personal, communal and world problems. It will be up to congregations to make clear their investment in the creation of a better world.

On a larger social scale, we are experiencing a Great divide, and our nation is divided on what constitutes a better world.

THE GREAT DIVIDE

Super nationalism took office with Donald Trump's Presidency which began in 2017 and ended in 2021. He affiliated with the extreme Christian right. A nation and a Christianity already divided became fractured. He and his followers were anti-abortion and among his adherents were white supremacists who were now emboldened to come out of the shadows.

With Trump's election, backlash against the social movements of earlier years was in full swing. Authoritarianism became a threat to democracy. Police brutality against Black Americans took place. Sexual infidelity seemed irrelevant to Trump supporters. Truth seemed unimportant. And women's right to choose abortion or not was revoked.

When Trump lost the election to Biden in 2021, he did not go quietly. His assertion of election fraud culminated in the Insurrection of January 6, 2021, which protested the election of President Biden.

Ex-President Donald Trump continued to marshal his followers for another run for President.

While Trump was still President, Covid hit, and life changed for everyone as we went into lockdown. Most religious communities stopped worshipping in their sacred spaces. We learned to use and lean on Zoom. What personal interaction there was took place on the internet. And we cannot forget that by 2024, 1,104,00 people died.

Now that we have vaccinations against Covid and we are trying to get back to normal, the old normal is gone. It is as if we are beginning again at all levels of social life including church life.

In our churches which were already facing declining membership, all of this had a serious impact. A few people have taken the opportunity to drop out of regular worship permanently, at least for now. Some others have begun to attend church, needing community after the isolation of Covid while others continue to worship on Zoom.

I am now Pastor-ex-officio at Clarendon Hill Presbyterian Church. Our services are both in-person and on Zoom and we, like many other churches, are working to get back to full strength numerically. Our commitment to our mission is as strong as ever. Our dedication to being both locally focused and engaged in the world has not wavered. And there are churches all over the nation in the same situation. Just as the world is feeling very unstable both politically and environmentally and is in transition as we move into a new era, churches continue to experience the pressure of social change on many fronts.

As is obvious in my reflections on the changes in the church that I have experienced in my professional life, declining church membership is a reality. It is a reality in my own family and in the families of relatives and friends. Many of us could not give our children the experience of church or Christianity that we had growing up in the church's hey-day. We could not give them the deep sense of taken- for- granted belonging in Christian community we once had in America, and some wish we still had in our growing religiously pluralistic country. That is not all bad. Our horizons are expanding.

Like many in coming generations across the nation, the young people we know have a strong sense of social justice. They have awareness of the precious and often precarious nature of life. They have a deep capacity for love and compassion.

My fear for new and coming generations is that if the religious roots on which life-saving ethical sensitivity is built are lost, the roots of ethical sensitivities will wither as generation succeeds generation. My hope is that, by the Spirit's grace, they will find a way to express their ethical sensibility in community somehow. Maybe even in some form of church.

THE FUTURE OF MAINLINE CHRISTIANITY

> *Our role is to provide the hands and hearts that will enable the universe's energies to come forth in a new order of well-being. Our destiny is to bring forth a planetary civilization that is both culturally diverse and locally vibrant, a multiform civilization that will enable life and humanity to flourish.* Journey of the Universe by Brain Thomas Swimme and Mary Evelyn Tucker p.117

When the early church emerged, its purpose was to continue the work of Jesus Christ, his teachings, his healing, his message of God's love. It was called to proclaim and live the Good News of God's coming realm on earth, in a violent time when the Romans Empire ruled the Western world.

Living in the flame of the Spirit and the power of resurrection, the early church brought odd assortments of people together, often people incompatible with each other, beginning with Jews and Gentiles. They had many internal issues to work out and yet, they managed to bear witness that God's living presence was at work in the world.

The mission of churches has not changed much from that of the early church but there is a new urgency about it. We are rediscovering Christianity on the brink of everything.

The very earth on which we live is in precarious condition. We watch wars rumble and know that some of the nations involved have nuclear bombs and we could all be blown up as lives are gambled with in the Middle East and other places. We know that people are starving in the world as a result of raging conflicts and poverty.

We know that Russia's Putin has started a war with Ukraine that could have implications for other parts of Europe. Israel's war with Gaza is turning into a genocide of Gazans and fear that a wider conflict in the Middle East could develop. Ukraine along with Israel needs weapons from the United States and our Allies. We are part of the war machine.

Meanwhile, while all of this is going on, much of the news focuses on the weather, car crashes and shootings, and sports with tidbits thrown in about our latest idols and the royal family in England. And at the end some feel good story about the rescue of an animal or the valor of someone helping someone else, or an impressive feat accomplished. We all know the script.

The world needs to wake up. I am not talking about the much overused and debated concept of being "woke." I am really talking about coming to, caring, saving the future for new generations, and transforming our lives, yes, those of us now living, recovering our humanity and healing our souls. Seems like this is church work. Not exclusively, but surely.

Those of us in the church or somehow marginally connected can claim this as our mission. Of course, it helps if we know the basics of our faith which I have laid out in this book from my perspective. Beyond that, the future of Christianity has to do with our own experiences and beliefs about God and God's coming Realm in our time and in the years ahead.

Christianity has to do with caring about and valuing life, all life. We live in a world in which we can all be very wrapped up in our own lives and can worship a God or not who is also focused on us and not our neighbor.

Christianity is about a God who cares about the whole world and is deeply embedded in it. As Christians we believe in both the historic Jesus and his resurrection and transcendence. We believe in the Spirit who breathes life into the world. And since we are heirs with Christ, we are challenged to believe that in our humanity is a capacity for transcendence. These beliefs matter in a time of changing eras.

We are witnessing tumultuous times, and our feelings can be all over the map. Some of the changes seem dangerous and could throw us into despair so we distract ourselves. Sometimes change seems dysfunctional and confusing and causes us to withdraw into our own little worlds, some changes seem so threatening that we lash out at each other, cling to the past, or become totally hedonistic.

There are also changes that promise a better world and bring hope that enlivens us and sends us seeking out more light to guide us into the coming age with creativity and expectation. What we have learned from the past is that God is with us in our darkest times and in our times of promise and celebration.

As we enter a new era there are divisions among us that are critical and deep. We have to sort them out. In the best of all worlds, we would respect each other as we seek life-giving ways forward. That is getting harder as major ethical divisions intensify.

The agenda of the Movement years is incomplete as old issues resurface and new challenges emerge. The backlash is fierce against the human rights agenda of the late Twentieth Century in which mainstream Christianity was so engaged. As all the old 'isms" assert themselves again, it is time for Christianity to confront them with clarity and recover the power of our moral voice for justice and peace enveloped in love and grace.

We have gotten very good at identifying problems, very legitimate problems of the past, and establishing blame or accepting guilt for them. In the new era, we need to do more than identify sin and address it and seek forgiveness and reconciliation, important as that may be. We need to develop new ways of being. We need to mature in faith.

Building God's realm in the new age entails finding ways of being in the world that make relating to one another with integrity real. We need to create ways of living on the firm foundation of God's creative and life-giving love. We need to figure out what love really means. If we leave patriarchy, militarism, classism, and all divisive isms behind, how can we reconfigure and reconstruct our social order?

And, underlying the social ethical agendas of Christianity there are faith questions that need to be addressed. What do we mean by God's power? How can we replace religious sacrifice with mutual service? How can the Holy Spirit become more central to our faith?

The Spirit is leading us back to God's "I am who I am," to addressing the God who is the "I am who is becoming," We need God's creating energy to lead us into the future, into a new future beyond the brink of everything that threatens life.

With Moses, we need to ask God again, "Who should we say you are?" And with Peter we need to ask Jesus, "Who should we say you are?" And of the Spirit, we need to ask, "Where is your Breath blowing?"

We need to ask ourselves who we think we are. Are we created to be in relationship with a sacred force beyond and within our world? Do we have the capacity to love? Are we inherently violent, competitive, and prone to love power above all else or can we be transformed to find the power of love and seek peace with justice?

Is every single human being in this world valuable or are some disposable? When did it happen that a few human beings came to hold most of the world's wealth and to make billions of more dollars than the majority of people who just get by (or don't) on a daily basis. How can we take back our world for God's sake and our own? How can we take back our minds and souls by expecting those who are entitled to serve the common good and not by trickle-down economics.

I pray that we are ready to open our lives to new revelations of the Spirit. We, and those before us have worked hard for this day of moving into a new era and exploring a holy, wholly new creation.

Tradition is very important in Christianity and continuity is a key to movement from one generation to another. We are not called to throw out all that is a great resource from the past. But we must know that God cannot be limited by tradition. God's call comes to religious communities across racial, national, and ethnic lines to pursue and ensure the future, a future that is life-giving for everyone.

Present generations who have some affiliation with Christianity keep the faith alive and bear witness of its foundations and future. Many of us have been part of either liberation movements or ministries of healing and hope. We have faith that the Spirit who has been a silent partner all of our lives is there for coming generations.

New generations cannot help but be aware of the connectedness of all humanity. We pray that they are prepared to accept responsibility for the earth and hold it in their hands close to their hearts. From a religious perspective, they are not alone. God is with them as are generations who have gone before them in faith. Many of them are, at least partially, rooted in religious values absorbed from those past generations.

The future of the church rests with the perseverance of current generations, and new generations whose spirituality and ethical values are coming to life in the power of the Spirit. In Christianity and other world religions they can find a foundation on which to build as people of faith come to terms with the past and accept responsibility for the future.

CHURCHES AND AN ELECTRONIC FUTURE

Now and future religious communities will have to continue to address societal ethical issues of justice and peace, an end to war, and a solution to environmental issues in a new electronic, technical age that is already upon us.

In the new era there are and will continue to be new technological developments in society's future which have enormous social implications and raise new ethical questions. These developments will only grow in importance for coming generations. What will the church's response to them be? What does God have to do with this new world?

The growth of Artificial Intelligence is raising ethical questions such as the place and power of truth, propaganda, appearance, and reality in personal and public life. Will competition between human beings and machines, including robots, turn into a concern. It raises the question of who controls the robots. What is the role of government in regulating new technology? What will be the role of religious communities in identifying ethical challenges and providing avenues for human beings to address them? Will religious communities provide an alternative to computer reality?

The ability to gather on Zoom and other media platforms that developed during Covid has already affected the religious community. It has enabled people across geographic lines to gather at the same time that in-person community is possible. This ushers in new challenges and possibilities. Where does it leave in-person connection?

How does religion, which while dealing with material reality deals with faith in that which is real beyond material reality, deal with that which is not real in material reality?

Many children already have electronic communication at their fingertips. Electronic media is ubiquitous. Electronic developments are trending toward individual connections and mass participation with social influencers gaining in importance. How can religion compete for the attention of young people?

The new Techtronic, Cosmic age that is exploring new horizons on earth and in space is our future and comes with both danger and promise.

Technology has already developed atomic and nuclear weapons that changed our lives. Humanity enters a new age with power never held in human hands before. We can wreak havoc on the world with our weapons of war and with the exploding use of electronic technologies of all kinds. All of this is leading to an anxious undercurrent that could sweep us away if we are not grounded in our humanity and passionate care for the world. If we are not, in Christian terminology, grounded in God's creating love.

The new age also has great promise. Human beings enter a time in the history of the world when we can be a creative force as never before. We are on the forefront of new discoveries in technology, medicine, science, and other human endeavors. We are making great progress in human rights. We continue to be engaged in all of the activities and relationships of life that give us meaning. Do we need God anymore?

Life and death once assumed to be only in God's hands is now also in human hands. Many theologians have identified humanity as co-creating with God. It is our relationship with the Holy that allows us to see the whole of life beyond ourselves and to not think the whole revolves around us. The Spirit of God can empower us to harness our energies toward a more humane future. If we ground ourselves in the Holy, the ancient of days, we can connect to the past for the wellbeing of the future. We can be prepared to build societies committed to human wellbeing at all levels of life. Religious communities have a significant role to play in the coming era.

In an age when high technology is allowing us to create human-like robots; through AI, to create reality stories through machines, and to develop images of human beings, and new creatures on the internet and screens of our minds, we have power to safeguard our own reality and marvelous diversity.

Human beings have a life force and consciousness and conscience and connection with the heart of the Holy that no machine can ever have. We have an ability to love. We are coming of age in the era of the Spirit when we can explore more fully how love can cast out fear.

In the future we need the ability to combine a perception of God that does not limit God to our parochial images of Divinity, and a perception of humanity that does not limit us to stereotypical images of who we are.

No robot or form of artificial intelligence can match the complexity, depth, and spiritual potential of human beings or our need for one another and love, our emotional intelligence and flexibility and even fickleness, and our ability to connect with a Wisdom beyond our own, a Holy Spirit that is not human made.

In spite of, or perhaps because of, the great power humanity now holds in its hands, life sometimes seems and is very fragile to ordinary people. Human beings need one another more than ever to celebrate and protect our humanity.

One thing that is missing in technology is face-to-face relational connection and community. We text in brief comments rather than have conversations. Most of us are attached to our computers and tablets and phones and are content with brief human encounters. This is a wide-open door for the church that is built on community to provide a place for relationships to form.

In the future we will need to value more than ever being connected to one another as real, complex human beings, to talk to one another, to share more of ourselves, to take time to be together, to build relationships. All of this to hang on to and celebrate our humanity. And we need to see a transcendent Reality that is more significant, more influential, more able to work with the human side of life, to save humanity. A Divine Reality with a loving and deep relationship with Creation who can help us forge our human connections.

RELIGIOUS AND SECULAR JOIN FORCES

As we look toward the future of Christianity and indeed of religion, the relationship between religion and the secular world is important. Secular is not the opposite of religious. It is simply the wider world in which the religious resides. It does not imply any particular value. Profane is the opposite of religious and does imply value.

The future of the church lies with our ability to translate ancient and advancing Wisdom to meet today's needs. The world is a shrinking community, and we are all interconnected. Most of our lives touch many cultures. We are aware of humanity's dependence on the earth and our existence on this planet in a wide universe.

As we stumble, slip, or are dragged into the future, we go with a prayer on our lips for the Spirit to guide us and those who come after us in the ways that lead to life. Trying not to fall prey to the sins of the past or the temptations of the future, we go with boldness and discernment into a new era as part of secular society and for some of us, as participants in religious community.

As we do, there is a need for all Christian churches who carry Jesus' name to carry his message of loving God with heart, mind, and soul and neighbor as self, into the world. Christians who live with open minds and hearts will breathe in the Breath of God along with the air they breathe. The One we call Holy will be with us.

In the Holy Presence we can seek out common causes with common sense in our secular context. The Holy is at work in the secular world as surely as in the religious world. The challenge for all of us is to join forces with all who care about the salvation of the world and all in it. The religious and secular are meant to interact and reform each other. Both secular and religious society need to have the courage to reject tyrannies that kill.

We need the intellectual, emotional, and spiritual capacity to endure the dislocation we feel as we address, with the rest of the world, the issues of change in our times. The Spirit is calling us into the unknown even as it supports our living in the present and remembers with us lessons from the past.

Christianity is not dead or even dying, it is evolving. In some places, its adherents are a precious remnant. In other places they are thriving. We are rediscovering Christianity.

In this book, we have set down some basics of Christian origins and looked behind the curtain at some theologies born in another time to follow the God beyond time who is still creating with humanity in time from generation to generation. The God of ages is making all things new.

We live in a world in need of holiness and compassion that religious communities and secular organizations of goodwill can foster together. None of us has complete knowledge or full awareness of God or the Divine by whatever name or names.

We enter a new era in which we are all called to reform our own faiths, not convert other people to them. We are all looking at life from many angles through many different lenses. We all have gifts to share with one another. We need a common vision of goodness and righteousness as we seek for a moral compass and sanity for today and coming times.

Religions at their best will remind us that even though evil is ever present, it cannot and will not prevail for the Good will not die. Religions call us to listen for the songs of angels and believe the voices of prophets and embrace the unfolding of creation.

The Spirit of Holiness is in motion and being unveiled before our eyes in human faces, in all of creation, in the stars, if we have hearts and minds to see. The Holy goes with us into the future, into sacred spaces and into secular places that are infused with the sacred.

Having written this book about the basics of faith and its future, and speaking very directly about God, Jesus, the Holy Spirit, Scripture and the Church, I end with a quote I came across in my book, "Button Reflection."

My faith has been a central part of who I am as is my feminism and is an integral part of my reflections. I do not often talk or write in religious terms. I see all of life as religious and religion a part of all of life. I have a strong proclivity for both mystery and common sense. Sometimes I see the Spirit at work in our lives and world and the way ahead seems clear. Sometimes I know the Spirit is moving in ways that elude me and I move forward in faith. I assume the Spirit to be present and prodding in all of life even when I or any of us is not noticing." p. x and xi

I obviously have departed from not writing in religious terms. However, I still see God as alive in all creation and remain committed to mystery and common sense.

CHURCHES AS A LIGHT IN THE FUTURE

All plants tilt toward the light of the sun. In the same way, we tilt toward the Light of God.

Christian faith and the churches that carry its message are called to be instruments of life, of light and love, to be people of goodwill called to honor the basic ethics of human relationships and the essential moral laws of creation. We are called to fully embrace the sacredness of creation for a sustainable world.

While we cannot see the future, we have learned lessons from the past to guide us. We have histories, those recorded and those still being uncovered. We can speculate on how the things we do now will affect the future.

There are many Christians in the world, and we have each other. We in the United States are one small part of the picture. God is at work by whatever name, in other nations in religious communities and secular forces of good will, around the earth. They too are on the brink of everything because we are one world. We are creating the future together. It is time to mature in faith, for our faiths to mature, for our world to come of age.

Passing on faith to future generations is getting harder and that makes it all the more important for those of us connected to religious communities to be clear about what we believe and don't believe and are struggling to believe. And to act with integrity on what we believe. Only then will new generations know what faith means to us. Only then can they choose religious belonging for themselves.

I am always amused to hear atheists, journalists, and academics talking about what we believe as Christians, and then, trusting in their own assumptions, proceed to critique Christianity. I often wonder what or whose Christianity they are referring to. It is seldom mine.

In much the same way, mainstream media equates Christianity with whatever popular notion of "church" prevails in any given time. It is time for mainline churches, Roman Catholic, Orthodox, and Protestant in all of their diversity to become more visible as expressions of Christianity in the public eye.

Mainstream churches, even in their diversity, are oriented toward the sacredness of life, and in varying ways try to serve the common good and human survival. They cannot and should not be involved in partisan politics, but they must be involved in humanitarian and environmental issues.

While church bodies have their own deep institutional networks, theological positions, and forms of worship, they are, in the end, not at the heart of faith. In society, the belief in a Holy Presence that churches share is what gives strength to, informs, and transforms human spirits in all of cultures turning, from generation to generation.

In 1976, Sister Concilia Moran made me a banner when we were working together in the Women's Coalition for the Third Century, that says, "Sing to the Lord a new Song" from Psalm 96. It hangs in my entry way as a reminder to always sing a new song to the Holy One who moves with us into the future

Religious communities and the theological schools and related religious organizations that help create and sustain them, can be a gift to the world in the future if they educate leaders who can give courageous leadership to religious communities and their constituents that lead to healing the world, working toward establishing peace with justice in society and affirming rich spiritual lives open to God's amazing and sustaining love.

The fact is, however, that we cannot take our human need for spiritual expression and services as for granted as we take our need for physical, psychological, educational, legal, and economic services. Religious community is optional. My profession as a clergy person is non-essential. I smile because there are times when this is hard to accept. I look at other members of my family and they are all engaged in essential work. But I get it. I have to live with the fact that I am in a dispensable profession. Spirituality and faith are matters of choice.

Religious communities will have to adapt to a new era in the years ahead and in so doing, they will have to negotiate an often-bumpy road. We live in a time of great transition. We know that life is complex, and churches have always had to struggle to discern God's will and participate in drawing closer to God's Realm on earth. As we gain in wisdom, we must speak truth to power as never before in the knowledge that we do not face the challenges before us alone. The Spirit is already there.

As new changes are taking place in congregations, unresolved old issues both theological and ethical will surface. These old issues are insidious. We have all been influenced by them and have remnants of them in ourselves to deal with. And we have passed some of those remnants on to new generations. It will take those new generations to sing their new song to and with the Spirit, a song prior generations have just begun to hum.

The churches of today need to take a deep breath as they move into the future and face new theological issues, leaving behind doctrines and beliefs that have outlived their time and follow where the Spirit is guiding.

"What do we mean by God anyway?" How seriously do we take the teachings of Jesus? Are we open to a living God who through the Spirit speaks anew in every time and place? We cannot remain caught in the imagery of a patriarchal, militant, controlling, parochial God.

Diane Butler Bass raises a related question, "Where is God?" In her book, *Grounded*, she talks about a spiritual revolution and the end of God sitting on a throne, high above a three-tiered universe with earth in the middle between heaven and hell. She says:

"God is the grounding, that which grounds us. We experience this when we understand that soil is holy, water gives life, the sky opens our imagination, our roots matter, home is a divine place, and our lives are linked to our neighbors and with those around the globe. This world, not heaven, is the sacred stage of our times." p. 26

All generations of Christians living today and those to come need to address the questions, "Where is God" and "What do you mean by God? They are connected. Just asking them opens the door for new insight and revelation.

God is our source of vision, creativity, strength, and courage. The Spirit who is beyond time and breathes life into all that is, and the risen Christ who is one of us, is our guide as we face the daunting yet amazing gift of being human in this age, in the era that lies before us.

This book has no conclusion. Future generations will continue the narrative in the power and love of the Spirit in the context of the religious communities and the secular world in which they are set. God will be there and the Spirit will breathe life.

I leave those of you who are and will choose to be part of a church, a prayer from Ephesians.

> *I pray that, according to the riches of God's glory, God may grant that you may be strengthened in your inner*

being with power through the Spirit and Christ may dwell in your hearts, through faith, as you are being grounded and rooted in love. I pray that you may have the power to comprehend, with all the saints, what is the breadth and length and height and depth, and to know the love of Christ that surpasses knowledge, so that you may be filled with all the fulness of God.

Now to the One who by the power at work within us is able to accomplish abundantly far more than all we can ask or imagine, to that One be the glory in the church and in Jesus Christ to all generations, forever and ever. Amen. Ephesians 3:14-20

To all I leave this simple poem as I stop writing.

When the sun is rising
And its rays cast rainbows
Hope is there
When the moon is rising
And it lights the night
And shines on the ocean,
Love is there
When gardens are growing
And flowers are blooming
New Life is there
When ruble is smoldering
And lives are shattered
God is there.
In the greening of spring
In the heat of summer
In the colors of fall
In the cold of winter
The Earth is turning
When a baby cries,
A toddler toddles

Children play
Young people explore
Adults create and mature
And everyone reaches for love
Jesus is there
As we find our way
In our labyrinthian world
The Spirit leads the way
As the wheels of life turn.
And when things and life
End as they will
And what is visible changes
An unseen energy emerges
And Holliness is there.
We have barely dared to believe
When it rises to make all things new
And life continues
People and all creation
Keep going on
Grounded in the flesh
And all the dailiness and wonder
The mystery of it all
Shines under the stars in the sky.

It becomes clear over and beyond time
That the dividing, divining line
Between heaven and earth is porous
And in endings there are beginnings
And we are at home in it all.

So I stop writing
On the pages of this book
It is not finished, it has no end,
And that is as it has to be. PBK

In Gratitude for Saints

MODERN DAY SAINTS

Through all the changes that have taken place over time in my life, I have seen the face of God in many people and have been touched deeply by them. They have helped shape my life and that of countless others. People like them are the heart of the evolving church and world. They are saints whose name will not be known by many.

I am eternally grateful for them. As you read about these saints, I invite you to think of those in whom you have seen the face of God.

The people I mention are no longer with us. They were the modern-day Marys, Peters, and Marthas, and Pauls of our time. Our communities are full of them. They lived the teachings of Jesus as best they could and followed the leading of the Spirit. People like them will populate the future church.

I give endless thanks for them.

Phoebe Giddings was an elder in Westminster Presbyterian in New Jersey. She was an effective, inspiring, and faithful leader. I was privileged to be her Pastor. She raised six children as a single employed parent after her husband died when their youngest was small. Her three sons served in the Vietnam War. She came through that time with great resilience and strength. Two of her sons, one was so traumatized by the war and probably affected by agent orange, died an early death. She never wavered in her commitment to racial and gender justice and saw all people as God's children. She was incredibly strong and kind. As a

Black woman Elder, her acceptance of me as a young, inexperienced, White woman Pastor was a gift that enabled me and encouraged me throughout my ministry and life. Her daughter, Elenora Giddings Ivory became a Minister and prominent church leader.

The Rev. Dr. Beatrice Melano Couch, an Argentine, was, if not the first, one of the first women liberation theologians in South America. Bea was educated in both France and the United States. She was truly a citizen of the world. As a pioneer, she walked a rocky road. Bea was a Seminary classmate and in the groups that went to Mexico in our second year. She was a dynamic speaker and brought faith to life. She spoke on behalf of women at the second General Assembly that raised the women's issue in the church. She was very impressive and persuasive. She married an American and they returned to Argentina for their ministry. She was never fully appreciated for her great faith and mind. But she opened doors for others and was a prophetic saint and devoted friend.

The Rev. William Hervey was the Pastor of a Presbyterian Church in New Jersey. I have already mentioned his involvement in the Civil Rights Movement. When the buses began to roll into the south to advocate for the rights of African Americans to vote, Bill felt called to go.

When I first began to preach at Manalapan, I felt I could not get ordained. I was the mother of three young sons, and I felt that mothers could not make that kind of life-long decision. Bill, visiting one day, told me he thought I needed to be ordained. I shared my reservations. "Patty," he said, "Your people need you to be ordained now. Leave the long term up to God." A wise and open perspective. And that is just what I did, I got ordained.

Bill was totally committed to Jesus' way of life. He was a good and faithful Pastor who inspired his congregation to commit their lives to pursuing justice and the abundant life for all promised by Jesus.

Wilma Scott Heide was a leader in the feminist movement and one of the most ethical people I have ever known. She was a person of faith though never an official member of any church as an adult. As a young woman, both her family and her church had rejected her aspirations to become a Lutheran Minister and sent her to a therapist instead.

She was an informed activist, insightful in her critique of society and clear that prejudice of any kind is wrong. Beyond society's sexism, she perceived the possibility of a new creation and saw and encouraged the good in everyone she met and saw all causes for social justice as one. Before the word came into being, she believed in and practiced "intersectionality."

Embracing love in profound ways and having great integrity was part of who she was. In her later life, we worked together on feminist issues bridging church and society. When we spoke as a team, she would introduce us with good humor, saying that I was a minister of the church, she was a minister of the truth.

My grandmother, Marie Dick, an immigrant from Germany, came to the States when she was fifty. She had planned to come with my grandfather, Xavier Dick, but he died a few months before sailing time. She and her husband had seen Hitler rising in their part of Germany and they had nothing but disdain for him. No one in our family ever talked about her parents or any other relatives. She was a mystery woman who belonged solely to us as family and to the church she attended faithfully. She became a citizen late in life.

Marie Dick came alone to join my mother who had immigrated alone herself a few years before her at the age of seventeen. She took care of me until I was two when my mother was working to put my father through school. As I got older, she became a port in every storm and a dear confidant.

My grandmother and mother lived through the great depression in Germany, they understood that conservation is essential. They never wasted anything. They taught me about faithfulness, courage, and thrift long before the environmental movement took hold.

My mother married Harold J. Budd, son of Mary Budd, who gave birth to nine children, five of whom lived beyond twenty-two. Her husband died when my father was five. They lived in the anthracite coal region of Pennsylvania and two of her sons were involved in coal mining. By any standard they were poor. My father, being the youngest, was encouraged by his mother and siblings to be the first in the family to attend college. The family were faithful and active members of the Methodist Church except for Uncle George who married a Catholic woman and returned to his paternal grandfather's faith. He was the most saintly and down-to-earth person I ever knew. Hearing him laugh always brought joy.

Dr. Barbara Krasner, a Jewish theologian and therapist helped Harvard Divinity School students and some of our faculty, understand the dynamics of family systems when she led a symposium for us in our continuing education program.

On a personal level, she helped Tom and me sort out what really mattered in our personal lives. She emphasized the importance of seeing reciprocity in relationships as essential to love and reworking injustices. She saw this as humanity's and God's creative work. She had no tolerance for Christians who spoke freely of love but never stopped to figure out what it means to practice it.

The Rev. Fuad Bahnan, a Palestinian Christian, and a Pastor in the United States, was a living example of continuing the teachings of Jesus. He had experienced racial discrimination in Palestine/Israel as had many of his friends and family. His people were persecuted, driven from their homes, ghettoized, imprisoned without trial. He witnessed innocent lives lost. When several of us went to the Middle East with him, he was not allowed to return to the place of his birth. He stayed in Lebanon when we went to the West Bank and Israel and then joined up with us in Egypt.

Later, when we were at a Synod conference on the Middle East where he spoke, amid a call to justice for Palestinians, he called for compassion for Israelis, as he prayed for peace with justice.

Fuad had been a Seminary classmate at Princeton Seminary. It was not until years later that he became a mentor and a truly holy man for me as a friend and Christian prophet.

Betty Lin was a dear friend whom I first met in High School. She joined our class in our sophomore year after immigrating from China in 1949 when the communists took over. We were members of Miss Duncan's Peace Group, a commitment we carried throughout our lives.

Betty went on to become a social worker and therapist. She married Poping, an accomplished scientist, and they had two sons. They settled on the West Coast.

After we moved to the Boston area, Poping had a several year assignment here and we reconnected and renewed and deepened our friendship with the help of another dear friend, the Rev. Charles Munion. Betty was a deeply committed Christian and more on the conservative evangelical side than I was. We respected and cared for each other in spite of our theological differences, of which we were well aware. Our faith transcended them even when we disagreed.

Betty welcomed me into her home many times after they returned to California. She introduced me to her church, and to Stanford University. She lived her faith both in her family life, in her work as a therapist, and in her friendships.

Doris Fisher was one of the early members of Clarendon Hill Presbyterian Church. She was one of the Nova Scotians who established the church and built it up over the years. She worked as a receptionist at a Boston hospital while raising six children, four of whom were deaf. By the time I knew her, she was retired. Doris was hospitable, strong, and deeply committed to the church. She welcomed everyone. She nursed a daughter who died of cancer. She dealt with other difficult life events including losing a granddaughter to addiction. Through it all remained steadfast and positive. She accepted change in the church and actively contributed to its future.

Espedito Liberace, an elder was a contractor by trade and our church building's expert fixer. He was a kind, generous, and inspiring member of Clarendon Hill without whom we could not have functioned during our development years.

He came from the Italian Presbyterian Church in Somerville which eventually merged with Clarendon Hill. He and his wife raised four children, two of whom are vital members of CHP today. In his later years he took up ball room dancing! Espedito was a saint who truly lived a full and inspiring life.

There are so many more saints. Beth Yolton, a young elder who had to deal with mental illness throughout her life showed great stamina and artistry and commitment to social justice. Maggie Kuhn who worked for the Board of Christian Education of the Presbyterian Church and was a great mentor. In her later years she founded the Grey Panthers.

Ching Ling Kung, a doctor and acupuncturist from China shared her many gifts and her culture with me individually and with our church as a faithful, loving member. Judy Lambert, a creative, faithful, fiercely ethical woman was welcoming of everyone. She survived a lung transplant with great courage.

My brother, Harold, who faced many health challenges in his life also met them with courage and the help of his wife, Fran, who was always by his side. They were examples of determination and grace. Together they provided a gathering place for our family and was our mother's caregiver. They were active in the Methodist Church when they retired to Williamstown, PA. My brother-in-law, John Erdman Kepler, who served in the military and sang in the church choir and was in the bell choir of the Presbyterian Church in Fairfax, Virginia. He and his wife, Toyoko, had four sons. John kept family ties alive with great love. His parents, Margaret Blain Kepler and Raymond Kepler, also the parents of four sons, were missionaries in China and saints, whose story would require a book.

There are so many more.

So many people through the years have born witness to God's presence in their lives, sometimes professing their faith, sometimes expressing it only by example. They spread God's love and hope through their integrity and compassion, the sharing of their gifts, and their great faithfulness. They make up the church and religious communities of all kinds. They energize movements for human rights and create friendship circles that enhance life.

All these people have had an impact in the world though they never made the news. They were never called Saints. They are human beings, through whom God's light shone. The miracles they performed took place in the way they met the challenges of being human. These saints prepared the ways for others to carry the Spirit of God into the world.

BIBLIOGRAPHY

Ahmed, Leila, *Women and Gender in Islam*, New Haven, CT, Yale University Press, 1992

Alves, Rubem A. *A Theology of Human Hope*. Washington, DC: Corpus, 1969.

Armstrong, Karen. *The Battle for God*. New York, NY: Random House, 2001.

Barrett, Charles Kingsley. *Paul: An introduction to his thought*. Louisville, KY: Westminster John Knox Press, 2005.

Bass, Diana Butler, *Grounded: Finding God in the World A Spiritual Revolution*, New York, New York, Harper Collins, 2017

Brasfield, Alice, and Elisabeth Lunz. *Voices of Experience: Life stories of Clergywomen in the Presbyterian Church (U.S.A.)*. Louisville, KY: Women's Ministry Unit, Presbyterian Church (U.S.A.), 1991.

Brock, Rita Nakashima, and Rebecca Ann Parker. *Saving Paradise: How Christianity Traded Love of This World for Crucifixion and Empire*. Boston, MA: Beacon Press, 2009.

Brock, Rita Nakashima. *Journeys by heart: A Christology of erotic power*. Eugene, OR: Wipf & Stock, 2008.

Chittister, Joan. *The Ten Commandments: Laws of the Heart*. Maryknoll, NY: Orbis Books, 2006.

Chotzinoff, Robin. *Holy unexpected: My new life as a jew*. New York, NY: PublicAffairs, 2006.

Coffin, William Sloane. *Letters to a young doubter*. Louisville, KY: Westminster John Knox Press, 2005.

Coffin, William Sloane. *The Courage to Love.* New York, NY: Harper & Row, 1982.

Costa, Ruy O., and Lorine M. Getz, eds. *Struggles for Solidarity: Liberation Theologies in Tension.* Minneapolis, MN: Augsburg Fortress, 1992.

Douglas, Kelly Brown. *The black christ.* Maryknoll, NY: Orbis Books, 1993.

Ela, Jean-Marc. *My faith as an African.* Maryknoll, NY: Orbis, 1995.

Fowler, James W. *Becoming adult, becoming Christian: Adult development and Christian Faith.* San Francisco, CA: Harper, 1984.

Fox, Matthew. *A New Reformation: Creation Spirituality and the Transformation of Christianity.* Rochester, VT: Inner Traditions, 2006.

Fox, Matthew. *The coming of the cosmic christ: The healing of mother earth and the birth of a global renaissance.* New York, NY: Harper & Row, 1988.

Friedan, Betty, and Brigid O'Farrell. *Beyond gender: The new politics of work and family.* Washington, DC: Woodrow Wilson Center Press, 1997.

Gamble, Eugenia Anne, *Words of Love: A Healing Journey with the Ten Commandments, Louisville,* Kentucky, Westminster John Knox Press, 2022

Gomes, Peter J. *The good book: Reading the Bible with mind and heart.* New York, NY: Avon Books, 1996.

Harris, Maria. *Dance of the spirit: The seven steps of women's spirituality.* New York, NY: Bantam Books, 1989.

Heide, Wilma Scott, *Feminism for the Health of It*, Buffalo, New York, Margaret Gaughters, Inc. 1985 Christian 1958.

Hendry, George S. *The holy spirit in Christian theology.* Philadelphia, PA: Westminister Press, 1956.

Hengel, Martin. *Between Jesus and Paul.* Philadelphia, PA: Fortress Press, 1983.

Hinn, Benny. *Welcome, holy spirit.* Nashville, TN: Thomas Nelson Publishers, 1997.

Hogan, Linda. *Dwellings: A spiritual history of the living world.* New York, NY: Touchstone, 1996.

Hunter, Archibald Macbride. *Paul and His Predecessors.* Philadelphia, PA: Andesite Press, 2011.

Ivory, Elenora Giddings, Worldview from Elenora Giddings Ivry Tower: The Life and Times of a Religious Advocate, Christian Faith Publishing, Meadville, PA, 1918

Jacobs, A. J. *The Year of Living Biblically: One man's humble quest to follow the Bible as literally as possible.* New York, NY: Simon & Schuster, 2007.

Kepler, Patricia Budd. *Button Reflections.* Philadelphia, PA: Xlibris Corporation, 2015.

Kepler, Patricia Budd. *Work after patriarchy: A pastoral perspective.* Philadelphia, PA: Xlibris Corporation, 2009.

Kidd, Sue Monk. *God's joyful surprise: Finding yourself loved.* New York, NY: Guideposts, 1987.

Kim, Grace Ji-Sun, *Spirit Life,* Minneapolis, MN, Fortress Press 2022

Kim, race Ji-Sun, *The Homebrewed Christianity Guide to the Holy Spirit*, Minneapolis, MN, Fortress Press 2018

Kushner, Harold. *When children ask about God.* New York, NY: Schoken Books, 1971.

LaCugna, Catherine Mowry. *God for us: The Trinity and Christian Life.* New York, NY: HarperCollins, 2006.

Lamott, Anne. *Grace (eventually).* New York, NY: Riverhead Books, 2007.

McBride, Hillary L. *The Wisdom of Your Body.* Grand Rapids, MI: Brazos, 2021.

McFague, Sallie. *Models of God: Theology for an ecological, nuclear age.* Philadelphia, PA: Fortress Press, 1988.

Palmer, Parker J. *The Active Life: Wisdom for Work, Creativity and Caring.* San Francisco, CA: HarperCollins, 1990.

Panikkar, Raimon. *A dwelling place for Wisdom.* Louisville, KY: Westminster John Knox Publishers, 1993.

Placher, William Carl. *The Triune God: An Essay in Postliberal Theology.* Louisville, KY: Westminster John Knox Press, 2007.

Richardson, Alan, ed. *A Theological Word Book of the Bible.* New York, NY: MacMillan Company, 1957.

Rohr, Richard. *The universal Christ: How a forgotten reality can change everything we see, hope for, and believe.* New York, NY: Convergent, 2021.

Russell, Letty M. *Household of Freedom: Authority in feminist theology.* Philadelphia, PA: Westminster Press, 1987.

Russell, Letty M., ed. *The liberating word: A guide to nonsexist interpretation of the Bible.* Philadelphia, PA: Westminster Press, 1976.

Senior, Donald, *Jesus: A Gospel Portrait,* New York, Mahwah, New Jersey, Paulist Press, 1992

Shaull, Millard Richard. *Heralds of a New Reformation: The Poor of South and North America.* Maryknoll, NY: Orbis Books, 1984.

Spong, John Shelby. *Eternal life - A New Vision: Beyond Religion, Beyond Theism, Beyond Heaven and Hell.* New York, NY: HarperOne, 2009.

Spong, John Shelby. *Here I stand: My struggle for a Christianity of Integrity, Love, and Equality.* New York, NY: HarperCollins, 2000.

Taylor, Barbara Brown. *Always a Guest: Speaking of Faith Far from Home.* Louisville, KY: Westminster John Knox, 2020.

Thurman, Howard, *Jesus and the Dispossessed,* Beacon Press, Boston, MA., 1996

Tutu, Desmond, and John Allen. *The Rainbow People of God: The Making of a Peaceful Revolution.* New York, NY: Image, 1994.

Vahanian, Gabriel. *The death of God: The culture of our post-christian era.* New York, NY: George Braziller, 1961.

Vaillant, George E. *Spiritual Evolution: A Scientific Defense of Faith.* New York, NY: Broadway Books, 2008.

Wright, Robert. *The Evolution of God.* New York, NY: Little Brown, 2009.

Printed in the United States
by Baker & Taylor Publisher Services

Printed in the United States
by Baker & Taylor Publisher Services